# ...AND THERE I WAS!

## A PILOT'S MEMOIR

by

**J. M. (Mike) McEniry**
Author of *THE JANITOR*

*To LAURI — great FAMILY! Fun times & ... Mike McEniry*

ISBN – 13   9781535313155

# ACKNOWLEDGEMENTS

The author wishes to acknowledge the assistance provided to this narrative by fellow NavCads Benjamin F. King, Delbert L. Peterson and Ric Novak for their contributions to this effort and their life-long friendship.

I would also like to thank my Editor, Kyra Tyler for making publication possible. Without her effort it would not have happened. A sincere thanks to her father, James Tyler, a fellow novelist who was a major help in the publication arena of formatting and prepping for print.

To my sister, Patricia Adele Love, a fellow writer and critical mentor, a special thanks. Her literary guidance reminded me of our early childhood.

Many thanks to Karen Kucera, my "non-military" proof-reader who pulled me back to reality when my writing got too 'techy'. And to Steve & Lisa Hilbert for dragging me, screaming into MS-10 for publication.

And a thanks to my son, Scott who came up with the title, which is a great deal more suitable than what I had in mind.

And finally to my bride of seven years, Catherine Ann McEniry, who's proof-reading and patience kept me at it. Thank you, Catherine. You're a blessing!

# DEDICATION

This memoir is dedicated to all Navy and Marine pilots that managed to get through the Naval Aviation Cadet Training Command. Well done, Gentlemen. (And also to the Lady pilots that came later.) Your commitment to service is applauded. It is that commitment that has made this the great nation that it is.

And to my fellow Marines….."Semper Fi"!

*IN LOVING MEMORY*

Peggy Lou McEniry

April 26, 1933 - to- September 20, 2008

# PREFACE

This is a story about a young boy's dream of becoming a pilot. Growing up in the depression years the chances of realizing that dream were poor to impossible. And then World War II opened a possibility, and enforced by our entry into the Korean conflict. Our country needed pilots. A visible path to achieving the dream presented itself. A series of twists and turns slowed the progress but eventually the goal was achieved.

It is a story, and one extracted from a biography out of necessity, but the details of the Navy flight training wouldn't have been possible without the assistance from Ben King and Del Peterson. We shared e-mails back and forth, pulling out the little vignettes' covering the human side of the eighteen-month Naval Aviation Cadet experience. I copied all of those e-mails and they would make a good book of themselves. Some of the tales told were not suitable for publication however. That portion of writing this narrative was the most enjoyable.

I was forced to spend a great deal of time pawing through the archives of my being. I learned a great deal about myself. Some things, not so good and others a joy to re-live.

I'll share them with you now.

# ONE　　　THE BEGINNING

$\mathbf{I}$t all started sometime in August of 1931. Probably too hot to sleep, so what the 'hey'. Anyway, the results culminated in my birth, the 27$^{th}$ of April 1932 at two-thirty in the morning to Betty Marie (Braga) and James Arthur McEniry. I was given the name of '*James Michael McEniry*', named after my paternal Grandfather, Michael Stanislaus McEniry. The momentous event occurred at Virginia-Mason Hospital in Seattle Washington.

This book is about my difficult and convoluted road to becoming a pilot. It is about the driving force that one puts into a passion of striving effort to realize a goal. Some of this will be in a form of biographical segments that contribute to the story regarding the travel to reach that goal. But the key point, or 'core', of this narrative is "*passion*". –with it you can achieve anything. Without it, everything you do is *work*.

My sister, Patricia Adel, was six years older and enjoyed her role as 'Mom'. Early-on the family was well off enough to afford a permanent Nanny. She was actually a nurse, having come out of Russia through China during the Russian Revolution. She wasn't able to practice nursing because of license requirements. Not that it matters, but I spoke Russian before I spoke English, or so I've been told.

The Depression was in full swing and had made its way across the nation to the west coast. We had to move into humbler quarters and the Nanny had to go. I have a few fragments of the life around me. One of them was a vague memory of being seriously ill with pneumonia. The

1

closest hospital was Catholic and when the Sisters discovered that I hadn't ever been baptized made that happen. Not soon after I was given 'last rites'. (It was an open 'n shut case and has served me well since.)

I was a little over two years old when my Mother divorced my Father. I have memory glimpses of being on a boat going to visit my Father in prison. He was in the Federal Penitentiary on McNeil Island located in the south Sound area of Puget Sound. The boat was transportation to and from the island. My memory-fragment of the boat was that it was painted white and had green trim. I don't remember visiting with my Father.

There are other fragments of our life, more like short videos that show bits and pieces. My Sister, Patsy, being six years older has more memory of those early years and has told me a lot. My Father took to drink quite a bit...was always broke and the family moved often, usually in the middle of the night to avoid rent payments. All of the problems finally drove my Mother to divorce him in 1935.

Patsy has told me more of my early years. I was born with very blonde hair. Both of my parents had black hair. It seemed that our 'ice-man' was a big strapping blonde-haired Swede. My folks took a bit of a ribbing about that. Within a year my hair started turning brown.

She also told me that my introduction to "show biz" took place when I was three and a half years old. She and I had been attending a church on lower Broadway, Capitol Hill. Patsy had been working with me on "It Came Upon A Midnight Clear" and I was to sing it solo during the church's Christmas Program. When it came time to perform I refused until she came up to stand beside me. She did come up and I took a very relaxed position, leaning on the alter and gave forth my song. I didn't get any other offers from that early exposure until much later in life. And then, it wasn't for singing. We'll talk about that down the road.

The church is still there on Capitol Hill, lower 10th Avenue.

We were living in a large yellow house on Boylston Avenue that had been converted to apartments. I think it was called "Mrs. Engles". I went to Kindergarten at Seward Grade School. We then moved down to an apartment house at 916 Yale North. I attended the original Cascade Grade School from the First to the Fourth Grade.

My fondest memory from that period is winning a 'food-battle' with my Sister and Mother.

I did not care for cucumbers, especially slices soaking in some kind of vinegar. I had been told time and time again how *"good"* they were for me and so I had to choke them down. Well, I was in the Second or Third Grade and our textbook in Health Class stated that *cucumbers had absolutely no food value!* Hoo-RAH!

I was elated. Normally the school did not allow books, at that grade level, to be taken home. I had to get special permission in order to do so. It was the first battle against 'authority' that I won in my early life. I haven't knowingly eaten a cucumber since!

The routine, during this period, required that I come directly home from school and 'report-in' to Seattle Day Nursery. I would have to remain there until such time as my Sister or my Mother would 'bail' me out. Sometime later I graduated. I didn't have to go to Seattle Day Nursery. I had my very own front-door apartment key. I must have been about six or seven by then. I would come home, change into my 'play clothes' (school clothes had to be carefully hung up to keep them presentable…I was to learn about uniforms in the same way later in life) and stay close enough to be able to hear a call to come in around dinnertime.

When I was about six we visited my paternal grandparents in Pasadena. My grandfather, Michael Stanislaus McEniry sat me down and explained that my father had been his eldest son. He said that I was the 'eldest-Son-of-the-eldest-Son' and that all titles and claims would go to me when he and my father died. He explained the family history to me.

*Our clan lived on the east coast of Scotland. We were seafarers and raiders. Most of our raiding supposedly took place across the channel. When Stuart the First made his push our clan supported the "other" side. Wrong thing to do. It wasn't a 'two-party' system and the losers had to hide. They faced arrest, imprisonment, sent to the Colonies indentured, or death. We chose to not go across the channel, there being folk that would remember us. Way too much "rape, pillage and burn", and by the way it took three generations to get the order right! So instead, the clan went over the top of Scotland to Ireland. It was there that the family did well, built a castle and acquired large land holdings. Grandfather said that it would be my responsibility to reclaim the titles and holdings. (My mother had always thought him to be a bit of a storyteller.)*

A few years ago my son Scott was doing some family research and came across a book called, *"A MARINE DIVE BOMBER PILOT ON GUADALCANAL"*, written by Colonel John Howard McEniry, USMC, –a relative from the east-coast side of the family. Scott contacted the family only to be told that John Howard had died a couple of years prior. Scott talked with his son,

5

who had recently returned from Ireland where he had visited the family castle!

I guess my Grandfather was right. Hellava deal.

We had a piano. Both my Sister and I took lessons. I like to think that my taking lessons were all due to my sister, Patsy's, insistence. –Thank you, Patsy.

She was also nice enough to include me in many of her teen-age activities like skiing parties, picnics, with her contemporaries, and other such events. One of her 'beaus' had a yellow 1932 Plymouth convertible that had a rumble seat. There's something magical about riding in a rumble seat. Young or old it's just plain fun!

That 'beau' also had a niece that was about my age and the niece and I got to share that rumble seat on a few of my sister's dates. It wasn't until later in life that I really learned to <u>fully</u> appreciate her, my Sister that is. Now we're tighter than paint!

During the depression my Mother worked at a few meaningless jobs. One of them was a woman's store of some kind. She would bring damaged or dirty handbags home, repair or clean them in order to sell and earn a greater commission. Supporting my Sister, our Nanny and me during the depression had to have been difficult. But the funny part was that I don't remember being denied much. We were close to poor but I didn't know it.

I had an early interest in aviation. Seattle was an aviation town due to Boeing's activities. The 'Twenties and Thirties' were the golden years of aviation. Records were being set and airplanes were all over the sky. The Boeing Company airplanes could be seen in the skies over Seattle. And now, living near the south end of Lake Union, there was also a lot of seaplane activity.

On Saturdays I was given an allowance of eleven cents, the price of admission to the weekly matinee at the Uptown Theatre located at the foot of Queen Anne Hill. At age seven I was allowed to walk to the theatre. My route took me past Kurtzer Flight Service, located at the south end of Lake Union. Kurtzer was a seaplane operation. On one of my Saturday trips the street-side door of the main hangar building was open. I could see an airplane being worked on. I got as close as I dared when one of the mechanics noticed me.

"Hey Kid...you like airplanes?" He called out.

I quickly answered in the affirmative and he motioned me into the hangar. "C'mon over here."

Wow! --I was able to walk into this 'Temple of Aviation'...real airplanes! As I approached him I noticed the name *"Bud"* sewn on his coveralls.

"What's your name, Son?" ( --he called me 'Son', Wow again!)

"*James-Michael-McEniry*", I mumbled, running all of the words together.

"What does your Mom or Dad call ya?"

"My Mom calls me Michael and I don't have a Dad."

"What happened to your Dad, Mike?"

"He's in prison, Mr. Bud," I replied.

"Oh. –you can just call me Bud, Mike. So, you wanna be a pilot, huh?"

"Yes Sir!" Looking around I added, "--what's that funny smell?"

Bud took a moment to answer, realizing it was something that he took for granted, said, "its dope. It's like paint on the fabric of an airplane like this one that I'm working on." He motioned to the side of the  small seaplane mounted on a rolling frame, for me to feel it. He

7

continued, "When dope is painted on the linen fabric that covers the wings and fuselage, it shrinks and tightens the fabric…here, feel it."

I reached up and felt the side of the small two-place airplane's fuselage. ( I found out later that it was called a Taylorcraft.) I could feel the smooth, hard surface, like a thin metal skin.

It was the first input of my learning process that was to soon become a major part of my life. My early interest was intensifying. Bud Swenson taught me many things over a period of time, spending many Saturday mornings with him instead of going to the movies. He was patient, taking the time to answer my many questions, and a wonderful Mentor.

Bud had been a "Bush Pilot" in Alaska. He told me many stories about his experiences. Bud wasn't very tall, a little on the portly side, but there was something just *"airplane"* about him. I had always thought of pilots as being tall and dashing…but Bud was the real deal!

Over time he encouraged my reading, directing me to books about early aviation, the rapid development of airplanes during World War I, and the Aces of World War I. Books about the glamour and chivalry of the 'knights-of-the-skies'. The books didn't talk about a pilot's short life expectancy flying the early fighters. Their life could be measured in days and flight-hours. –only the glory was talked about in all that I read.

The top of the list of World War I Aces was the Red Baron; Manfred von Richthofen of the German Army, with eighty confirmed kills, followed by Ernst Udet with sixty-two. The French aces included Fonck, Guynemer and Nungesser, with over twenty victories, the British added to the list with Bishop, Mannock and McCudden, the American Eddie Rickenbacker, later

founder of Eastern Airlines, with a bunch of kills and Elliot White Springs, who gained notoriety in the 40's and 50's with his 'suggestive advertisements' for his "Springmaid Sheets". (The ad depicted a well-endowed Indian maiden climbing out of a sheet-hammock with a knocked-out, wasted Indian buck hanging half out and the slogan, *"A Buck Well Spent On A Springmaid Sheet!"*) Shocking, I tell you…simply shocking!
–he also shot down a few, sixteen in fact.

My boyhood hero was the Red Baron.

On one side of the Kurtzer hanger was a large cabin monoplane, with the wings off and still on 'landing-gear' wheels. It had a big round engine on the nose. Bud told me that the airplane was a Bellanca CH-300 that he had flown over many parts of Alaska. It had the distinction of being able to carry just about anything that could be put into the cabin…whether the airplane was on wheels, skis or pontoon floats. He let me sit in the cockpit and I could pretend I was flying the much needed serum into the ravaged Eskimo village suffering from some dread disease. Sometimes I didn't ever go to the movies but played in that airplane all day or listened to Bud's life-stories in Alaska. (My initial exposure to "war stories".)

But it wasn't all play. Bud taught me many things starting how the wing shape created lift and made flying possible…the instruments, and what they told the pilot. The only one I had trouble understanding was the Outside Air Temperature instrument. The mysteries of *Adiabatic Lapse Rate* would come later in my life. (--look that one up, Guys & Gals)

Bud was a major influence on me. I often wished he was my Dad…he came very close to filling that need.

9

Disaster struck in the third or fourth grade. My teacher sent a note home telling my Mother that she thought I needed glasses. I have no idea what prompted her to do that but it was what it was. My Mom somehow scrapped enough money together to pay for the eye examination.

When the eye doctor was filling out the prescription for the glasses I said, "NO!" I didn't say it disrespectfully, I just said it plain without inflection.

Some of you, who might know me, might be surprised to find that I was a polite, well-mannered young man not known to make a fuss about things. My outburst surprised my Mother, and the doctor as well. Mom gently asked me why I was acting like this.

I said, "Mom, I'm going to be a pilot and pilots can't wear glasses."

She thought about that for a moment and then turned to the eye doctor and asked him if there was anything that could be done. He said that eye exercises would help with my kind of condition, but being a child I wouldn't do them consistently enough to do any good. She asked for him to show them to me…which he did.

Mom decided to hold off on getting the glasses for the time being.

I'm glad that she did. I did as the doctor showed me, keeping in mind my goal. It worked because the teacher that was the cause of all this left me alone and later I didn't have any problems with 20/20 vision testing goals.

I've since wondered how many kids have been put into early glasses-wearing, causing more and more reliability on stronger and stronger lenses.

My Mom finally landed a decent job as a bookkeeper for Continental Can Company. There she met

10

and eventually married Jim Burchett. He also had an interest in airplanes and even knew someone who actually owned an airplane. He took me down to Boeing Field a couple of times to see this friend. I remember and recognized the smell of dope. It smelled like banana oil. Dope was painted on the fabric covering the airplane to 'shrink-wrap' around the framework. It was a unique smell that I had first encountered the year before at Kurtzers'. I loved that smell.

*Some years later I encountered the luscious smell of Castrol-R, the racing-car engine oil. It was close to the top of the 'special smell' list. –more would be added, until the top of the list was the smell of one's first baby! --a son or daughter, it didn't matter.*

Sorry, I'm digressing.

### I had my first airplane ride!

The airplane was a Piper J-3 Cub. I was to sit in front of the two-place airplane and the pilot sat behind me. That first take-off was almost a religious event. I was thinking about the things Bud Swenson had told me about how the wing works and I could feel waves of air lifting this small airplane. We flew around a bit and then the pilot asked me if I wanted to try the controls…I was thrilled. I had practiced this moment many a time in that Bellanca hangar-queen. It didn't take long to find the "sight picture" of the horizon in the *middle* of the windscreen and then I was able to actually keep control of the airplane, using small control inputs, like Bud had told me. The owner was impressed. ***And there I was***, I knew that this was for me. I felt at home….comfortable.

Jim Burchett had purchased a new 1940 Oldsmobile equipped with an automatic transmission.

We drove the car to the San Francisco World's Fair in 1939. I remember most of that trip; feeding the chipmunks at Crater Lake, going to the Fair site on Treasure Island, etc. When we started home the Golden Gate Bridge had recently opened. We drove over it and on up through the Redwoods, for our return to Seattle.

The years before World War II were highlighted by the Continental Can Company summer picnics. These were old-fashioned affairs at such places as Lake Wilderness, where a very large swing out over the water was a lot of fun and also Juanita Beach that had two very tall water slides. Those kinds of things are long gone now probably due to liability factors.

One summer, at Juanita Beach, Burchett (the asshole) threw me into deep water so that I would learn to swim. Nice. My Mother was furious! That family vacation also netted me a horrible, never-to-be forgotten, sunburn. But I survived the burn and did indeed learn how to swim.

Jim and my Mother bought a three-bedroom house at 8602-12$^{th}$ Avenue South West, in the Highland Park-White Center area of West Seattle. (Boeing Hill) The house abutted a grade school and a city park. They paid the exorbitant price of two thousand dollars for it. (1940 real estate prices.)

Moving into a new neighborhood I wanted to change my name to "Spike". I think it lasted for less than a week when my Sister, Patsy, called out, *"MIC-HAEL, DINNER TIME."*

I had to fight all the kids on the block!

My friends and I were playing Football in a vacant lot next door to my house on the Sunday in December when the Japanese attacked Pearl Harbor. My stepfather called me into the house to hear the broadcast, and

12

suggested that my friends should go home and listen to the radio.

The following day we listened intently to the President of the United States, Franklin Delano Roosevelt, as he addressed the Congress asking for a Declaration of War. –A moment in history not soon forgotten.

I had a Seattle Post Intelligencer morning paper route. I would sleep out in a room that was part of the garage and my District Manager would come by and wake me. It worked pretty well until I had to have an emergency appendectomy.

I remember it was 11:25 AM, almost 11:30, on a school day, when we would get out of school for lunch…with only five minutes to go for the bell I thought I'd escaped being called, but the teacher called on me to stand and spell 'oyster'. I stood up and the movement caused pain of a burst appendix that was so intense I passed out. The teacher helped me to the nurse's office, and the nurse sent me home, a half block away. The following day or days, a doctor determined that I had appendicitis and told my Mother to get me to West Seattle General Hospital pronto. It turned out to be major surgery. The appendix had indeed burst the day or so before…peritonitis had set in and drains had to be installed to deal with the infection.

It was the end of my newspaper career.

# THREE THE ARMY MOVES IN

The United States of America was at war. It was determined that the Boeing Airplane plants would need protection from air attack and the Highland Park City Park was chosen as a site for a ninety-millimeter anti-aircraft gun battery consisting of four or five gun emplacements. They were disguised as house roofs, constructed of canvas and wood framing, that was on rollers to slide back uncovering the large guns. Barracks had been hastily thrown up…there were sentries walking the perimeter. For an eight or nine- year old this was heaven!

The Boeing Plant 1, on the Duwamish River and Plant 2 on King County Airport were both camouflaged with wooden frames covered with fabric disguised as streets and houses. The hill-top gun emplacements were for protection for this company building bombers.

The start of 'bomber-thinking' by the military culminated in a 1934 Air Corps contract to develop a long-range experimental heavy bomber. Boeing's answer was the XB-15, a monster with four engines, 150-foot wingspan and weighing close to 40,000 pounds empty! It was never intended to be a production prototype. There was a lot to learn in this scale and the XB-15 proved to be a valuable flying-laboratory. She was in the skies over Seattle in 1937…I had seen her since I was five.

The Air Corps issued a purchase order for 13 B-17's in 1935. The Boeing plants built bombers. Those plants needed to be protected. Hence the Army in my back yard.

I wanted to somehow be a part of this and decided to take a direct approach.

The quickly-constructed barracks were end-to the property line between 'city-park' and lots with houses, a pathway separating the two. I walked down the path until coming to the first barrack, opened the screen door and entered, saying *"I would like to run errands, ....be a mascot or something and I'll stay clear of the Sergeants."*

The room had cots down one side and uniform racks beside each cot. All of the uniforms had Sergeant Stripes. I was in the *Sergeant's Barracks!* As it slowly dawned on me I was preparing to bolt when one of the Sergeants, laughing, called me over to his bunk.

"What did you have in mind? --errands?

"Well yeah, that or clean your rifle and shine your shoes. Isn't that the stuff you have to do in the Army."

"Well, that's pretty much it. What's your name?"

His name was Sexton, Sergeant Sexton. He showed me his M-1 Garand, thirty caliber semi-automatic rifle. It was the Army's new primary infantry weapon, replacing the Springfield thirty-caliber single, bolt-action rifle. The Springfield might be replaced, but not forgotten, a favorite weapon of snipers. The Garand's eight-round clip, firing each time the trigger was pulled, was far superior in laying-down rapid-fire on an enemy target. I learned how to strip it down for cleaning and then reassembling. I was also learning the language of soldiering. The spit-shine shoe indoctrination would come soon enough.

As I soon learned, their primary task was the anti-aircraft functions protecting the Boeing plants. I asked Sergeant Sexton that if their 'main thing' was shooting down airplanes why did he have to have a rifle.

15

"Mike, I'm a soldier. My job is 'cannon-cocker' or artillery, as some say, but I'm first and foremost a soldier. Soldiers have rifles."

"Sergeant Sexton, I'm gonna be a pilot and when I'm flying over the bad guys will there be 'cannon-cockers' trying to shoot me outta the sky?"

"Mike, I think you've got it figured out. That's why they call it War."

My Father, James Arthur McEniry, came to visit. He was in an Army uniform, having enlisted. As a convicted felon he had lost all of his citizen rights. When our country entered the war President Roosevelt offered a Presidential Pardon to those convicted felons who chose to volunteer for the armed services, thereby restoring their citizenship rights and honor.

I took him over to the Sergeant's Barracks and introduced him to the guys. As it happened, he did run into one of the sergeants he had met, when he visited Seattle on leave. (Or so he told me after the war, as an "*Oh, by the way*" thing*.*). Small world. At the end of the war he was Honorably Discharged, with the rank of Technical Sergeant.


Jim Burchett, my stepfather, had elected to accept a civilian contract as a machinist and went up to Dutch Harbor, in the Aleutian Islands. My Mother divorced him. I never knew why. He was a real jerk. I never forgave him for one of the most embarrassing moments of my childhood.

I had really missed having a *father*. Other kids had fathers that took them fishing and hunting. Burchett took me hunting one time. I don't know why he and his friends called it 'hunting'…all they did was sit around in the cabin drinking beer and playing poker. I finally got up enough nerve to ask if I could at least shoot at some targets. The guys set up some beer cans on a fence in the field. I was about to shoot when Burchett told me to wait. He ran back into the cabin and returned with a roll of toilet paper in case I soiled my pants. Like I said, I never forgave him for that.

During this time-frame my Sister, Patricia Adele McEniry, moved in with the Isham family. She didn't get along with Burchett, either. She had been a baby-sitter for the two Isham children, Donny and Sandy. Their home was next to the Volunteer Park Cemetery on Capitol Hill. Patsy didn't come out to the West Seattle house very often.

My Mother married Martin Nelson.

He treated me okay, but not like a dad would. For some unknown reason we moved to a two and a half acre mini-farm in a suburb of Sacramento called Carmichael. It was out in the country. Martin was burning off some grass near our nearly-new chicken coup. The fire got away from him, burning the chicken coop down and almost our house, plus a neighbor's house. The heat was so intense that candles in the house melted, just laying down.

I attended seventh grade at Carmichael Grade School. The country school auditorium was also used for showing movies on Friday and Saturday nights. Like I said, this was 'out in the country'. I had a neat girlfriend, Floynell Soper. Her Father's name was 'Floyd' and her Mother's name was 'Nell'....hence the name Floynell.

Significant things happened while living at our farm. Martin had bought a 1928 Studebaker that had been converted to a pick-up. It had a 1940 Studebaker pick-up bed on it. (More about this in a moment.)

17

One afternoon I heard Martin and my Mother arguing upstairs, followed by a scream and a loud thump. I went dashing upstairs only to find my Mother on the floor crying. He had struck her. I was furious. I told Martin to get the Hell out! I was a pretty good-sized kid and he elected to not oppose me, and left. They were later divorced.

My Mother and I had gone into Sacramento to attend a movie. It was the 'something Sisters' (Dolly??) with Betty Grable and another blonde. I don't remember how we got into Sacramento...but it turned out to be the end of World War II.

When we came out of the theatre the town had gone crazy....the war was over. It was V-J Day, August 14, 1945. (That was the other significant thing.)

Shortly after war's end my Father stopped by to visit, having just gotten out of the Army. My Mother suggested that he stay with me while she returned to Seattle to settle some real estate issues. He took a job driving a water truck on a freeway construction site, bypassing Sacramento. This freeway later became part of the I-5 Interstate Freeway System.

It was great. Here was my real father and all. He taught me how to drive that Studebaker Pick-Up. He spent time with me...listened to me and told me a lot about his life in the war. He didn't talk about prison.

*(I didn't find out until many years later the facts surrounding my father's felony conviction. He had been convicted of "Postal Fraud". He and a couple of others had been developing and selling mining stocks. They were probably worthless, but apparently they sold some through the mail. He was convicted and served eighteen months in prison.)*

My Mother returned. Father moved on. My Mother decided to sell the farm and return to Seattle. She also sold the truck, much to my disappointment. I was sent back to Seattle early in order to not miss any school. I boarded-out with the Eldreds, neighbors from our old neighborhood in West Seattle. I attended Eighth Grade at my old Highland Park Grade School.

My initial interest in sports was baseball. In grade school I was playing center field and after retrieving a ground ball I threw it *over* the backstop, allowing all of the bases to empty. That was the end of my baseball career. I became interested in track, and specifically, the pole vault.

My Mother bought a house on Capitol Hill, 228 Boylston North, two blocks below Broadway and near the intersection of East Thomas and Boylston. (The house is now gone, having been replaced with an apartment complex.)

Okay enough of that.

# FOUR     THE JOURNEY GETS SERIOUS

**L**ike many before me, the high school years created turning points in my life in many ways. It was the start of the pathway that would lead to Naval Aviator Pilot, "Wings of Gold" and a commission as a Second Lieutenant in the U.S. Marine Corps. It wasn't a smooth pathway. Much had to happen before reaching that goal.

During World War II the Army Air Corp's Aviation Cadet Program only required a High School Diploma and some college-level tests and a 'flight physical'. Eighteen months later came silver wings and commission as a $2^{nd}$ Lieutenant in the Army Air Corps. The war was over, the market was glutted with returning pilots, the Army Air Corps became its own branch of the service…now called the U.S. Air Force. The 'cadet' program now required two years of accredited college credits. I was too late, --still a Junior in high school when that change took place. I couldn't see how it would be possible to get the required college. I was old enough now to recognize the real challenges I faced if I was to realize my passion. Okay there it is. Well, let's get on with it.

It was 1946 and I thought I would be attending Broadway High School as a Freshman. But some folk in authority decided that Broadway should be turned into an adult technical school that provided a high school diploma and college prep courses, for the returning veteran, who had left high school in a moment of patriotism, and joined the armed forces. The school was renamed "Edison Technical School", offering high school grades and some first year college courses, providing a path toward college entrance and a degree for these deserving souls.

I met my first 'girl-friend', a trim little blonde by the name of Beverly Barron, while attending E.S. Meany Jr. High for my Freshman year and then it was on to Garfield High School for Sophomore, Junior and Senior years. It was at Garfield where my love, and participation, in jazz was born. I owe many thanks to the help received from a fellow classmate, Quincy Jones. We'll get to that in a bit.

Beverly Baron

A neighbor, two houses down the street was Tom Roselli. He became my best Buddy. We shared many experiences, some good...some not so good, but all memorable. One of our early efforts was a 'dance'. It required cleaning up a basement at my house, waxing the cement floor, moving record player and speaker downstairs and figuring provisions. Hey! We were fourteen and it was cokes and chips.

The party did well but one of the lads brought some wine. And then the party got noisy...the police came, the kids ran. It was my house, I couldn't run, and Tom was *resting*. The police thought the beverage was tainted and took Tom to the hospital to have his stomach pumped. Maybe it was to teach him a lesson. Police were different then.

## THE HIGH SCHOOL YEARS

A couple of things were eventful, romance and the military. Let's start with romance. Her name was Anita Dykeman and we met in the darkroom of a photography class. She was my first real love. This was different. This wasn't family love, sibling love, or the like, but something else. Our time together was special. We could just 'be together', not a lot of conversation and then speak for hours on the telephone. She taught me compassion and patience. I honored her all of our two years together. A beautiful memory now, and still friends to this day.

**Anita Dykeman**

My Mother didn't have a car. When I turned sixteen Anita's mother helped me get my Driver's License. Anita's father, Captain Dykeman was a retired Merchant Marine Captain, "All oceans, all tonnage" rated. Their home was on Hamlin Street, near the Seattle Yacht Club. He skippered a large private yacht in his semi-retirement years and would be gone for periods of time. I

22

enjoyed his company when he was home. He had many a tale covering the period of the Atlantic battle with the German submarine activity. Not too long later I was training on submarines. We talked about that and my serving in the Navy Reserve to earn a G.I. Bill to afford college and go to flight school. Anita was working part time as a waitress at Frederick & Nelson's Tea Room, in downtown Seattle.

Before I acquired my first car Anita could use the family Chrysler for our date. Rather than be 'dropped off' at my home I would go home with her for some 'cuddle and lickey-face' and then take a cab home to Capitol Hill. Farwest Cab Company had the first radio-dispatched service in Seattle. When the same cab picked me up twice in a row the driver and I became sorta friends. Jack Waterman, Cab No. 63 was the owner-driver. One night he asked if I wanted to ride along downtown...the night life is a different place in Seattle. I learned about the "Black & Tan", the "513 Club" and a couple other after-hour jazz clubs. (I looked older for my age due to a receding hair line caused by brain surgery.) It was an early education.

My sister's new husband, Henry King Love helped me buy my first car. It was a 1930 Buick Special sedan. The back seat was large enough to hold a dance. It didn't have a heater so it was best to remember to bring a blanket, especially ski trips to Snoqualmie Pass. I learned to love Classic Cars and had the good fortune to own a couple.

Roselli heard that the Sea Scouts had acquired a new boat and wouldn't it be fun to cruise the San Juans', and so forth. We attended our first Sea Scout meeting but it was too late for us. One of us said, "Well how about the Navy Reserve, they have a lot of boats.". Truthfully I can't remember which one of us asked the question, but we decided to do it.

At age seventeen, with a parent's permission, one could join the Navy or the Naval Reserve. I had a hard sell. The war had just ended four years prior and was fresh in my Mother's memory. It was difficult but I eventually prevailed. She signed.

Tom's job was easier. His older brother had joined the Navy and had nothing but good things to say about it. Tom's Dad thought it would be good for him.

With all of the paperwork out of the way we were sworn in to the United States Navy. I don't think either of us fully realized that we were, in fact, making a six-year military commitment. But, there you have it. (One should always read the fine print when signing anything.)

The Reserve program at that time in Seattle, offered destroyers or submarines. The surface contingent trained aboard a Destroyer-Escort and the submersibles aboard a Gato Class, Fleet-type boat of World War II vintage, called the USS Puffer. Both of these vessels were moored at the new Naval Reserve Armory located at the south end of Lake Union. (Kurtzer had been forced to move to another location on the south-west side of the lake.)

It was the adult world of performance, respect and accomplishment, plus a whole lot of fun in the process. Best of all, we were treated as adults!

Our annual ACDUTRA (pronounced: "act-due-tray") two-week Active Duty Reserve Training was performed at Hunters Point Naval Station in San Francisco. The base hosted a Sub School as part of its activities. The first week would be in class and simulator training then the second week, aboard a Fleet-Type submarine cruising out into the Pacific Ocean, in this case, the USS Sterlet. The sub had just completed a movie, starring William Holden and William Bendix called "Submarine Command". The crew looked like a bunch of 'recruits' in their brand-new dungarees, having sold their *salty* ones to the movie crew. We served a week with that crew enjoying many lurid tales of their time in "moviedom". The following year, another two week ACDUTRA, at Hunter's Point, this time included a week aboard the USS Baya. She was also a Gato Class Fleet-Type boat. (Submarines are always referred to as '*boats*'.)

The experience of submersing didn't even come close to the opposite experience of flight.

Just typing a few lines on a page doesn't tell the story. I really can't say enough good things about my military experiences. I was given many opportunities, including acquiring my boyhood aspiring goal of becoming a fighter pilot.

Entering the service at age seventeen was the best thing I ever did. I was taught discipline, respect for others as well as for myself. The training made it easy to accomplish practical goals, especially if done in *"The Navy Way"*. Best of all was being treated as an adult. (I think I already said that.)

It was along those lines that some of the things about high school bothered me. A lot of childishness was one. It may have showed because I wasn't ever asked to join the "boy's fraternity club". I bootlegged beer to them but wasn't asked to join. (Years later I asked a friend, who had been part of "the club", why I wasn't ever asked to join. He told me that they thought I wouldn't put up with the initiation for one thing.)

At age sixteen I applied for and received my FAA Student Pilot's Certificate. I also obtained a FAA

Medical Certificate. I had started taking flying lessons in Kurtzer's seaplanes. It was good seeing Bud again.

I could only afford thirty minutes of 'dual instruction' at a time. Bud told me that land-planes were a lot cheaper, by the hour, than seaplanes. He told me to go out to Lake Air Park and look up a friend of his, one Rudy Parpart. He owned a PT-19.

Lake Air Park was located at the east end of the Mercer Island bridge on Lake Washington. I met Rudy and he introduced me to other airplane owners based there. I traded 'washing airplanes' for flight time.

Most of my flight time was in Rudy's PT-19 and a Ryan PT-22, which was my favorite. I had seen a movie with the Army Air Corps showing extensive scenes with the Ryan PT-22. That airplane was their current trainer. It made me feel like the Cadet I wanted to become. Unfortunately, none of the owner-pilots were FAA Certified Flight Instructors, so I couldn't be turned loose to solo. Between the seaplanes and land-planes I had logged close to twenty hours. All 'dual', no solo flight time. (More about that later.)

At Garfield High School we had three lunch periods. I would always arrange to have all three. One day, during my junior year, I was up in the music room playing the piano for my own enjoyment. (I had music class right after the last lunch and would often go up to the classroom and play during the lunch periods.) One day I was playing a Bach Two-Part Invention, when I finished I heard the sound of one person clapping. I turned to find Quincy Jones sitting over in the corner of the room. He was the person clapping.

He said, "Man, I didn't know you could play like that."

26

I replied, "Thanks, but I would like to play your kinda music, Quincy."

"Hey, if you can play Bach, you can sure as hell play Bop!" was his reply. He proceeded to teach me two tunes; a Blues in 'C' called "Red Top" and "Lullaby In Rhythm". It was the beginning of a beautiful relationship. We're still friends to this day. I became his piano player for the better part of a year. The first time that I received money for playing music was at a black club called the "Washington Social Club", located upstairs in a building on the corner of 23$^{rd}$ and East Madison. That night I was not only the only *'fay* in the band, I was the only *'fay* in the house. Quincy was progressing at a very rapid pace; I couldn't keep up and was eventually replaced by Johnny Morrison.

There was a some-time singer in the band called Neddie Valentine. She was very attractive. I think every member in the band had dated her. I finally got the courage to ask her out. She said, "I suppose you want to take me to a drive-in movie."

I told her that I would take her wherever she wanted to go.. As it turned out, we did go to the Duwamish Drive-In where "Young Man With A Horn" was playing. We both wanted to see that picture. After the movie I took her to the XXX Drive-In on Olive Way, where all of the kids hung out. I then took her home. When it became apparent where I was headed she started to cry. When asked, she said that I wouldn't understand. She told me to ask her out again and she would show me a good time. We went together for a while. (We ran into each other in Southern California some years later.)

I then joined a band called the Norm Calvo Quintet. Norm was well connected in the Jewish community and I think we played for every Bar Mitzvah and Jewish wedding in Seattle during that period. It paid at least five dollars a man and all the booze we could steal…anyway at least a bottle apiece. We played a lot of gigs. I think that it really seasoned me as an accompanist and helped in my infrequent solo choruses since the quintet hosted both a sax and trumpet player that did most of the soloing.

In fact, nothing used to piss me off more…the horn player would do his thing and then look down asking me, "Hey, wanna piece of this?" --would come his droll inquiry. (What'd he think I'd been doing?) And, not to mention, the damn soloists got all the girls. Not unlike the football quarterback. The poor piano player was just like a line-man holding back the masses.

During Christmas break I got a part-time job at the Bon Marche as an "escalator guard", helping little old ladies off and on the moving stairs. Right in front was an island-counter displaying jewelry. Manning this island was a striking blonde that appeared to be in my zone. Her name was Donna Shrewsbury and she was Roosevelt High School, Class of '50. I made my move and for once it moved on at a nice comfortable pace. Her father had died not long before. Her mother had their house up for sale and they would be moving down to the Bay area where she would soon assume the position of Head Nurse at the Oakland Army Hospital. I would be able to spend time with Donna when I did my summer active duty at Hunter's Point, in the Bay area.

Donna was quite attractive in a blonde, Scandinavian way, and was filling the gap left behind when Anita had found the love of her life. Things were working out for me.

**Donna Shrewsbury –and Ryan PT-22**

The Navy offered many opportunities to Enlisted men. For example, they were currently encouraging applications for taking the Entrance Examination to the Naval Academy at Annapolis. My Leading Chief encouraged me to apply. I did and was scheduled to take the test in the fall, allowing about three months to prepare. I was sent a 'home study' course. (If I had been a Congressional applicant I would have been sent to a prep school for six months just to take the test.)

This was a very busy time in my life. I was attending school and then going to work at Harborview Hospital from three to eleven and playing music on the weekend, and attempting to have some sort of courtship with Donna. Life, at the moment, was stretched pretty thin.

I was having trouble paying for school, a Step-Father that wanted me to 'forget all this school crap' and go get a real job.

Becoming more familiar with the Reserve programs I learned that serving two years Active Duty could earn me the G.I. Bill benefits that would pay for college and meet the new requirements for military flight training. I went in on a non-drill day to discuss it with my Leading Chief.

I asked him, "How do I go on Active Duty?"

He was up from behind his desk in a flash, walking me down the hall with his arm around my shoulders and I truly believe that I was processed in a matter of minutes. It seems that the Korean conflict had just started, and the Navy needed men.

After the paperwork was complete he told me that I'd have to wait for the results of the Academy exam before orders would be issued.

Soon the exam was over and the results posted. I had failed one of the four batteries.

I met a chap, Ric Novak, a Reservist from Alaska, currently serving as a Station Keeper at NAS Seattle (Sand Point) when he reported with some others to take the exam. He would play a significant part in my life to come. He told me a few years later that he had passed the test but wanted to fly and didn't want to wait four years to do so. He had put in for the NavCad program.

With all of that out of the way, my orders to Boot Camp in San Diego were activated. I was handed my orders and a train ticket, including meals, and included a compartment. Wow! --the Navy was treating me pretty good!

Much to my surprise, a Reservist going on active duty *re-took* the General Classification Test (GCT). That test determined one's total Military Occupational Specialty (MOS) eligibility. I damn near four-oh'd the thing. Keep in mind, I had recently taken, probably the

30

hardest test devised by mankind; the U.S. Naval Academy Entrance Exam, plus I had just come out of an intense academic school environment, and probably more importantly, by this time I knew the importance of the GCT test.

Since I hadn't completed the requirements for Submarine Qualification, I was exposed to "the needs of the service". The Korean War was in full swing and the Navy didn't need more submariners but they sure as hell needed Hospital Corpsmen. Because of my civilian work experience at Harborview Hospital, I was given orders to Naval Hospital Corps School, in San Diego. But first the interview.

(It would have been great if I had completed Submarine Qualification. I would be entitled to wear *Submarine Dolphins*, a very distinctive uniform badge, similar to pilot's wings. i would have probably been the only Marine Corps Officer wearing Dolphins along with Wings Of Gold. I have since seen a Navy Pilot with Wings and Dolphins, and a Marine Pilot with the Army Combat Infantry Badge, but never Dolphins on a Marine.)

During my military occupation selection interview my high GCT score opened up many opportunities. Among them was "NavCad". The acronym stood for "Naval Aviation Cadet". I asked, "Is this flight training, Sir?"

The interviewing officer answered in the affirmative but pointed out that if accepted I would have a full four-year commitment. My current commitment was only two years Active and four years Reserve.

NROTC was also on that list. I probably should have opted for that one since the Navy would have sent me right back up to the University of Washington and paid for my college degree. Then I would be able to apply for flight training.

Nope. I didn't want to wait. I couldn't believe that this was happening! I had wanted Active Duty to earn G.I. Bill college expenses to meet the school requirements for flight training **and there I was**, staring at the NavCad Program, right there in front of me. There really is a God and *she* sure has a sense of humor!

I asked the interviewing officer, "Do you have a pen, Sir, and where do I sign?" I didn't mind the four-year commitment. He told me that it could take up to a year for the NavCad processing and in the meantime I would complete my Recruit training and then expect orders to Hospital Corp School.

# FIVE    MILITARY ACTIVE DUTY

**B**oot camp was a 'walk in the park' for me. To begin with our boot-class D.I. (Drill Instructor) was a Navy Chief and we were his last class before his retirement. He assembled the class and told us that this boot training could be easy or hard. He would prefer it to be easy, so what we had to do was just get it done without any drama. Help any slackers, take care of any problem-folk and don't let any problems come to his attention or things would get 'hard'. The Chief was patient and helped us with the academic side of the training, easy with the physical side and since we were all Reservists with some military experience he left out the bad parts. We only had one "problem child" that we had to deal with, but after some *counseling* he straightened up. It never came to the Chief's attention.

When I was in high school my Mother had encouraged me to take a typing class. I was a tad reluctant until she pointed out that the majority of the students would be female. As it turned out I really enjoyed the class and ended up taking two semesters. So, of course, I ended up the Company Clerk. It got me out of a lot of troop and stomp and other unpleasant assignments like Mess Cooking. Like I said, --a walk in the park.

One of my high school friends, Sarge Allen (His real name; Thomas Sargent Allen) was also in the service. He had joined the Marine Corps and was attending *their* training process's on the other side of San Diego…a totally different experience. (I don't even want to think what problems his name caused with his Marine D.I.'s!)

Close to a year later we would be enjoying Laguna Beach's lovelies' for a couple of months.

Soon it was over and I reported to the San Diego Naval Hospital to start my Hospital Corps training. I was surprised to learn all of the things a Navy Hospital Corpsman was allowed and trained to do, like invasive procedures, normally reserved for at least a Registered Nurse, or higher, in the civilian sector. It was excellent training.

During the school period, my NavCad application paperwork was catching up with me. The first step was the 2CX Two-Year College Equivalency Examination. I passed it.

Oops, I was informed that the requirement had been changed from the 2CX test to the GED Col Level 1 Test. Since this was supposedly an easier test, I probably took it with the wrong attitude and anyway, failed the English portion of the four-battery examination.

I could not believe that I had been that stupid. All was not lost, I was informed that I could repeat that failed one battery test after a six month waiting period. I wouldn't have expected that much latitude.

The six months went by quickly, I had spent time with the English Study Guide and felt ready. I sharpened up, stayed alert, and passed. Whew!

*This fixation and passion that I had found in aviation was my center core. This is what I've wanted since I was seven. Don't screw with it, McEniry! Get, and keep, your head out of your ass! --OVER!*

I met two fellow-musicians at Corps School, who would become life-long friends. They were Dennis Jack (Dee Jay) Lynch, tenor sax, and Chuck (Hambone)

Hamilton, trombone. I performed with DJ a couple of times. I don't remember ever playing with Hambone.

D.J. and I ended up jointly owning a 1932 LaSalle drop-head coupe with a body by Fisher. It had a rumble seat and a golf-bag door on the right side. The heads and manifold were black porcelain-ized. It was a beautiful car, my second 'Classic'. The top needed replacing and the shop where we decided to have it done was operated by a neat middle-aged couple. He designed the top so it could be retracted part way, leaving the seats open. DJ and I were invited for, I think it was Thanksgiving or Easter Dinner...anyway some special weekend. We dressed sorta "30's era" to honor the occasion. (Jackets with vest and school-tie.) The rumble seat was still a lot of fun. We called her "The Countess".

We weren't ever able to clear the title on the car and eventually lost her. We both felt that we had gotten our money's worth out of her though. She made me feel like Gatsby!

Upon graduation from Hospital Corps School Hambone drew San Francisco for a duty station while D.J. and I got assigned to the Corona Naval Hospital, located near Riverside California. It was a beautiful setting having once been a very private, very exclusive resort. The Navy had taken it over during World War Two.

Some of our Hospital Corps classmates pitched in and bought us a case of thirty-weight oil for the hundred mile drive from San Diego up to Corona. We had enough left over for many weekend trips down to Laguna Beach and back. It didn't take long to use it all.

I learned that my friend Sarge Allen was stationed at Camp Pendleton and we arranged to meet in Laguna. After the second weekend Sarge and his friend

35

George Sterk, DJ and I decided to rent a house. With the four of us kicking-in it was affordable. Weekend activity in Laguna Beach was something to write home about. We didn't have time to do that with all the pollinating required that was taking up all of our time. The lovely little 'beach bunnies' just loved "The Countess" and wanted to ride in her rumble seat...naturally, we prevailed. Those were wonderful days.

While stationed at Corona Naval Hospital, working 'Officer's Country' at my job as Corpsman, I encountered a Navy Lieutenant-'aviator' in for ulcers. I told him that I was in the process of applying for NavCad. We spent a lot of time talking about the program since he had been through the program about a year and a half prior. What really thrilled me was his flying the Grumman F6F Hellcat in 'advance'. He 'carrier-qualified' in it as well. (After getting his "Wings Of Gold" he transitioned into jets, flying F9F Panthers.) The Hellcat was the Navy's primary fighter during War2. I used to have pictures of that bird on my wall, as a kid, during the war. He loved that airplane and would describe, in detail, flying it. He cautioned me to the fact that there is about an eighteen to twenty per cent drop or wash-out in a class of thirty. —study, learn and pay close attention to everything. He reminded me that being 'former enlisted' like I was would be a help. (I forget his name...other than "Sir", but he was a real help. When I did get to Pensacola I remembered our conversations and it gave me a real 'leg-up'.)

Meanwhile, back at the beach, I was getting tired of 'playing the field' with the beach-bunnies. I was seeking something a little more permanent and decided to venture north to see Donna Shrewsbury, up in Berkeley I managed a five-day basket-leave. (It is essentially a three-day Pass with provision for taking *Annual-Leave-Time,* day or days, if I didn't make it back in the three-day extended Pass.) I decided to hitchhike up to the Bay Area. In those early 50's hitch-hiking in uniform worked pretty well. People were a lot more trusting than today.

−well sorta. Read on.

I was picked up by a bunch of soldiers, from some Army base nearby, when hitch-hiking through Santa Barbara. I should have become suspicious when they told me to sit in front. (Three of them were in the back seat.)

They turned off Highway 101 and the next thing I was hit on the back of my head. The blow didn't knock me out and I turned, grabbing the weapon used (a jack handle). I immediately slashed at the nearest soldier, opening a long cut on his cheek. The driver stopped the car and I threatened him. Nobody else wanted anymore. I got out of the car and smashed the windshield with the jack handle. The driver had the gall to ask for it back, so I threw it on the floor of the front seat and they sped off.

Shortly after, a Police car came by. I flagged him down and told him what happened. I said that one soldier would be requiring medical attention and the windshield condition would make them fairly easy to spot. The Policeman drove me back out to Highway 101. The rest of the trip went okay.

My big Saturday night with Donna turned out to be a real disappointment. She had a 'Sorority-Fraternity' date thing *"she just couldn't break"*. Okay, WTFOver.

Her Mother, Shoes, and I went out to dinner. I've always gotten on well with Shoes and our medical commonality had a bit to do with it as well. I enjoyed her company.

We shared "hospital jokes". Her joke was the nurse that returned to the Nurse's Station, reached in her rolled-up hair for her pen....extracted a rectal thermometer and exclaimed, "Oh dear, some asshole has my pen!"

(Waiting for the applause to subside, I ventured forth with my contribution: )

The Charge Nurse of the Officer's Ward at the Naval Hospital was passing the Admiral's room and stopped short, going in to the room, saying, "Just what's going on in here?"

The Admiral responded, "Haven't you ever seen a patient getting their temperature taken?"

"Yes, many a time, but never before with a daffodil!"

(What? –the agony of silence. Oh well, I better keep my day job.)

In the meantime, the NavCad selection process was grinding on. I received orders to report to MCAS El Toro for a Flight Physical and Officer Selection Board. The Marine air base was located about half way between Corona and Laguna Beach. I drove The Countess down for the appointment. Driving on to the base, past the Flight Line I could see the Banshee's and Grumman Panthers that were the hot machines of the time. (I would be out here again in about two years assigned to a squadron flying the Grumman F9F-5 Panther.)

The Flight Physical included being strapped into a chair that was mounted on frame-work in such a manner as to allow the chair to be tumbled, rotated in any and all axis to test spatial disorientation. It was quite an introduction to vertigo. The physical itself, other than the usual 'turn your head and cough', not to mention the 'just drop 'em and bend over', --paid particular attention to eyes, the eye examination was a far cry from what I remembered during my grade school days. However, the eye exercises that I practiced from that period worked because I passed the eye test with flying colors.

I was shown to the chow hall by a corpsman. He was curious about Corona Naval Hospital…. was it really some kind of mental-care re-hab, a resort? What was it like? I lied a lot but he seemed to enjoy it.

After chow I had to appear before a Selection Board that consisted of five Marine Officer-Naval Aviators. They were seated comfortably in a semi-circle while I stood at ram-rod attention and parried questions that were fired at me from all sides; one coming close on the heel of the last.

This went fairly well until one question was asked pertaining to my early interest in aviation.

My reply was that my boyhood hero had been Baron Manfred von Richtofen. I was asked why it wasn't the American, Eddie Rickenbacker.

I quickly replied. "Rickenbacker was a racecar driver and 'Soldier of Fortune' whereas Richtofen was a graduate of the Prussian Officer School and a professional soldier."

It got quiet for a moment and the officers looked at each other, then I was dismissed.

My lunch-mate Corpsman told me that he had heard the officers' talking in a favorable manner and thought I had passed. I thanked him profusely and added that I had told him a fib about Corona…we sailors didn't really eat our meals off of linen tablecloths.

It looked like I'd made the grade. I wouldn't be notified officially for another week or so.

I would soon be on my way to NAS Pensacola, home of the Naval Aviation Training Command.

**M**y twenty-first birthday was celebrated aboard a DC-3 flying from San Diego to New Orleans. When I told the stewardess it was my twenty-first birthday, she brought me a couple of drinks. I then repeated that story, with the same reward coming again, aboard an almost empty Lockheed Lodestar out of New Orleans, landing in Pensacola Florida. NAS Pensacola was the home of the Naval Aviation Training Command. *–and here I was.*

I got off the Lodestar and walked into the terminal and made my way over to where the baggage would be brought in from the plane. I was in my 'Enlisted Blues', a fairly heavy wool uniform, and was beginning to get uncomfortable from the heat and humidity. (Military regulations state "--when checking-in to a new command, dress-code is *Dress Uniform of last command*.") The airplane hadn't been very full, just five other passengers, so the wait for the baggage didn't take too long.

I soon had my sea-bag and decided to take a cab into downtown. I wanted to look over this Navy-Town of "*Penis-cola*", with its signs here and there proclaiming "Dogs And Sailors Keep Off The Lawn". Good, bad or indifferent, it would be my home for a year or so. Wandering around town with a sea-bag over my shoulder wasn't such a great idea, the three or four drinks had worn off and the heat and humidity…even though it was the end of April, was getting to me. I figured I might as well go on out to the base.

The town people were friendly enough and when asked, directed me to a bus-stop where I could catch a bus out to the base. One came along shortly, I boarded, paid my fare and started 'scootching' my sea-bag to the back of the bus. I found a seat near a window and was looking around when I noticed some commotion up at the front of the bus. It didn't take long for me to realize the driver was yelling something at me. WTF! It seems that I was to move back up to the front of the bus, that the back of the bus was for 'colored'.

Welcome to the South, White-boy. Racial equality had not come to Florida yet. My upbringing and early exposure to the Negro community, through school and music, hadn't shown me "color". I didn't see color. I still don't see color. This was a new experience. I don't think I much cared for it.

Arriving at NAS Pensacola I turned in my orders, was directed over to an 'Incoming Barracks', informed of chow time and told that my processing would start in the morning.

I met my first, soon to become a life-long buddy, when I returned from chow. I noticed that he had, what had to be, a music case with his luggage. I approached him about the case and we struck up a conversation. His name was Ben King, from Chicago, and a saxophone player. We talked about Chicago jazz, "The Deuces", "Harry-the-Hipster Gibson" and other musicians. Seattle had Ray Charles who would soon rise to stardom, and Quincy Jones. –but it wasn't Chicago.

Ben was tall, one could say 'skinny', well-spoken and like myself, had been a Reservist for some time. He was interested in aviation but hadn't fallen into the passion pool like I had. Aviation was just one of many things that were of interest to him. It would bite him when he got to shoot at things and drop bombs…. all the good stuff. But that was almost a year away.

We exchanged stories of how we got here. Ben told me that he had graduated High School in 1950 and was looking forward to earning some money during the summer following, to earn college money. He had received a scholarship to University of Chicago which he was going to attend while living at home. Summer of 1950 was pretty scarce for teenagers and he and his friends had heard about a pretty sweet deal at the nearby local Naval Air Station at Glenview, a suburb of Chicago. If they joined the Naval Reserve, went through an eight-week boot camp they would be paid $250. In 1950, to a teenager, it was all the money in town. He, and some of his buddies, took the oath on Saturday, June 24th, 1950. No one really thought that they were committing to serving for six years.

The very next day North Korea invaded South Korea and the "Korean War" began.

(As it turned out few Reserve Units were "called up" during the Korean War. A far cry from the current situation in Afghanistan, and Iraq. There was a picture in the news of a National Guardsman driving a truck in Iraq, holding up a sign in the window, *"One Weekend a Month, MY ASS!")*

Ben and I were assigned to Class 19-53. (The nineteenth Naval Aviation Cadet Class of 1953.) The first day was a short examination and educational resume to determine military knowledge. Uniforms were issued and a welcoming class lecture, delivered by our Battalion Commanding Officer, Major Squires.

The make-up of our class consisted of lads fresh from college, some enlisted Reservists, English Midshipmen and French Cadets…. about thirty-five all told. Our Battalion Commander stressed the fact that we were less than one percent, of the ten percent military-age male's eligible, health-wise, to be accepted into the flight program. (It wasn't until 1974 that females would be accepted into Navy Flight Training.) We were told that to have made it this far makes us exceptional, --one in ten thousand. We were not to gloat but to live up to the status of earning and wearing "Wings Of Gold". That was what we were here for. The Navy was investing a great deal of money in our training. Looking out over the class Major Squires paused and then went on to say that five or six members of this class would not complete Pre-Flight, and some more would not make it through the whole eighteen-month program.

"Look around you...think about it. Know that this is what you want to do." He finished by adding the chilling news, "NAVCADs who fail to successfully complete flight training are contractually obligated to enter 'fleet service' as undesignated enlisted personnel".

"Those of you who successfully complete this program will, in all probability, remember this as the best period of your life!"

Next event brought a week-long Speed Reading Course. Flight training was expensive for the Navy. A lot of new material must be absorbed in a relatively short time. The Speed-Reading Course would have been quite expensive in the civilian sector. It was a smart move on the Navy's part.

Pre-Flight consisted of class studies in Aerology, (the "mystery hour") Flight Dynamics, Navigation, North American AT-6/SNJ Aircraft Systems and military courses. And yes, there was a lot of physical fitness included, and, of course, 'guidance' from our Marine Drill Instructors.

One of the military classes was 'aircraft identification' from silhouettes. I did pretty well in that class but Ben King was exceptional. His mother had been an Air Raid Warden in Chicago during War2 and Ben had all the flash cards nailed. A clerk would say, "Ready...Now", and then flash, for a mille-second, a given airplane. Near the end of the class there would always be a nude slide slipped into the slide machine. This was to keep us awake and attentive. It worked.

We had Marine Drill Instructors as part of our 'military indoctrination'. These were the real thing. They were to help us learn the military way and would work with us until we got it right. Sometimes it took some 'special counseling'. There's nothing quite like being on the wrong side of a pissed-off Marine Sergeant Drill Instructor, –about in the same category as the pleasures of a root-canal, or colonoscopy.

Our PT Instructor was Lt. Bustard. Lt. Bustard was a Navy full-lieutenant (equivalent to a Marine or Army captain) and a fighter-pilot. He had been shot down over enemy territory during the Korean conflict. He *ran* some twenty miles, evading enemy troops who were looking for him. Needless to say he was a firm believer in physical fitness. He was our Physical Fitness Officer during Pre-Flight. Oh yes, we did run. And then we ran some more. (The second letter in his last name changed frequently.)

Smitty, one of our lads, was appointed Cadet Commander of our Class. He broke his leg while playing soccer with the French and English Cadets that grew up playing that game.... their national sport. Hello!

(It's interesting to see that soccer is gaining in popularity in our country these days. It must be

45

remembered that soccer is the 'baseball & football' all-in one throughout most European and Latin American countries…. like I said, their national sport.)

Ben King was appointed in his place when Smitty was taken to the hospital. Ben always insisted that it was only because of his class grades. He was loath to accept the fact that it was his charm and military-bearing that awarded him the honor. (Due to his thin build he was frequently admonished for his military bearing.) Whatever the reason, he made a good class officer. During parades he marched at the head of the Class-platoon, officer's sword in hand, and calling out the 'marching' orders as applicable. He knew his stuff. (Smitty had screwed up a couple of times, so us folk in the ranks, knew when it was done right. –you can't fool the troops.)

One such time, on passing the Reviewing Stand, Ben called out, "Eyes right!" and the cadet officers drew their swords to render the "sword salute". Joe Dill, immediately behind Ben, caught his thumb on a belt loop as he drew…lost his grip on the sword, causing it to do a complete somersault in the air. It tumbled high then returning, slashed the back of Ben's shirt and also bloodied his back. Somehow Joe recovered and caught it.

*Major Squires told Ben later that the Admiral, who was sitting in the Reviewing Stand with him, turned and said, "Jesus Major, what in the hell was that fancy maneuver? I've never seen anything like it!"*

Hey! --it's the old- *"Don't-Run-With-Scissors!"*-story. The pointy end of Joe Dill's sword did draw blood on Ben's back as it totally trashed the shirt.

Another Joe Dill story.

Joe dill was a real good ol' 'country boy' from some little town in Texas. He received his home-town newspaper every week. Back during the Korean War, the home-town papers would have a column of "Hometown boys in The Service". Well some wags in our class snuck into the Battalion Commander's office and typed out a "News Release" on official stationery, embossed with the Navy Seal, placing it in the "Out-going Mail" box. In a few weeks Dill received his newspaper and there it was, in blazing headlines, *"JOSEPH DILL PROMOTED TO CAPTAIN OF THE HEAD"*.

We could only imagine how proud his mother must have been.

The NavCads had their own club called ACRAC, for 'Aviation Cadet Recreational Club'. It served beer and soft drinks and had a dance floor and a piano. Ben and I got involved with some other cadet musicians to see what we could put together. When it was still in the planning stages I was over at the club by myself, a mid-week night, playing some blues. Earlier that day at Mail Call I had received a Wedding Announcement from my first real love, Anita Dykeman. As I was playing, out of the corner of my eye, I noticed a guy carrying a stand-up bass, tuning it as he carried it across the darkened dance floor. When he got to the piano he "came in, on-time, on-pitch" nailing the key and the top of the twelve-bar blues. This dude knew just what the hell he was doing. (Maybe *"cat"* would be a better word for the era.) We didn't say anything, just played. He was damn good. We had to break early since it was a school night. We introduced ourselves; he was Jack Sutter from Chicago. I couldn't wait to get back to the room and tell Ben I had found us a bass player.

"Sutter? --you must be kidding. I knew him at the University of Chicago, and one of his Dads owned the "Sutter Brothers Ball Room", Ben told me. (Wow! The world gets smaller every day, but as Steven Wright would say, "I'd hate to have to paint it.".)

Later, when he was playing in our combo he told us some lurid stories about the 'ball room'. He'd dance with the old ladies for tips and loved telling tales about getting blow-jobs behind a curtain by some elderly widow or another. That was a typical 'Jack Sutter' story.

Our jazz quintet, (trumpet, sax, piano, bass and drums, augmented at times with a trombone) played at some Friday and Saturday night dances at the ACRAC. It was productive…lots of girls and some good playing.

There was an abundance of Southern Belles in the area and many would attend the dances at our club. A Naval Officer was considered a "good catch" but Officer rank was over a year away. A cadet had to stay single for the eighteen-month training period or if caught 'married', was washed out. This was long before "the pill" and there were a few *"oh damn's"*, or, *"—are you sure?"*…along the way. I wanted to fly so decided to keep my pants up and zipped.

Pre-Flight is known for some significant 'events' that stood out beyond the norm. The military indoctrination, was difficult for some. A few of us were Reservists and had experienced Boot Camp, so the military part was easy for us. But we're talking about *'events'*. The first eye-opening 'event' was the "Step Test". This was one of the first things at the beginning of Pre-Flight.

Now pay attention, Jocks, here's one for you. –try this. A fifteen-eighteen inch or so, high step, you're stepping up then down at 180 steps per-minute cadence for five minutes. Let me tell you, people were throwing up, passing out and, or simply falling out. Near the end of Pre-Flight we had to do it again in order to graduate. We were in much better shape then and most passed without any problem. Our eighteen weeks of Pre-Flight had beefed us up pretty good. As usual, there would be a couple of guys that would have to take it again, you had to pass or wash out.

The next 'event', under discussion, is the "Dilbert Dunker".

Swimming was emphasized. Navy pilots operate off aircraft carriers…on the water…and sometimes airplanes crash into the water and the Navy has a lot of money invested in the airplane pilot so he had better be able to return and fly again. That said, swimming was emphasized.

My buddy Ben King was <u>not</u> a swimmer. He had to take an extra 'Sub-Swim' course   Lt. Bustard was his instructor and Ben had nothing but nice things to say about him.   In fact he told me a story to illustrate that fact.

*He, and some of the lads were having way too much fun downtown, dancing on tables and raising general hell. The Shore Patrol arrived and five or six cadets, including Ben himself, were picked up and thrown into the Paddy-Wagon. The SP's went back to get some more and Lt. Bustard, dressed in mufti, had observed the activity so when the SP went to fetch more,  he opened the back-door of the Paddy Wagon and said,  "Run Cadets…Run!"*

Ben did well enough in 'Sub-Swim' to qualify for his AAA Red Cross Life-Saving Qualification that we all earned by completing the requirements.  He was pretty proud of that accomplishment!

Okay, but getting back to the "Dilbert Dunker". This was a training device consisting of an SNJ cockpit mounted on forty-five degree rails, ending in the deep end of a swimming pool. Most of us hadn't even been in the SNJ cockpit yet. A student would be strapped in, seat belt fastened, and head-phone cords connected…then the cockpit was released, hurtling down the rail, splashing into the water and promptly tipping over, as it was hinged at the bottom of the firewall of the cockpit. Now upside down in the water, the student had to unfasten his seatbelt, unhook head-phone and 'mic' cords, swim <u>down</u> to clear the up-turned cockpit and then rise to the surface. It can be very disorienting. One must learn to remain cool and follow the bubbles that are always rising to the surface. It could be dreaded or fun, but it was realistic training for a real life situation. There were divers standing by if a student went the wrong way or got tangled up in belts or cords.

The Navy had learned that a fighter-plane, when ditched, skips a couple of times then stops, tipping up and over, turning upside down. The Dilbert Dunker is not just a training device, it's <u>life-saving</u> training device.

Then there was "The Tower". It was pretty high, we were told that it was about the same height as from a carrier deck to the water. Anyway it looked and felt quite high. You had to jump, with your legs crossed, (protecting future generations), from that tower. Most didn't have a problem but there were a few where height was a major issue. Ben told me that when he was attending 'Sub-Swim' there were students, officers or cadets, that would climb the tower, stand for a while and climb back down. It was another one of those 'events' that had to be marked off as completed. (When Ben and I were reminiscing he said there might be some still standing on the top of that tower.)

50

The main base at NAS Pensacola (where we were undergoing Pre-Flight Training) was also the home of the Naval Aviation Cadet Choir. The choir had national recognition, having appeared on the Ed Sullivan Show. I heard rumors they would be going to Seattle for Sea Fair so decided to audition. It would be a free trip home. Luck was on my side and I was accepted.

It was a wonderful experience. Everywhere the choir went by bus or airplane we would be singing. What fun. We did Seattle, Minneapolis, New Orleans and a couple of others that I can't remember. (–big surprise, memory is a real challenge in our later years, be nice, I'm old now.)

The sixteen weeks of Pre-Flight over, and most of the 'chicken-shit' behind us. We've been issued our flight gear and we're on our way to NAAS Whiting, an auxiliary field where we would undergo our initial *actual* flight training. (By the way, included in our issue of flight gear was the cloth helmet of WW2, I fantasized about being a replacement pilot on my way to "the Canal". We were issued the new 'hard' helmets later at Whiting Field.)

# SEVEN     FLIGHT TRAINING

Upon completion of Pre-Flight we were transferred out to NAAS Whiting Field to start our flight training. Primary A Phase was done in the Navy SNJ. (North American AT-6 Texan, Navy model SNJ.) They didn't use small airplanes like 'Piper Cubs or Stearmans'. The SNJ was equipped with the Pratt & Whitney R-1340, nine cylinder, 600 hp radial engine. She was equipped with fully retractable landing gear, flaps and variable pitch propeller. We had studied the hydraulic, electrical and fuel systems of this complex airplane in Pre-Flight but now comes the practical application. We had to be checked out in "Bail-Out" procedures; diving out of the cockpit onto a trampoline. This wasn't an easy thing, standing up in the cockpit, with parachute seat-pack strapped to our back and butts, then diving over the side. We were told it would be easier in an actual bail-out due to air-flow carrying us over the wing. We were told that if actually bailing out, just dive for the wing, you'd never hit it. I believed those words but it was an experience I hoped to avoid.

Regardless of anybody's prior flight experience a student was locked into the Navy's specific training syllabus. One of the cadets was a former crop duster and another was a lad from Texas that had flown his Howard DGA-15P, single-engine, high-wing, large cabin monoplane from his family's ranch. It was tied-down at the Pensacola civilian airport. Sometime later another buddy, by the name of Delbert Leroy Peterson, had joined our group. Del knew some history about the Howard, that the DGA-15 had won both the Thompson and Bendix Trophy's in 1935. The only airplane to win both. –he wanted to have an up-close look at it. It was a beautiful airplane and faster than the DC-3 airliners flown by most airlines of the day. Del had driven his 1950 Ford two-door to Pensacola from Minnesota. We had wheels! Del and I checked out the Howard. The big radial engine on the nose reminded me of Bud's CH-300 Bellanca in the hangar at Kurtzers'. God! –I love round power!

Fresh out of two years of college, Del had started NavCad training in Class 16-53. He was awakened one night, in his first week or so of Pre-Flight, with the loud, crashing sound of a Pratt & Whitney R-1340 engine hitting the ground right outside of his barracks first-floor window. A couple of SNJ's had collided right overhead and pieces of the 'mid-air' collision landed all around the building. There were no survivors.

Del became ill and spent a couple of weeks in the hospital. Now recovered, he had joined our class to continue his journey. (However, I will mention here that we were not going through the program as a "class", but by individual progress. As we moved through the eighteen-month program the class spread out to a degree.)

My first flight instructor was Navy Lt. Ellis. After our first hop he asked me how much flight experience I had before entering NavCad. I didn't want to lie and told him about the few legal 'dual' seaplane hops that I'd logged, plus rides and stick-time with the two War2 trainers, (PT-19 and PT-22) that I had washed and waxed in exchange for 'stick-time'. He said that it showed, but we had to do things the "Navy Way".

53

**My first Flight Instructor, Lt. Ellis**

There would be twenty training hops in this first 'A phase'. My A-19 hop was my 'check-ride' with a different instructor. He signed me off. I was released to solo. *–let me say that again.....*

### I WAS RELEASED TO <u>SOLO</u>!

Writing this I checked my Log Book to confirm the details at the time of accomplishment. I had 28.7 hours of military dual time when I soloed. Adding my civilian 'stick-time' to that total, it had taken me close to some forty hours to solo.

Let me take a moment to reflect. The Log Book showed that it was October 5th, 1953, I don't recall the hour. I had overcome, what I thought would be impossible odds, to meet the requirements of military flight training. I had joined the Navy Reserve, chosen active-duty to earn G.I. Bill college benefits in order to meet those requirements and that decision had led to the

54

path that delivered me to this momentous occasion. Hello? Thank you Lord!

Student pilots, in the civilian sector, talk about soloing in seven, eight, ten or other low-time hours. So I must have set some kinda record.

This solo was done out of a grass-covered mile-square field. The SNJ was equipped with a full swiveling, locking tail-wheel. One of the procedures was to unlock the tail-wheel after landing in order to taxi around easier. When the instructor climbed out of the airplane and told me to go ahead.... this would be my first solo. WOW!! What a day! Except for one small item. I forgot to lock the tail-wheel for take-off. It got pretty interesting when the torque of that 600 hp Pratt & Whitney engine made my take-off run a bit 'swervy'. I was hoping that the instructor wouldn't see it, but he did, and commented on it after I successfully returned to earth. The importance of this occasion defies description. As a young person growing up there are many "firsts" in one's life. Some are more significant than others. This was one of the "major" ones'.

The landing was satisfactory.... the airplane could be used again.

The current "Solo" tradition was that I got to buy the beer and someone would cut-off my necktie. That was it. More memorable occasions were in store.

Next came B Phase; Aerobatics.

It started with reviewing spins and spin recovery and then maneuvers wilder than spins. This phase was conducted with a dual-hop to illustrate a given aerobatic maneuver or maneuvers, and then two solo hops to practice what had been demonstrated. That solo time was truly *at the foot of the cross*...a righteous experience. The

55

freedom of just flying around…. paying attention to avoid other aircraft, and looking around at the country side. You've got work to do but this was a few minutes of just flying free. Okay, funs' over Let's try a barrel-roll or Loop. We also learned and practiced the chandelle, full Cuban eight, half Cuban eight and the "Immelmann Turn", a maneuver attributed to the World War I German Fighter pilot, Max Immelmann, holder of the Pour le Merit or "Blue Max". The maneuver is a loop, rolling over upright at the top. It requires a high degree of energy at a place where the aircraft is losing energy which means higher entry speed and Gee forces to complete the maneuver. This can cause 'grey-outs', then 'black-outs' followed by un-consciousness, from the blood leaving the brain and pooling in the lower torso from the "G" forces.

That is what I was dealing with. When I would lose consciousness the airplane would just continue on over the top and on down. Strangely enough, vision returns to your senses before sound. I would regain consciousness looking straight out the windshield that was filled with the earth coming straight-up at me, followed by, what seems like a half-minute later, the engine roar and high-screaming wind noise of the dive that the plane was in.

Knowing that it shouldn't be like that I discussed it with Lt. Ellis, my instructor. He told me that he'd had the same problem in his early flying career and realized he had been holding his breath as well while grunting to control blood flow. It might be my problem. Loss of oxygen and loss of blood pressure at the same time was the cause. He also suggested checking-out the centrifuge at Aviation Medicine at Mainside. They're always looking for riders and I'd learn a lot. I managed to do that

56

sometime later and I learned quite a bit and enough to raise my Gee tolerance a significant amount higher.

This was very important since my choice was fighters. I understood full well the forces dealt with during "bank and yank" or "pull-out" that I was yet to experience. But soon.

There was a terrible airplane crash; a Marine C-119 Flying Boxcar, carrying, a plane-full of Navy NROTC students, back to their home base after completing their two week ACDUTRA here at the Pensacola training command. The C-119 had just re-fueled at Whiting field, and crashed shortly after take-off. There were only five survivors from the forty-six passengers and crew...

On top of that disaster there were a few student incidents that included two fatalities at about this time. The fact that aviation could be dangerous was becoming obvious. The crash site of the Marine transport was in our flying area, easily identified by the twin tail-booms.

Ben King had studied French in school and wanted to sharpen and exercise his writing and speaking skills so shared a room at Saufley with three French cadets. His room-mates told him about a French cadet in A Phase, that when the engine-driven fuel pump on the 1340 crapped out the instructor yelled at him, "The pump, hit the pump!" (--only the front cockpit was equipped with an emergency hand pump. This was emphasized in our studies.) The student, thinking the instructor was yelling, "jump", bailed out. The instructor had to then bail as well.

Ben told me that for a Frenchman to be able to apply for this 'exchange flight training' he had to have two years of high school level English. It was pretty hard for them. There are many stories, some we'll come to as this narrative progresses.

Our quintet kinda took root during this phase of training. In retrospect I can't believe we were able to fit it in. In writing this narrative, Ben reminded me that I had somehow squeezed him, Chuck LaBeau and me, named to the Advisory Board of the ACRAC club, by virtue of some attractive WAVE that I was hustling, who was also the local base radio announcer. I don't remember that. (I really try to remember them all.) Sorry Ben. Anyway that's how we got the ACRAC gigs.... I had forgotten the details. Ben tells me that we also played at the Whiting O-Club and a local downtown Arthur Murray Dance studio. (Ben, was the WAVE cute?)

A few words about Chuck LaBeau. Chuck was very good looking, charming and really attracted the ladies. He was happy to share any 'fall-outs' with the band. It was said that Charles got more 'tail' than a toilet seat!

The Pensacola area has many out-lying auxiliary fields. Primary training and aerobatics were conducted at NAAS Whiting Field, then on to NAAS Saufley Field for Formation & Night Flying. Then to NAAS Barin Field for Gunnery and Carrier Qualification. Next came NAAS Corry Field for Introduction to Instruments. That was the first twelve months of the eighteen-month program.

Then would come 'Advance' at NAS Corpus Christi Texas for fighters, NAS Hutchinson Kansas for multi-engine and somewhere else for helicopters. (I forget but who cares about helicopters?)

It isn't remotely adequate to comment on the NavCad Program with a simple listing of the training syllabus. The program was eighteen months' duration where one was totally immersed in all aspects of flying from the initial solo to jet fighters. In between came excitement, thrills, and occasional moments of stark terror, along with great satisfaction of accomplishments. Emotions and testosterones ran high!

Formation training started at NAAS Saufley Field. It was two-plane formations, (called a "section") then working up to four-plane formations (called a "division", consisting of two sections.) Military tactical maneuvers are built around this format. 'Division' training was done with four students, and the Instructor chasing, in a fifth plane, calling out maneuvers to be done and criticizing, etc.

There was one Instructor Pilot that was a real "screamer". He was brutal and investigation showed that he was failing too many students with other-wise excellent records. The other instructors didn't care for his attitude and decided to do something about it.

Imagine a very large field with hundreds of North American SNJ's parked in rows. A student is assigned a given aircraft and then he hops on one of the stand-up trailers pulled by a jitney, after telling the driver his airplane number. (The driver knew where all the aircraft were located.)

On the day that this incident took place four Instructor-Pilots intercepted the four students, taking their place. The flight that followed is still being talked about in Naval Aviation circles. Knowing what was to take place, someone in the tower recorded the transmissions, monitoring the tactical frequency assigned to the flight.

The four pilots did everything wrong, cross-over's that were unsafe, improper join-ups and more than can adequately be described here. It was a total FUBAR!

The "screamer" nearly had a heart attack! (There is a copy of the recording around. Check U-Tube, *'Navy formation flight training'* or something.)

Another 'jitney-pulled trailer' story.

Pilots have, or acquire "handles". For instance, mine was "Doc" (from having been a former Corpsman). We had a class-mate that was going to become a priest, but changed his mind before taking his final vows. His handle became "Padre".

Now imagine the Pensacola area in the summer time...hotter than the blazes of hell...students in a full-piece flight suit, un-zipped down to the waist...no tee shirt, and sweating profusely. Four or five students on the flat trailer, no place to sit, standing with seat-parachute on, and as each cadet stepped off, upon arriving at his airplane, Padre would reach into his armpit, grab a handful of sweat and hit 'em with it, making the sign of the cross and saying, "Pax Vobiscum" --or the like.

When it was just Padre and me, alone on the trailer, I asked, "Padre, isn't that kinda sacrilegious?"

"Doc, this way they accept it."

I got it. As I stepped off at my airplane, I turned and said, "Hit me, Padre....hit me" He did and, for some reason, I felt a little safer.

I really enjoyed formation work and got pretty good at it. The more you do it the more it becomes almost second nature. We were all capable of becoming a 'Blue Angels' team member.

Next came night flying.

It was okay, different, but okay. Things do look different at night and if it's a really dark night you can't see <u>anything.</u> You don't see many birds at night. There is a reason for that. They stay on the ground because they can't see in the dark either, --well, for the most part.

Part way through this phase I was on a solo, three-leg, night cross-country, flight. There were five or six planes launched, five minutes apart. I was assigned an altitude, let's say, of thirty-five hundred feet. On the middle leg a mist was forming on the ground and a broken ceiling was forming up high. Above the high broken ceiling was an almost full moon, the light creating a silver bowl that I was winging my way through. It was beautiful.

Our aircraft radios, at that time, were 'Low-frequency' coffee-grinders and subject to "skip", sometimes even picking up a foreign language. I don't recall it ever happening during the day…it was a night thing.

Tonight I was receiving some beautiful Bach-like music, that even though I had been a student of Bach, I did not recognize. It gave me the feeling that I wasn't alone in the cockpit. I spoke to *The Man,* as if speaking to a good friend that I hadn't seen for some time. It wasn't praying, I wasn't anxious or frightened, but it was certainly a spiritual experience. It made me feel good. After landing back at our base I asked the other guys if they heard any music on our frequency…none had. I choose to believe that it was a visit from my God.

You've heard the expression that *"there aren't any Atheists in a foxhole".* Well, there aren't many that drive airplanes either. You can't spend hours flying above the earth, seeing the beautiful world around you, and believe that it was all just an accident. Over the years my cockpit became my church. It was where I related to my God. Since I was born and raised in the 'Western World' I *choose* to accept Christianity as my religious label, but studying philosophy has led me to believe that Buddha nailed it.

When writing this memoir, I was in contact with Del Peterson and Ben King frequently. They reminded me of many things that I hadn't thought about. Ben reminded me why he considered me his very best, life-long friend. He wrote:

*Do you remember a certain prick, a ring-knocker (Academy graduate), Lt.(jg) Instructor that gave me a 'below average' in mental attitude because I climbed out of the SNJ before he did. (Enlisted men must always wait and let officers leave small boats first. –a Navy tradition, harking back to the days of sail.)*

*Later, you and I were in a bar in Mobile and I pointed out the culprit to you. He was sitting in mufti ogling some bimbo. You said, "Watch this." And then you casually sauntered by his stool, feigned having stumbled and poured beer all over him. I have never forgotten your great act of comradeship. A citation should have gone into your NavCad file!*

Thanks Ben, a great story. I'm putting it in the book.

I got into *BIG* trouble while at Saufley. One of my roommates, also a former enlisted man, and I ran a Poker game. The roommate owned a window air-conditioner that he took with him from training phase to phase. Our room was comfortable during the over-warm Florida nights. It became a gathering place. So, let's play some Poker. We used chips, since gambling was illegal in the Navy. One night when the Duty Officer was making his rounds, he came in, saw our game and asked if we were gambling. *Of course we weren't*. Right. So he said, in that case it wouldn't matter, as he scooped all of the chips on the table into a pile in the middle! That took a bit of straightening out.

We played 'payroll Poker', keeping track of losses to be settled come Payday. We were careful to not let anybody get into us too deep. But still someone wrote home for money since they had been "taken for a ride" in a Poker game by a bunch of enlisted men.

Well, somebody's mother had political connections and somehow complained to someone, maybe a Senator or Congressman, then on to the Navy Department. By the time this trickled down to the Commanding Officer of NAAS Saufley Field it had gathered massive momentum and in a very short time! (It had to have been a Senator's ear.)

The only thing that saved our collective ass was the fact that Saufley's Commanding Officer was a "Mustang" (former enlisted himself). He wanted to know how we ran our game, wanted to see our records and if we 'partnered' during play. The answer to the latter was a definite "NO", that usually the only time that it got to be fun would be if we were going head-to-head against each other. The problem was that these college Fraternity boys just didn't know how to play real Poker, honest Poker with no wild cards.

Punishment was quick, but we hadn't been 'washed-out'. We could forget about any weekend "Liberty"

We were both restricted to the base for the remainder of our tour at Saufley and our records were marked, restricting _all gambling_ for the remainder of our NavCad training. Being found in a football pool could get us dropped from the program. Oh, and there were a few thousand Demerits that had to be 'marched off'.

Donna Shrewsbury and her Mother came to visit me in Pensacola, Florida. We had been exchanging letters. They found their way out to Saufley, finally finding me. I was still restricted to the base, however. I toured them around the base. We had lunch at the ACRAC club and Donna took me aside and said that she was ready to get married. I told her that I was committed to the NavCad Program for eighteen months and so she could go ahead without me.

Saufley's Formation phase completed, it was on to "Bloody Barin".

# EIGHT     GUNNERY & CARRIER QUALIFICATION

**T**his is why we're here. Our job as fighter pilots will be to shoot down enemy aircraft attempting to harm our aircraft carrier or provide close air support to our fellow 'jungle bunnies' and by shooting down enemies attempting to harm our ground folk. The Navy's job is to protect the sea lanes of the world. The aircraft carrier is a vital part of that protection. Unlike the Air Force's ten thousand foot runways, we had to learn how to cope with, something like three hundred feet of 'postage-stamp', to operate off of.

I don't know why this base was called "Bloody Barin". Granted, carrier work is inherently dangerous, but all of us have had experience seeing or hearing about this crash or that one, and who died...every day Basic Training produced accidents somewhere. But now we were going to get to play around with <u>real</u> <u>live</u> <u>bullets</u>. This is far more hazardous than the pointy-ended class officer's parade swords.

I won't say that any of us have become hardened over the loss of life, or immune to acknowledging the dangers of military aviation. In our immediate greater group consisting of the classes behind and after us, there have been a dozen serious crashes that included six fatalities. It constituted an impressive percentage that couldn't be ignored. That said, this was the most exciting phase of our training. And we looked forward to it with gusto.

Shortly after arriving at Barin I ran into a sailor selling his car, because he had received transfer-orders to sea-duty. The car was a 1940 Lincoln Zephyr, V-12 convertible! --a beautiful car. This was long before classics were valued, it wasn't considered valuable, just an old car with lots of miles. I bought it for something like $125, with some financial help from Del. It lasted through our full stay at Barin, eventually losing the reverse gear in the transmission. It was left behind with the keys in it, paper-work in the glove compartment and parked just outside the Main Gate at Barin Field. (No insurance so it couldn't be brought on base.)

We were transferred to NAAS Corey Field, back in the Pensacola area. We had gotten our money's worth out of the Lincoln. Let someone else enjoy it. *(Another "Classic-car" in my collection-memory.)*

As mentioned somewhere earlier in this narrative Del had brought his 1950 Ford with him to Pensacola, but loved that Lincoln. We chose to use the Lincoln for our many jaunts over to Mobile, Alabama that was nearby. Mobile was rich in feminine pulchritude that were fond of cadets, and the Lincoln convertible was certainly an asset. –it really looked 'cool'.

NAAS Barin field was located near Foley, Alabama a short drive to Mobile. Ah yes, and we did make that drive frequently. Perhaps I should add, at this point, that we managed to hook-up with some really great ladies. I'll tell about mine first, since this is my book....a lovely Alabama girl, red hair and the name of Gerry. Del fell into the arms of one Shirley Mae Morris, equally lovely, dark-blonde hair, somewhat wholesome in a well-stacked way and a wonderful attitude toward life in general.

As guys talk, and we did, I had learned that my dear friend Delbert Leroy Peterson was a virgin. WTFOver! This was a matter that should be addressed.

66

The two girls, along with Del and me, spent a lot of time together and I got to know Del's Shirley pretty well. She was gifted with a free spirit and I suspected that she just might be the one to alter Del's chaste condition. With my girl-friend's permission I carefully approached Shirley with a plan to alter Del's status. After satisfying herself that this wasn't some new "Yankee's Way" of getting into a lady's panties, decided that it was, indeed, a "grand plan". –Gerry and Shirley took it from there. Del's fate was sealed.

(There's a follow-on to this event that I'm going to put in here.)

*A few years later, after Del was out of the service, back in Minneapolis and happily married to his child-hood sweet-heart, he took his wife, Audrey, down to Alabama on vacation, and introduced her to Shirley. He had told Audrey of his christening into the delights of the "two-humped" beast and how it had happened. Del got a hold of Shirley and Gerry and they all went out on the town, with Audrey thanking Shirley for her very excellent training of her husband!*

Del told me this when we were e-mailing back and forth during my writing of this effort. I told him that I was impressed. I went on to say that he had *"huevos grande"* (large balls), in fact, for telling his wife, and that was an under-statement!


Okay, okay, meanwhile back at the ranch, we were having a couple of beers at the ACKRAC and chatting about unusual experiences with the SNJ. Del told me about one incident...

67

It was at Whiting, after soloing. He was scheduled for a solo practice hop. When he strapped-in and was preparing to start the engine he noticed some unusual switches where the Start switch was normally located. The ground crew member, after sensing the delay came up on the wing and leaning in told Del that this SNJ was one of the few left on the field with an "inertial" starter. He pointed out that there were two switches used for starting, the first activated and 'spun up' the starter flywheel and after stabilizing at a high RPM, the second switch activated the clutch, engaging the flywheel to the engine. There would be the high pitched noise coming down to the explosive exhaust as the engine caught. (How do you write it? I'll give it a try…"*Pneu-u, cough, bang*!...bubba-la….bubba-la…? Or something like that.)

Del said that it made him feel like 'Captain Midnight' of radio and movie fame.

I remember Bud Swenson telling me about inertial starters that had to be <u>hand</u>-<u>cranked</u> to spin the flywheel up to speed and then engaging the engine, by a clutch, to the flywheel. Ah yes, the changing technology! Del's SNJ had an electric motor to spin the flywheel up, as it were.

As you may imagine, the Pratt & Whitney R-1340 engines in our SNJ's took a beating and kept on ticking, as the Timex commercial goes, but overhaul times come up pretty quick. When over-hauled the engines must be 'run-in' at a low power setting. This is the first base, or phase where students, with over a hundred hours, were eligible to fly the 'low-power settings', Slow-Time hops. These were very enviable hops and difficult to get your name on the schedule. I wasn't even aware of the opportunity, it hadn't occurred to me until Del discovered it somehow, brought it up. Okay, let's do it. I told him to come with me. Don't say anything, I'll show you how this is done.

We went down to the Line and wandered over to the line shack and found the Chief at his desk. I asked some pointed maintenance related questions and told him that it probably drove him to drink, or rather Scotch at the very least. True to form, the Chief responded with something like 'Nah, Bourbon was his poison of choice...something simple like Old Charter...not high-fallut'in Scotch...and so forth. We hung around chatting it up and then made our departure.

When clear, I told Del that now we would go to the package store and purchase a bottle of Old Charter. –and Del, it's your treat. I'll do the thinking and you can do the buy'in. (Just like Butch and Sundance.)

Having acquired the bottle, in a plain brown wrapper, we made our way back to the line shack. I took the package and made my way directly around to the back of the Chief's desk, opened the bottom left hand drawer and slipped the obviously-shaped package into the drawer and went back around to the front of the desk.

The Chief smiled, looking up he said, "And what could I possibly do to help a *Kay-det* such as yourself?"

I took a small piece of paper out of my pocket and placed it on his desk. On the paper were two names, 'N/C J. McEniry' and 'N/C D. Peterson. Without making a big deal out of anything, mentioned, "Well, we're looking for a couple of "Slow-Time" birds if you have the need for a couple of people to fly 'em."

"Well that doesn't appear to be any kind of a problem, we're always looking for people that don't mind smashing bugs just flying around." Was his almost casual reply.

69

The next morning Del and I were on the flight schedule when it was published. –and that's the "Navy way", Mr. Peterson.

**NAAS Barin Field**

Our flight was a thing of beauty. Well first of all this was a 'none-syllabus flight' for both of us. We haven't had this freedom since back in aerobatic phase. Remember?

We're flying out of a field, located in the finger of Alabama butting up against Florida, climbing out to the West and Mobile Bay. It's a warm, cloudless sky and over Mobile Bay, the air is like skating on glass. This is like eating some kind of mushroom and you're transported into another space...the Indians used those magic mushrooms for religious things, other tribes had "peace pipes"....Right! Whatever it was, this was absolute Heaven! Del was on my Port wing, and in close.

I gotta tell-ya folk, in my current life and the experience of seventy-five hundred hours driving airplanes, Delbert Leroy Peterson is <u>one</u> of the only <u>two</u>, *smoothest* pilots I've *EVER* flown with!   (--the other being Gene Wing, who I'll introduce to you later.)

Del moved in a little closer....our wing-tips were inches apart and over-lapping.   I believe that we "rubbed" wing-tips, being careful of the wing-tip 'nav' lights.   The smooth air made this possible.

I still had the 'Lead' and headed us up Mobile Bay where there were Liberty ships and some military ships, all "Moth-Balled".   We flew among them, avoiding tall masts. After that pass I then gave the Lead over to Del.   He managed to find Shirley's house and we flew by....it might have been a tad bit low and we didn't go back for a second pass in case people didn't get our 'numbers' the first time.

I've had many wonderful flights but that one ranks among the top ten in my memory bank.   A truly fantastic day!  --at the foot of the cross, righteous!

Our SNJ's were equipped with a cowl-mounted 30 caliber machine gun.   The ammunition for each of the four planes had the bullet-noses dipped in different colored paint.   A fifth, instructor-piloted SNJ, would be towing a fifteen foot, fabric banner.   As the bullets passed through the banner they left a trace of the colored round.   After landing the pilots would inspect the banner, counting the four different colors (hopefully everybody had gotten hits).

My buddy Del did really well.   He was an Ace.   My efforts were a disappointment.   Pushing my ego aside, I asked him the secrets of his success.

"McEniry, I merely followed the teachings of the German Aces, Boelke and Richthofen, who said 'don't fire until you're close enough to guarantee a hit',  --that's it, get close."

71

I tried it and my number of hits improved a bit but I wouldn't have lasted long in the war-to-end-all-wars. Avoiding flying into the banner also became an issue. Seeing the banner as my enemy…target or the like, just wasn't making it into my persona. It was just a banner. (If it had been a Tri-Wing red Fokker I'd a nailed it! I did much better with bombs, rockets and strafing. I had real targets in that scenario. –this sounds like a 'snivel', sorry.

We joined Ben at the club for some beers. He was pretty happy. It seems that the ground folk ran out of yellow paint, so told him he would be 'no-color'. The tow plane was late returning, after the hop, so the same ground crew decided to check the sleeve the following morning, leaving it lying outside. It rained that night. Ben said that it was possible that some of his hits had been colors that washed off some of the other bullet-holes. Ben said that he tried to protest. (--the honorable thing to do) Oh well. He was an Ace as well. I wasn't an Ace, but managed to struggle through the phase without shooting down the tow-plane, or flying into the banner. In fact, I had made it all the way through Basic without a "down" so far. Advance would be another thing.

Now to get ready to become a real Navy pilot; carrier landings. We started FCLP's (*Field Carrier Landing Practice)*. These were conducted at an outlying site called "Canal Field". It had the outline of a carrier's flight deck painted on the tarmac. A LSO (Landing Signal Officer) would be standing on the left corner signaling the pilot with hand-held fluorescent paddles. Arms held *shoulder high, straight-out,* was indication of an "okay" approach, Arms *lowered* indicated you were too low, and *raised*…too high. Paddles *waved over-head* was a mandatory "Wave-Off", and when the LSO brought his right hand to his chest, was a <u>mandatory</u> "Cut" of engine power and land. Those two mandatory signals one did not think about or hesitate…. you just did.

The carrier-approach is flown at a 500-foot altitude, a relatively flat approach, gear and flaps down and enough power to hold the 'dirty-configuration' at a controlled airspeed of 58 knots and the 500-foot altitude. In that configuration the stall speed was 56 knots. This could be dangerous. If you stall or have an engine problem, you're too low to recover or bail out.

There would usually be four aircraft at a time in the pattern, spaced apart, landing and taking-off for another pass. Each student would shoot five to seven or eight passes. Taking off, after touching down, it was gear-up and flaps up, then turning down-wind 'dirtying up' again.

Del was following an SNJ, in the pattern, when he noticed that the flaps were not down on the plane in front of him. Del was reaching for his microphone to warn the pilot, when he saw the airplane snap-roll and plunge to earth. Just an explosion and ball of flame followed. The pilot did not survive. (Not that it matters, but the pilot was the first Negro NavCad to make it into the program.)

Checking my Log Book I see that I flew fifty-seven FCLP approaches but now it was time for the real thing. We would be qualifying aboard the USS Monterey, a small 'jeep carrier", built on a cruiser hull. The jeep carriers were built in War2 for the Atlantic Ocean German submarine action. They could operate anti-submarine, single-engine dive bombers, patrolling ahead and around the convoy. They were part of the success in combating the German threat.

It is an interesting fact that FCLP's are more dangerous than the actual carrier approaches and landings. Water crashes are a lot more forgiving than dirt…. you can drown instead of burn. But remember? --we have learned

73

how to swim and how to survive a water crash, so called, but usually results in going straight-in from a stall.

One of our guys, Dinsmore by name, went in from the "forty-five" degree portion of the pattern…wings level, into the drink, due to an engine failure. He was picked up by the destroyer almost immediately. He was back in an airplane the following day.

I had gotten pretty good at this and felt comfortable with the FCLP's so the actual qualifying aboard the USS Monterey was accomplished with six "okay" approaches. It was March 11th, 1954. I was a qualified "Navy Carrier Pilot". A happy day.

Del and Ben qualified without any problems, in fact as I remember, also with all "okay" approaches. We were having some beers at the club and Ben had some comments,

"Well Guys, that was a lot of fun, and as the Brits like to say.. *"A Piece Of Cake"*. But keep in mind…that took place on a nice sunny day, the Gulf was as flat and calm as could be. But just think, how about a Med Cruise…snotty weather, or night and the ship is bouncing thirty or forty feet, and you have to either get on-board or you're going to get wet. –I think I'll apply for 'Multi-Engine', you guys can go fly fighters."

"Hey Mr. King, that's one of the reasons I've elected to take my commission as a Marine. We operate on land, for the most part, and can even keep a bottle in our tent to enjoy upon returning from a "pucker" hop. You Squids can't have booze aboard ship except the shot of Brandy the Flight Surgeon gives you after they fish you outta the drink."

Del didn't say anything…he was probably thinking about Shirley.

All the fun and exciting stuff will have to do for now. We were being sent to NAAS Corey Field, over near 'Mainside' Pensacola, for Instrument Training.

# NINE    INSTRUMENT TRAINING

$\mathbf{E}$d Link had always wanted to be a pilot, but fate and circumstances kept that from happening. We should be thankful because he turned his interest, and the assets of his family's business of manufacturing music-organs and nickelodeons into, what became known as the "Link Trainer". Ed Link used his knowledge of pumps, valves and bellows to create a flight simulator that responded to the pilot's controls and gave a reading on the included instruments. Ed developed the trainer in 1929 out of the need for a safe way to teach new or old pilots how to fly by instruments, in part due to the heavy losses by the early mail pilots, when encountering weather. Then in early 1930 he founded and headed Link Aviation Devices, Inc.

The original Link Trainer was a ply-wood box with instrumented controls plus stick and rudders and large enough for the pilot. The box was mounted on a universal joint, allowing movement in all planes, up to a limit. Control inputs by the pilot were transmitted to a three-wheeled 'crab-on-small-wheels', electrically, and the crab (with a red pen attached) could move over a desk-mounted navigation chart, covered by a sheet of plastic, tracing progress. The Trainer operator would give instructions to the pilot by microphone and the pilot, wearing headphones, would perform accordingly.

The box was later painted blue and became known as Link's "Blue Box". Over 500,000 United States pilots were trained on Link simulators, as were pilots of nations as diverse as Australia, Canada, Germany, United Kingdom, Israel, Japan, Pakistan and the USSR over the years.    The company continues to make aerospace simulators, now a far cry from the original 'Blue Box".

Once the pilot climbs in and closes the hatch he can't see anything until the instrument lights are on, and then only the instruments, of course.    It can be a bit claustrophobic, to say the least.    The box's movements could be jerky and not very realistic, but it was a good training device for Instrument Approach Procedures and helped in developing "scan" patterns.

I knew well what "Link" time was worth in the civilian sector and availed myself of extra link time some evenings when not chasing girls or drinking.    The building housing the trainers had watch-standers that had to be there anyway and they were always ready to give a cadet extra training time.    I was really beginning to enjoy the challenges of instrument flight and was getting pretty good at it.

Flying in the clouds without any visual references to some kind of horizon requires learned skills.    Our mind plays tricks on us and developing vertigo can send us plummeting toward earth in a spin.    The need for 'visual reference' led to the development of Gyro-stabilized instruments like the "Turn & Bank", which was the first and followed by Directional Gyro and Artificial Horizon. It took learned-skills to accept the instrument readings instead of our senses.    Believing our senses leads to a "Death-Spiral", ruining your whole day.

I should add, at this point, that I don't know of any birds that fly in the clouds either.    Something to keep in mind.

Our syllabus training covered Low Frequency Range Approaches, Automatic    Direction    Finder    (ADF) approaches and quite possibly some Ground-Controlled

Approaches (GCA). The Omni Range, or VOR was not in general use yet.

Our training included 'under-the-hood' flight in the SNJ, along with the Link Trainer hops.

It was a much longer drive to Mobile now. Del had found love so he continued. I hung back spending more time with Ben, music and ACRAC beers. Basic was soon over and we would be receiving orders to Advance.

# TEN    ADVANCE FLIGHT TRAINING

Corpus Christi, Texas surrounded by beautiful beaches, sunshine, and humidity carried in from the Gulf and the throaty sound of 'round power' accompanied by the high-pitch whine of jet engines.   "..*here I was!*"   --and I was in heaven.

I was checked in, assigned a room in the BOQ and directed to the Navy All Weather Flight School.   Upon arrival I was 'paired-up' with another NavCad and introduced to our Instructor.   His name was "Butch O'Hare"...not the Hero from Guadalcanal, but anybody with the last name "O'Hare" automatically got "Butch" attached to it.  It was the same with "Ritter"....it got "Tex" attached.  There are probably more, but those two come to mind.

Lt. O'Hare was a good instructor, patient, and knew his job.  Once into the program, usually at least a three-hour scheduled hop, it went something like this:

The training was done in a SNB, a twin-engine twin-tailed small transport, similar in appearance to the twin-tailed Lockheed small transport that Amelia Earhart was known to be flying when she disappeared.  It had Pilot and Co-Pilot in two front seats, then four to five seats in back.  When the first student was in the left front seat the second was in the back cabin right behind the front student.  His job was to scan out to the left side of the airplane since the front windshield was covered on the left side with a louvered panel, allowing the instructor to view through the louvers, clearing the left side.   And, of course, the Instructor kept the right side clear.

79

**Beechcraft D-18 ( SNB-5)**

The purpose of all that allowed the student to fly by instruments, not being able to see out, and the instructor, with the help of the other student, could avoid running into another airplane, in the crowded skies over the Corpus Christi area.

The SNB was kinda tricky to land and the Navy didn't want to take valuable training time teaching landings. In fact, our Log Books were stamped, *"Completion of the USNS (AWF) Advanced Flight Syllabus, in itself does NOT qualify this pilot far a CAA Multi-Engine Class Rating."*

It was an excellent instrument training aircraft and used accordingly.

Butch liked to listen to Paul Harvey's noon broadcast, so when coming up on noon, whoever was in the left seat was told to proceed to the Aransas Pass Beacon and set up a 'standard' holding-pattern. It was a fifteen-minute reprieve and one we looked forward to. (Some years later I wrote to Paul Harvey, thanking him accordingly. He returned a nice letter commenting that he was also a pilot and did indeed remember his introduction to instrument flying. —and "That's the rest of the story", a Paul Harvey saying.)

And speaking of stories, Del had one that he saved for me. Pretty well along in the All-Weather Flight syllabus he was chugging along in an SNB-5 doing LF ranges, looking for 'cone-of-silence' and all that old stuff. On board was the instructor (a LCDR, name available upon request) in the right seat, Del's partner Cadet in back, Del flying in the left seat, and a 'white-hat' (enlisted sailor) along, riding in back just to get his flight hours in for pay purposes

Now, the Navy Twin Beeches had something like five gas tanks, strewn about wherever they could stuff them in. In order to keep track of things the idea was to use all the gas in each tank before starting with another tank. The tank we were on, at that time was what Del believed was the smallest of the bunch, at about 18 gallons.

The procedure was to have one of the pilots watch the fuel pressure gage as the 'duty' tank approached zero fuel. When the needle began to flicker you would switch to a tank known to have fuel, and simultaneously work the wobble pump energetically to keep gas headed for the engines.

"We pilots got a little slow this time, and, sure as hell both engines sputtered and quit dead! SILENCE!! The 'swabbie', who had been sleeping soundly in back, was, in mere seconds, wide awake, strapping on his parachute, and ready to go out the door. Just as the engines caught, my partner Cadet stopped the sailor before he could get the door open." Del was still laughing as he told this story.

"The flight then continued with restored calm and without further incident. It was only a 'laundry-issue' for the 'swabbie'."

About forty training hours later I was deemed qualified for, and issued, a STANDARD Type Instrument Rating, that was recognized by the CAA as an "Instrument" Rating added to his or her civilian Pilot's License.

A few years later I ran into Ben and I asked what happened to him when he went to Multi- engine Advance at NAS Hutchinson, Kansas. What was his experiences?

Here's what he told me:

*"We didn't have anything at Hutchinson called All-Weather Flight Training. Do I assume correctly that you mean some kind of instrument flight training? That was included as part of our later syllabus in the P2V. After the usual classroom stuff on systems, we started learning to take-off, fly, and* <u>*land*</u> *the twin Beech. We did not have chutes to sit on and when a plane had been sitting in the hot Kansas sun the metal in the cockpit was as hot as steel in a rolling mill. Until we got airborne we sort of had to suspend our butts above the seat and hold the yoke with our fingertips. That summer of 1954 I learned that taking a photo of a Navy cook frying an egg on the tarmac was a yearly tradition for the local newspaper.*

*After showing that we could land the SNB without either driving the wheel struts through the wings or ground-looping off the runway, we graduated to the P2V-3. It was really a fine aircraft in many ways, especially because it was really difficult to break it no matter how lousy a student airman one might be. I may have already written about Floyd Barkley, my mean and sadistic instructor. It was said that one reason that he was such an SOB was that when he got his wings just after World War II, the Navy had so little money that he was made an "Aviation Midshipman" instead of getting a commission immediately. So for a couple of years, at least until the Korean War was going on, his salary was still $90 a* *month, although he may have received flight pay. His bitterness was especially directed at student officers that had come to flight training either after the USNA or OCS. My flying mate was an Ensign. (We trained as pairs, trading the left seat back and forth, with our instructor in the right.) Thus he bore the brunt of Barkely's nastiness whereas he tended to go easier on me, a lowly NavCad. Other students who had the bad luck to get Barkely as a 'check pilot' would ask us how we could endure the SOB screaming at us all the time but they missed the beauty of our situation. --that since he was our instructor we could not get him on a check ride, and hence our examiners seemed like 'Santa Clauses' in comparison. The final two weeks of the syllabus at Hutch was long range navigation in the PB4Y-2, with little yoke time, just dead-reckoning and shooting stars with a sextant. We actually learned quite a bit about astronomy. In answer to whether or not you could choose your ultimate type of aircraft, it is "No". I certainly expected to be flying in a P2V rather than off of a carrier in an AJ. I had never even heard of our nuclear weapons or how they were delivered until I got to my AJ squadron. I had never heard of the airplane or what it's function was! Remember, I had selected 'multi-engine' to avoid carriers!"*

For the reader's benefit, I'll explain. Remember, this is 1955, we still lead the world in atomic weapons. The USAF has the B-36. Soon to be replaced with the Boeing B-47. The Navy needed a carrier-based 'bomber' that would be capable of carrying an atomic weapon.

In the late 40's the Navy contracted with North American Aviation to develop the large AJ Savage. She was powered by two Pratt & Whitney R-2800 piston engines and a third engine, an Allison J-33-A10 turbojet buried in the fuselage. All three engines burned the same

83

fuel to simplify the fuel system. It would be the largest, heaviest aircraft to be used on aircraft carriers. And like Ben said, he had selected "multi-engine" to <u>avoid</u> carriers. –and here he was flying a *'Truck'* aboard, not an enviable task, especially in night or nasty weather conditions.

There was a full-size auditorium-theatre on the base that had a grand piano. I used to drop in and play. I met the theater manager, a 2$^{nd}$ Class NCO sailor, Ricky Stearns by name. One day he told me that the Admiral wanted a talent show of sorts and had tasked him with putting something together. He asked would I perform. Of course, no problem-oh.

Ricky was putting together a dance routine based on the "Frankie and Johnny" stage standard. His female dance partner was a cute thing that I was trying to get next to but Ricky had that all locked up. Her girlfriend, however, equally ravishing, I did manage to get next to. Her name was Barbara Trench. She was an Arthur-Murray Dance instructor. We became seriously tight.

The other male lead dancer dropped out a week before show-time and I offered to try to fill in if Ricky could choreograph a routine within my ability. (My sister Patsy had been a serious dancer; ballet, tap and modern and wanted me to work with her. I sure wish I had done Tap, which is very cool, but thought dance was too girlish at that time in my life..)

Anyway, between Ricky and Barbara, I managed a *'Gene Kelly'* type thing and made it happen. –just another 'notch' in my budding show-biz life.

A former Navy pilot, now an Insurance Salesman, held week-end BBQ things, open to students in the training command, trying to sell life insurance. He was a neat guy and arranged for me to buy a 1951 MG-TD 'Sports Car' from a Navy pilot that had received over-seas orders. More about that in a bit.

Our next phase, following All Weather Flight, was "Fighter Tactics" and performed in the Navy's new Advance Trainer, the T-28 Trojan, designed and built by North American. There weren't enough in the program yet so the Navy decided to pull some F6F Grumman Hellcats out of moth-balls. Every other class got T-28's or Hellcats. I made certain that I was in the F6F Hellcat group. I really wanted to fly that airplane!

Growing up during War-2 I had maps and pictures on my bedroom wall. In a place of honor were pictures of the Hellcat, considered at the time to be the Navy's answer to the Japanese Zero. It was credited to having shot down the most enemy planes than any other model of aircraft in the Pacific Theatre. The ones pulled out of moth-balls were still in their WW-2 colors; dark Blue. –it would be my first "Blue" fighter!

The Hellcat was absolutely totally _righteous!_ No words can adequately describe it. You pull out onto the runway, advance the throttle to 36 inches of Manifold Pressure, clearing the plugs....then advancing the throttle to 60 inches while the P&W R-2800, 2,000 hp engine literally slams you against the seat-back and throws the fighter into the air! Hey! –we're talking serious 'dampness'...even wet here!

My Log-Book shows **35.0** hours in the F6F Hellcat and I remember it as if it were yesterday....chiseled in granite. However, I did encounter a problem that could have caused me to 'wash-out'.

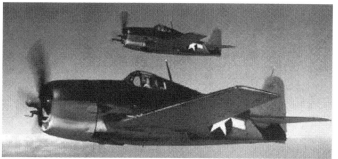
**Grumman F6F-5 Hellcat**

It was my first night cross-country in the F6F. I had launched first, leading a flight of about eight, in single file, maybe five minutes apart. Upon returning I mistook the commercial airport for NAAS Cabanas Field and did touchdown, then immediately added power and took off, realizing my error.

It didn't escape notice and I was in a world of Yogurt. I had to appear before a Review Board and was nearly 'washed-out'. My "Guardian Angel" stepped in again and I made it through the board. I was allowed to continue my training. –*whew*! It was my first, and only "down" going through the program.

Before leaving the F6F Hellcat scene, an incident took place that is now a legendary part of Naval Aviation History.

As I have noted before, we shared the NavCad Program with English Midshipmen and French Cadets. (I can't imagine having two years of high school French and then going to France and through a military flight-training program! Those poor lads had one hellava mountain to climb.)

Well, this French Cadet took off in a Hellcat without adequately 'clearing' his engine. He no sooner got his landing gear retracted, when the engine started backfiring and struggling to keep running, when it was just too much --the engine quit. He was too low to bail out so stuffed it into a farmer's field a couple of miles from the runway.

In the military, there has to be an Aircraft Accident Review Board. If the pilot survives, he must add to the final report a statement of *what could he have done to prevent the accident.*

The French Cadet made the following statement: *"THIS ACCIDENT WOULD NOT HAVE HAPPENED IF I HADN'T FLOWN TODAY."*


I was given orders to NAAS Kingsville, a few miles south of Corpus Christi, where I would train in the single-cockpit F9F-2 Grumman Panther. When I reported in, the Duty Officer, a Navy Ensign, put me "on report" for being "out of uniform". (I had exchanged the Navy belt buckle with a Marine belt buckle on my tan web trouser belt. I had made it past the U.S. Marine Corps Selection Board and was proud to wear any identifying article.) However, I was still a NavCad and should be in a Navy uniform, including the proper belt buckle... Let me see, hm-m…how do you spell *"Chicken-Shit"*? Oh yes, I remember.

That Navy Ensign (same as 2$^{nd}$ Lieutenant in the Army or Marines) did cost me a bunch of demerits that had to be 'marched off', and here I thought I was through with that stuff for the most part. Reason number four-thousand and six why I swore I'd never be one, an Ensign that is. In fact, I saw a ship's dog piss on an Ensign's leg one time and thought it so proper! I find Ensigns to be lower than 'whale shit'…. which is the lowest thing in the ocean.

Since I was applying for a Marine commission, our Marine D.I.'s told me, and others also going that way, when commissioned a 2$^{nd}$ Lieutenant, keep one's mouth shut...listen to the NCO's and just maybe one might live long enough to make 1$^{st}$ Lieutenant. Good advice.

I was told that it might be a week or so before a jet class would start so decided to take a five-day leave and take Barbara down to Monterey Mexico in my newly acquired car. We almost made it.

I had met a Navy Instructor-Pilot who owned a 1951 MG-TD. He was being transferred back to the fleet and offered to sell me his MG. We had put together an agreement where I would pay him $25 a month until commissioned and then $100 a month (my Flight Pay) until it was paid off. I was about four months away from commissioning. His car had an Officer's Base Sticker, giving me open-gate liberty. The gate sentries never questioned the driver of a car with an Officer's Base Sticker. They merely saluted and waved you through.

Barbara and I drove down to Brownsville, over to Reynosa and then Highway 40 to Monterrey.

Near a town called China the English *LUCAS* electric fuel pump gave up the ghost. Ah yes, Lucas, *"The Prince Of Darkness"*, supposedly the reason that the British like warm beer, since Lucas also manufactures refrigerators!

We were out in the middle of nowhere, broken down and no relief in sight.

After a while a stake-bed truck came along with a load of farm workers in the back. They were all dressed in white shirts, pants and straw hats. The driver stopped, without being flagged down, and speaking very broken English asked our problem. He insisted that I go with him and he would leave two of his workers with Barbara and the car for protection. It was then that I noticed some of the workers were armed. The driver said that this was not a very good place to be.

Reluctantly I agreed, after conferring with Barbara.

The ranch owner spoke very good English and was very helpful, sending a mechanic back and quickly got us back on our way with a temporary fix. It was good enough to last until a new fuel pump could be ordered from "Jolly old". –which only took a month or so.

Upon returning to Kingsville there were still no class openings, so I was transferred back up to Mainside at Corpus Christi and assigned to a class that would be flying the Lockheed TV-2. (Air Force designation, T-33.) This was not a fighter but a training airplane. If I had stayed in Kingsville I would have flown the F9F-2 Grumman Panther Jet. (That was to come later.)

Lockheed TV-2 (T-33)

This final Jet phase was done with an instructor, Navy Lt. Streeter, and three students. We would fly as a "Division", a flight of four. Lt. Streeter told us to just call him "Coach", to start living the part of fighter pilots, the relaxed 'rank' attitude of the Pilot's Ready Room. The

89

three students were Cono R. Borelli, Harry Worth and yours truly.

During one of the early hops I was to go through a series of maneuvers listed on a Syllabus Card while being covered by another aircraft. On this hop I had drawn the instructor as my plane-guard. As we were walking out to the two aircraft he asked me what we usually did after completing the required maneuvers. I mentioned that perhaps a hassle (--dog fight) would be in order.

With the syllabus out of the way I rolled in on him and the hassle began. He soon tired of shooting me down so we went on to other maneuvers.

He did a barrel roll, I did a barrel roll. He did a loop and I, -- attempted a loop.

The Handbook says to do a loop one must be indicating 300 knots and pull a constant four "G's", over the top. (I hadn't read that part of the book yet.) Well, I wasn't fast enough and I didn't pull the proper number of G's so the airplane wouldn't go over the top but continued going straight up, with my attempting control inputs to no avail. Finally, it ran out of airspeed and energy, whereupon it tumbled, end-over-end down until reaching enough airspeed for recovery. (Thank God that occurred pointing 'down' and not 'up' or the elevators could have been ripped off.)

During my recovery efforts the instructor transmitted, *"Easy...easy...now just fly that airplane straight and level until you know how!"*

Later research disclosed that Lockheed's Chief Test Pilot, Tony LeVere, had encountered the tumbling phenomena and referred to it as "the J.C. Maneuver". Very aptly named!

Both Harry and Cono were former enlisted Marines. We soon learned that Harry Worth was the worst pilot that we had ever flown with. A real "plumber"! He was really a nice guy and Cono and I both felt for him, but he was truly dangerous. For example, like I said, we flew as a Division, trading Division-Lead and Section-Lead, rotating positions within the division. Returning to base after completing a training hop, we would enter the "break" in a very tight formation, in right echelon, until over the center of the runway at 1,000 feet altitude, then peel-off individually, ('break' up the formation), entering down-wind, in file, preparing to land.

I hope I've explained the picture well enough.

So anyway, this specific day Harry had the lead. We took off on a heading of 270 degrees (West) climbing out with Harry in the lead, Cono on his wing, I had the Section (2 airplanes) with Coach on my wing. Coach always flew "tail-end Charley" to keep an eye on the formation. However, when we were returning and heading for the 'break', we always closed-up tight....*ala "Blue Angels"*, at which time only the Lead had "eyes," since the rest of us would be concentrating on holding position.

The training hop over, Coach told Harry to take us home.

Harry did that, *HOWEVER*, the wind had changed and so had the "Duty Runway"....now it was runway "9" (090 degrees) the reciprocal of runway "27" (270 degrees) There just happened to be a flight of F9F's coming into the break at the proper altitude and also in a right echelon...the tower was screaming...Eight jet aircraft were in a "HEAD-ON" collision course, a thousand feet above the runway...Oh my God in heaven......somehow the two flights barely missing each other.

Harry got a "**Down**" for that one. (No shit!)

There were other incidents, none as dramatic as that, but Harry was dangerous.

91

Coach tried to get Harry washed out. But the Review Board decided to give him one more chance. Don't ask...but maybe it was based upon 'need of the service'...maybe since he was former enlisted...maybe because he had made it this far...Hello? Whatever. –only the Shadow knows!

Cono and I tried to take out a Life Insurance policy on him, but apparently this isn't to be done. The tragic thing is that both Harry and Cono received orders out to Marine Corps Air Station Kaneohe Bay, in Hawaii. They were both assigned to the first Marine Corps squadron flying the FJ-4, Navy-Marine version of the North American F-86 Sabrejet. This was one of the hottest aircraft in the fleet! Harry lasted three months, crashing to his death.

The crash investigation raised many questions as to his ever being commissioned and designated a Naval Aviator. There was quite a write-up in the Naval Aviation News magazine, covering Harry's poor performance all the way through the training command.

Our last flight was a 'cross-country' up to Memphis, Tennessee. I had an Uncle Bob there in the welding supply business. I got involved and spent too much time with them. I was late getting back out to the airport...the flight was late getting back to Corpus, arriving after dark due to my dalliance, and Coach was chastised, taking the heat for me.

Having drinks at the Officer's Club (allowed during this final training phase) with Coach Streeter, he suggested that before heading home for a well-deserved Leave we stopped by the PX and pick up some miniature Navy wings. The idea being that when out on a date with some cutie, tell her that '*I brought these wings home to give to my mother but I want you to have them....*'

92

Sorta like being engaged. Coach referred to them as "leg spreaders". (I bought six pairs but it didn't work for me. –oh well.)

-o-

This was completion of our final phase of training, then will come Graduation, *"Wings Of Gold,"* and Commissioning, as a 2nd Lieutenant in the United States Marine Corps!

**September 7th**, 1954 - I flew a jet for the first time, the TV-2 (T-33 USAF designation).

**September 23rd, first jet solo**. This was final phase before Commissioning and 'Wings of Gold'.

Total Jet time, **57.1 hours**,

NavCad Graduation: **October 23, 1954**.

My Mother flew down to Corpus Christi to pin the wings on my chest. Barbara met her at the airport and we had dinner together that night. The following day she was to bring Mom out to the base on the day of my commissioning. They were late. The Admiral pinned my wings on, and then Barbara and my Mother arrived. The Navy photographer took pictures with my Mother and Barbara posing with me, marking the occasion. It worked out…it was fine. The prideful look on my Mother's face, as she pinned them on, was worth all that anyone could ever ask for.

I wore Navy Wings of Gold! I was a military fighter pilot. It was a dream realized. There is a God!

**Lt. "Coach" Streeter, my last Navy Flight Instructor with me, then the Coach, Harry Worth and Cono Borelli**

-o-

Mom and I drove the MG out to California. The MG had a rack over the rear spare tire, holding my Val-Pack with my new Marine Corps uniforms, and my Mother's suitcase. There was a small space behind the seats holding our smaller luggage pieces. We looked like something out of The Grapes of Wrath.

It would be a long drive so I went to Sick Bay and got a bottle of Dexedrine pills. (You could do that in those days.) My Mother didn't drive and I would be doing all of it. She was having a problem of some sort, not feeling well, *so I gave her a couple of pills.*

The combination of coffee and Dexedrine made her very 'talky'. It got pretty interesting. She would read aloud one story after another from RED BOOK or another magazine! It made for an unusual trip. If I had known about English cars, then I wouldn't have attempted that long trip. To my surprise we made it. –Mom was a little hoarse though.

We met my step-dad, Art Weishart, in San Francisco. Then the three of us drove up to Seattle in Arturo's new 1954 Volkswagen. –I was impressed with handling and performance, having been "a race-car driver" ....and sensitive to those kinda things. Right?

I was on a well-earned leave before reporting to MCAS El Toro. (near Santa Ana, California)

95

# ELEVEN THE DEATH RATTLERS

**R**eporting in at MCAS El Toro, the first step was being assigned a room in the BOQ and then told to report to building number something or other to start Leadership School. The purpose was to turn a bunch of 'snot-nosed', butter-bar $2^{nd}$ Lieutenants into something resembling a Marine. Those of us that hadn't been through OCS, in Quantico, would participate in a shortened course to learn the responsibilities of a Marine Platoon Leader. The school was run by some senior Marine Master Sergeants and a couple of Gunnery Sergeants. They were always respectful but quick to council us. We did a lot of running around in the woods and eating snakes, that sort of thing.

After some days and nights our 'Drill Instructors' decided that we at least looked like Marines, you know, filthy dirty, unshaven and in need of a haircut. When finished I had some idea of how to move a Platoon, while covering our flanks.

So the D.I.'s finally turned us loose. We could sleep indoors and eat real food…that sorta thing.

Returning to El Toro I found that I could 'live ashore' and draw housing benefits. Two other Seattleites, Pete Lottsfeldt, Ric Novak and New Yorker Cono Borelli and I found a neat house in Laguna Beach. It started life as a "guest cottage" behind a somewhat stately edifice, currently housing four BAM's (female Marines). It did provide company from time to time for our group…. sorta like "Friends", (the current TV show). In fact, I was seeing quite a bit of one of them. She was the Base Librarian and drove an Austin-Healey-100. We read a lot, held hands and that sort of thing…

I was assigned to my first fighter squadron, VMA-323, the Death Rattlers. The squadron was flying the F9F-5 Grumman Panther. There weren't any two-place versions. So, once again it was a matter of reading the Pilot's Operating Handbook, a cockpit check and off you went into the wild blue. It was all very exciting, to say the least.

The *dash-five* was near the end of her service life and the squadron was being groomed for a new airplane in about a year or so. In the meantime we had to live with this tired old bird. There were a lot of maintenance issues and in-flight emergencies were not uncommon.

**Grumman F9F-5 Panther**

I had opted to be assigned to the Maintenance Department. The squadron Maintenance Officer was a grizzly old Warrant Officer. I became his assistant. I loved to fly and there is only one other department that offered unlimited flight time, and that was the Operations Department. I had noticed that the department already had a plethora of "butter bar" lieutenants, so chose the

Maintenance Department. In the Maintenance Department one had test flights, ferry flights to Overhaul & Repair facilities, etc. It provided lots of flight time. Our Commanding Officer was Lt. Colonel Rick Hey. He wore Canadian wings as well as Navy wings, having joined the RCAF during War2. He was a great pilot and encouraged us to look for ways to get better. He drove a red 1953 or '54 Jaguar XK120 roadster. (–more on that later.)

The pilots were encouraged to do things 'outside of the box'. I decided to try for a non-stop flight record from MCAS El Toro to NAS Corpus Christi. It was beyond the normal range of an F9F. My crew helped me prepare a bird for the attempt. We removed the eight rocket rails, the other hard points, and waxed the airplane.

I had waited for weather conditions, primarily for the jet stream to swing to the south and assist my eastward flight. I would have to be above thirty thousand feet.

When the conditions were as right as I could hope for, we topped off the fuel tanks, towed the airplane out to the end of the runway with the Start Cart that was also supplying electrical power, got my flight clearance, started the engine and took off. (A jet does not require a lot of ground run-up procedures.)

The climb-out went according to flight plan and once at my cruise altitude I was making the above average ground speed required to make the record flight. The jet stream was doing its job.

As I was approaching El Paso Texas, however, it went away. My ground speed dropped to normal. I wasn't going to make Corpus Christi, but I pressed on.

Sure enough, passing San Antonio I flamed out. It came as a surprise, I had miscalculated. I was tempted to try to stretch my glide to Corpus, then thought better of it. I turned around, contacted San Antonio's Randolph Air Force Base tower requesting a "flame out" approach to their long runway. They said that they had heavy student traffic and couldn't allow a practice approach of that type. I informed them that it wasn't *"practice"*. The tower asked if I was declaring an emergency. I replied that I wasn't...that I wanted to land and refuel. They were very nice about clearing their traffic and allowing me to land.

I don't know how the Air Force does it but we practiced flameout approaches frequently and sometimes to touch down. (--not me, but I'd heard others say they had) I didn't think it was anything special, but the operations folk at Randolph were pretty excited...they had crash trucks, etc. near the runway until I touched down then followed me on the rollout. I turned off on a taxiway while I still had momentum so as not to block their duty runway. It was okay. Randolph AFB has a runway that is over ten thousand feet long. It wasn't like it was a hairy thing.

I proceeded to NAS Corpus Christi and RON'd (Remain Over Night). The flight back would require a fuel stop, since I would be fighting the normal west-to-east winds aloft. Upon my return the CO congratulated me on the attempt and my decision to land in San Antonio. He was amused over the Air Force's attitude about my request for the approach.

As mentioned, the F9F was nearing its service life and we were experiencing various problems. Most noteworthy were 'fuel-control' issues.

I had a period of about four or five weeks where I couldn't have a flight without an incident. One such actually had nothing to do with the Holly Fuel Control.

I was scheduled to fly Louie Farrell's wing. Louie

was a senior Division Leader (Flight of four aircraft, made up of two Sections.)

Louie took the Division over to the Lake Ellsinore area. We went through the scheduled syllabus and when finished, had time for a little "grab-ass". On this occasion, Louie chose to do some very low level flat-hating over the dry lakebed. (Lake Ellsinore was dry six months out of the year.) The normal formation position was a slight step-down and back about ten feet. For this event Louie signaled me into a step-up position and indicated a spread. We had started down to the surface. Louie went low enough to create a "rooster tail" over the dry lakebed surface, crowding 400 knots! He pulled up and did an aileron roll. Not to be out done I decided on a four-point aileron roll as I came off the deck. The sudden force of the four-point roll caused a hydraulic line that ran along the cockpit floor to rupture. The spraying hydraulic fluid blinded me. As they say, *"—so there I was, flat on my back, 400 knots and way too close to the ground and blind!"*

I yelled over the radio, "Louie I'm blind." He was on my position instantly and talked me into an upright, climbing attitude. He sent the other Section home to El Toro. We climbed out and I was trying to clear my vision. I even cracked the canopy, trying to get airflow to help. I could finally make out shapes…but that was about it. Just shapes.

Louie flew my wing, talking instructions for power and wing attitude. We returned to El Toro and Louie got us a long straight-in approach to the runway. It worked out fine. The ground crew got me out of the airplane. Then took me over to Sick Bay where the Flight Surgeon cleaned out my eyes and got most of my vision back. My laundry was another issue.

100

To be sure that my vision was okay I was grounded for a couple of days. I bought Louie quite a few drinks at Happy Hour that week.

I was out on a date with the BAM Librarian, who lived in the house in front of our bachelor digs. She had become my drinking buddy. I was pissing and moaning about missing Barbara and the BAM had heard enough! She said, "For Christ's sake, why the hell don't you call her and ask her to marry you...I'll even pay for the call!"

Well, the next day I called (--but I paid for the call). I arranged for her to come out to Laguna Beach. We would be married in the base chapel. So, it became a busy time; primarily finding a new place to live. . Getting rings would have to wait until Barbara arrived.

I had always wanted a flying honeymoon so I had to fit-in going up to Orange County Airport and checking-out in a Cessna 140...then reservations at Palm Desert Fly-Drive Inn, in the greater Palm Springs area.

My landings in the Cessna 140 left a bit to be desired and my instructor suggested that I get a little more time in the model. The 140 is a tail-dragger. Hey, I was a *hot Marine Jet Fighter Pilot*, and wouldn't hear of it. (It is said that "you can always tell a Marine". You just can't tell him very much!)

I had found a neat little furnished house on Laguna Canyon Road, near the outskirts of town. It could be called "quaint"; two bedroom, small kitchen and bath, gas heat and Dutch doors at the entrance and dividing the living room from the rest of the house.

All the planning went fairly well. It was a miracle, just a miracle.

We were married at the base chapel. Ric Novak was my Best Man. (There weren't enough Officer Swords in the squadron to walk under, like I'd wanted.)

101

The reception was at the Officer's Club and attended by some of the McEniry clan from Pasadena and many of my squadron mates. I paid the bar bill in 'payments'.

The honeymoon was another matter, however.

A Cessna 140 has a pretty small, cramped cockpit. On the flight from Santa Ana to Palm Springs I tried to open a WAC Chart in order to locate Palm Desert, which is south of Palm Springs. Trying to open and fold the large chart to the area I needed was a hassle. The chart filled the entire cockpit including blanking out the windshield, forcing a couple of 'recovery from unusual attitudes'. Oh well, just one of those things. There was more drama to come.

Palm Desert Fly-Drive Inn has two small, "X-shaped" pair of runways.

My first approach was to the south. Just about ready to touch down I noticed the windsock. I would be landing down-wind. It is not a good thing on a short runway. I waved off and came around to land to the north.

This would be Approach #2. Upon touching down I hit wheels first, bouncing down most of the runway and finally waved off again. Approach #3 was about the same. At this point Barbara asked me if I wanted her to make the landing. (She had been taking flying lessons in a Cessna 140 back in Corpus Christi.)

I snarled a firm denial! *(The marriage was doomed from the start, and did indeed end a year and a half later.)*

Approach #4 finally was okay. We climbed out of the airplane to a wave of applause from the crowd that we had attracted from the nearby swimming pool.

A very embarrassing situation for a hotshot Marine Jet Fighter Pilot!

Normal procedures for landing at El Toro during VFR (Visual Flight Rules) operations was to arrive at Point X-ray (Dana Point) at fifteen hundred feet, flying up the valley to El Toro and "break" over the middle of the runway, descending to a thousand feet and coming abeam of the end of Runway 25. At the break one pulled the throttle back to a 'detent', opened the dive brakes and as the airspeed bled off, lowered the landing gear and flaps as airspeed limits allowed.

The final incident in this four or five-week period was about to happen.

I entered the break, pulled the throttle back to the detent, etc. and as I approached the abeam position, added throttle to maintain altitude and airspeed, and noticed that there wasn't any power, I had a flameout.

Now the F9F-5 did have an Ejection Seat, but it wasn't the Martin-Baker Seat (which is capable of successful operation from on-the-ground and with zero forward speed). Our older model seat required 5,000 feet of altitude and success further depended on nose attitude above the horizon. I was at 1,000 feet, losing altitude and airspeed and unable to eject.

I remember thinking if I could just get inside the airport fence so that maybe the crash crew would be able to get to me quicker. With that in mind, I cranked the bird hard-over in a tight turn.

The F9F has an "Emergency Start" "T" Handle, located in the lower left side of the instrument panel. It has two positions; pulled once and then twisted and pulled again. When pulled it fires a shotgun shell full of magnesium located in the plenum chamber of the P&W J48 jet engine, and another shotgun shell in the second position. If there is any fuel in the plenum chamber it will

103

be ignited. If there is too much fuel in the plenum chamber it could blow the tail of the airplane off.

As I was reaching for the "**T**" handle the engine "lit-off", surged to a "hot start" and then again flamed out. The gyrations of my turn-in had sloshed more fuel past whatever was blocking fuel flow. The 'hot-start' provided enough momentary thrust to lift me over the boundary fence and I hit the ground about fifty yards short of the runway, bounced up and onto the runway, blowing all of the tires, and slid down most of the ten thousand feet of runway, grinding the wheels down to the axles, causing the landing-gear wheels to catch fire. (The wheels are made of magnesium.) Exciting. I think I was out of the airplane and running before it came to a complete, sliding stop. Maybe not...it just seemed that way.

A short time later I was given six-week TAD (Temporary Attached Duty) orders to VMO-6 at USMC Camp Pendleton. VMO-6 is a composite squadron with *bird-dog* fixed-wing aircraft as well as helicopters. At this period of time a student going through flight training could receive a commission when selecting helicopters in a one-year period instead of the year and a half normally required for designation as a Naval Aviator.

The purpose of my assignment was to train those helicopter pilots that hadn't gone through the Navy All-Weather Flight Program (part of the additional six-month training) how to fly cross-country Radio Facility Air-Ways. When I wasn't taking them cross-country they exposed me to their chores. It was good experience working closer to the ground forces, doing artillery spotting and locating simulated downed pilots.

Cessna OE-2

Toward the end of my six-week TAD the squadron, along with the Division, was involved in a large MARLEX training exercise. The U.S. Navy had provided a small escort carrier for helicopter use.

One night at the Officer Club Happy Hour I thought that it would be a good idea for my helicopter pilots to get "fixed-wing carrier qualified". They were carrier qualified in helicopters, but not fixed wing. I suggested that we launch at zero-dark-thirty Saturday morning and fly out to the carrier that was at anchor off Camp Pendleton and shoot some touch and goes. It seemed like a good idea at the time.

Bright and early, but a bit hung-over, I took a division of four Cessna OE-2's, the military version of the Cessna 180, out to the carrier. I set up for an approach and was about to touch down when a radio transmission came over the Guard Channel saying that I would be fired upon if I touched down. I acknowledged and was then told to return to Camp Pendleton, *"Direct...do not pass GO, and no $200"*.

We were met at the airfield by two staff cars and taken up to the Commanding General's quarters. The General was not happy. An irate Navy Captain had gotten him out of bed. He wanted to know whose idea it was to do what we did.

I told him that it was my idea and, I thought, "fixed-wing" qualification would be a good thing for the helo drivers.

The General was not amused. If it hadn't been for the fact that the *"squid that owned that damn boat"* was being so obnoxious, thus pissing-off the General, it could have meant severe disciplinary action for the four of us. As it was he pointed out that maybe…just maybe it might have been within my sphere of instructor to *arrange with the squid* to use his boat for training purposes?

The General said that we were all in hack and that I would remain so until my scheduled departure back to my fighter squadron. I would take his personal report that would go to my Commanding Officer and again, be part of my Personnel File.

My Commanding Officer *was very* amused but had to respond back to the general. I was to remain a First Lieutenant for a long time.

-o-

I heard that the Hamp Hawes Trio would be playing at a jazz club in Long Beach. The Hamp Hawes Trio, had Hamp on piano, Red Mitchell on bass and Philly Joe Jones on drums. On a Wednesday night I made it up to Long Beach to take it in.

I went up and spoke to Hamp during one of their breaks. He was polite but obviously not really interested in carrying on a conversation with a *'White Boy'*.. I had asked him if they would be at the club come the weekend. He said, "No that they were going up to San Francisco for a stint at the Blackhawk".

106

Back at the squadron, I was scheduled to fly up to NAS Alameda that weekend, where the F9F Overhaul & Repair facility was located, and exchange two of our tired birds for two newly overhauled. My wingman was also a jazz buff so we decided to go over to San Francisco and catch Hamp at the Blackhawk.

Again I approached Hamp during their break. He was surprised and asked had I driven all the way up here. I told him no, that I was a Marine pilot and explained our reason for being there. Hamp had done his two-year stint in the Army, playing in the band. He was fascinated with military airplanes. I suggested that he give me a call when he got back to LA.

There was an incident that I'll share with you. It's about the flight back to El Toro.

When my partner and I walked out to the line to pre-flight our two freshly overhauled aircraft, all of the F9's on the line had their wings in the folded UP position. I noticed that the Pitot Tube on the wing, high and far out of reach, had a fabric cover on it. I made a mental note to make sure it was removed. (The Pitot Tube provides the air and pressure to the Altimeter and the Air Speed indicators, quite necessary.)

Pulled out to a clear area, I was signaled to 'spread the wings'. I couldn't believe how new, clean and good the cockpit smelled. You know, sorta like a *new car smell.* Okay…wing locking pins IN, good to go.

Three quarters of the way down the runway I realized that I didn't have any Air Speed indication, *DAMN!* …the fuck'in pitot cover is still on the Pitot Tube! I have to continue, I was committed. As I was climbing out over the East end of the Bay Bridge, I advised the Tower, requesting landing. My No.2 came along side and I transferred 'lead' to him. He would be my air speed and altitude.

I really hate screw-ups like that, especially on a Navy base.... but I certainly "molested the pooch" that time!

We landed, a ground crewman removed the Pitot cover, and we got out-of-there!

To my surprise, Hamp did call. We arranged to meet and I took him out to MCAS El Toro, toured the flight line, let him sit in the cockpit of one of our F9's and let him try to fly our simulator. I had earned a friend for life.

I asked him if I could study with him for a while. He agreed and I studied jazz piano with him over a three-month period the summer of 1956. It was awesome.

It should be noted that upon completion of flight training, Marines are guaranteed fighters for their first tour of duty. This was a good deal, but then one had to make room for others. The Marine Corps had some wonderful opportunities such as Helicopters, you know those things that go up and down, and then there was Forward Air Controller School where one could become an expert on Asian types of soil.... or as Instructors back at the Training Command...none of which would be to my liking!

In February of 1956 a request for pilots interested in transports was published. Remembering the summer I spent working for West Coast Airlines, and how much I enjoyed it, I decided to look into it. A short time later I received orders to the R5D School, located on the other side of the
base.

108

# TWELVE  MARINE TRANSPORT SQUADRON

The Navy-Marine Corps R5D is the military version of the Douglas DC-4. The R5D is a four-engine, non-pressurized, long-range transport. It has a gross weight of 72,000 pounds that is made up of airframe, fuel, freight and/or passengers. It is capable of west-to-east coast non-stop flight and can cross the Atlantic Ocean. Operation in the Pacific Ocean is subject to island hopping, once beyond Hawaii.

**Douglas R5D/C-54 (DC-4) Skymaster**

The R5D is a complex aircraft. The R-2000 Wright Cyclone engines require attention to detail in handling power settings. The engines aren't as robust as the R-2800. The 8-tank fuel system is augmented with a large pair of tanks carried in the fuselage. A third of the length of the bird is made up of cockpit, radio & navigator stations (across from each other), then a galley, head and bunks for pilot rest during long over-water flights. Next was the Gas Compartment, containing the two large cylindrical fuel tanks with berths above. The remaining two thirds is the passenger/freight cabin, which also had a head. The cabin could be configured with open freight tie-down provisions, and/or bucket seats along the two sides. Stretchers or passenger seats or any combination of the afore-mentioned could also be accommodated.

Besides learning the various systems, special attention had to be observed in the weight & balance factors of loading. Weights and placement of load was critical. The airplane even had a tail post that was attached during loading of heavy freight that would then be moved forward from the extra-large loading/Pax door. How much weight and where it was located in the cabin was critical.

Colonel "Whitey" Hobbs managed the school. The white hair was due to his age. It was rumored that he had given Donald Douglas his first Instrument Rating.

Whitey was a tall, thin person. He could reach across the cockpit and open or close the co-pilot's side window. His permanent rank was Master Sergeant and he carried a 'temporary rank', of full "bird" Colonel. This combination allowed him to stay on active duty far beyond normal retirement age. He was one hellava gentleman, knew the R5D inside and out, and had the ability to pass on his knowledge. It was a great school.

Flight training consisted of landings and take-offs followed by heavy instrument training. The airplane was non-pressurized. It had to operate in the 8,000 to 12,000-foot range or lower. This was also where most of the weather occurred along with accompanying icing conditions.

As a jet fighter pilot I was used to being rushed to an operating altitude of 20,000 plus feet. Any weather penetration was very short lived. This was not the case in the world of reciprocating engine operation. I'll never forget the shock of copying my first instrument flight clearance that consisted of some intersections of airways that I didn't even know existed. I had to look them up in the Radio Facilities charts. It was a rude awakening.

Upon graduation from Whitey's school I was assigned to Marine Transport Squadron VMR-352. The squadron's mission was to move Reservists around in the summer months and Trans-Pac (Transport flight across the Pacific) during the winter months, primarily to Japan and beyond.

It was interesting flying. The summer Reserve requirements took us to every city that had a USMC Reserve Training Facility. There are a lot of them. I certainly learned my geography lessons.

My first Trans-Pac was a real history lesson. Started from El Toro to Moffett Field (in the Bay area), picking up cargo & pax for a twelve-hour flight to NAS Barber's Point Hawaii. We had two days 'crew-rest' in Hawaii. We flew Trans-Pac flights with an augmented crew, using an extra pilot, extra Radioman & Navigator, plus Crew Chief and his assistant. This augmented crew was due to the long over-water legs.

From Barber's Point we proceeded to Midway Island for refueling. Before landing we had to put up windshield reinforcement panels to protect us from a possible bird strike with a "Gooney Bird". The Gooney Bird is a giant Albatross. Midway Island is their breeding grounds. This species is probably one of God's dumbest creatures. They can stay airborne for days. Returning to Midway they sometimes forget to lower their landing gear...bouncing along on their butt and then rolling into a ball.

111

The Giant Albatross is a strange bird. The first time that they take-off as a chick they take off into the wind and became airborne after eight or ten 'wing-beats'. They would always repeat the same directional procedure even though maybe on a given day the wind could have changed. Taking off downwind wouldn't work, after the eight or ten wing beats they would suck up their landing gear, fail to become airborne and crash, rolling into a ball again. They would get up, tuck their head under a wing and complain mightily. Then try again.

Midway Island is an eighteen-month tour of 'sea duty' for Navy enlisted personnel. One could usually recognize sailors that had been out there for a year or so; they started to look and act like a Gooney Bird.

We only stayed long enough to re-fuel and get a bite to eat. Then onward to Wake Island for another refueling stop, then Guam for an overnight crew rest and finally proceeding on to Atsugi, Japan.

The flight between Guam and Atsugi took us over the island of Iwo Jima, site of one of World War II's bloodiest battles. Mount Suri-Bachi is where the historic Marine Corps flag raising took place that is now memorialized in bronze with a larger than life sized statue, located in Washington, D.C.

As I said, my initial Trans-Pac was a real WW2 history lesson. This included seeing Pearl Harbor from the air, then on to the site of the Battle Of Midway, and the fall of Wake Island, capture of Guam and Iwo Jima and finally to Japan. Allied Forces never 're-took' Wake Island; by-passing it. Wake had originally been established as a fueling station for Pan Am's Orient flights.

Departing Japan, the return flight differed in that we could fly direct to Midway, taking advantage of the westerly prevailing winds, and then on to Hawaii and the Bay Area, eventually returning to MCAS El Toro.

On my initial Trans-Pac I purchased a 35mm camera in Japan, with a built-in light meter. During the flight from Japan I had placed the camera up on the glare shield of the R5D instrument panel. I noticed that our navigator was nervously checking the compass and taking frequent star shots. I asked him what the problem was.

He came up to the cockpit and noticed my camera in the proximity of the compass. He quickly grabbed the camera...the compass swung about 30-plus degrees! The built-in light meter really affected the compass. I thought he was going to throw my camera out the window (had it been open). My foolishness could have gotten us wet! It's a long way from Japan to Midway direct.

Usually we flew under the jurisdiction of MATS (Military Air Transport Service), under the control of the U.S. Air Force. Occasionally we were under NATS (Naval Air Transport Service) control. The NATS flights took us to places like Hong Kong, New Zealand, Manila and Kwajalein. Interesting trips. The Pacific Ocean is a very large place.

In 1956 we assisted in the support of the "Geophysical Year" in Antarctica. It was a multi-national scientific event. Our involvement was logistic support as far south as Christ Church, New Zealand. Then the Arctic-equipped aircraft would take the loads on down to the campsites on the ice.

Liberty in New Zealand was something else. It seems that the Marine Corps had kept the Japanese away from New Zealand during War2 and the populace hadn't forgotten. It had only been eleven years since the end of the war. We were advised to pull liberty in uniform. It was awesome. –free booze and other delights.

113

I have to admit that I really enjoyed my tour with VMR-352, and transport flying in general. The flights around the United States, in support of the Marine Reserves, were also interesting. Unlike airline flying, where a pilot flies the same route every working day, our support flights took us to different cities on a daily basis. And the instrument flying was some of the finest experiences one could ask for. Many an approach was to minimums and sometimes to GCA minimums. (Much tighter.)

The Chief Pilot for Western Airlines used to occasionally attend our Friday night 'Happy Hour' and recruit for his airline. Western was flying the Douglas DC-6 up and down the West Coast and transitioning from the DC-4 to the DC-6 was a short walk in the park. The dash Six had R-2800 engines and was pressurized, and a bigger airframe, of course. I thought hard about the Western Airlines offer but just wasn't ready for that decision. The idea of '*sitting sideways*' as a Flight Engineer for a few years before moving up to the 'Right Seat" as a Co-Pilot, just wasn't in my zone.

Some years later, flying in the Reserve with lads that had 'gone airline', the common thread was that the flying wasn't good but the money and time off allowed one to do what one really wanted to do. The money was real good in those days when one became "Captain".

It was during this period that my wife Barbara decided that she was in love with my best friend (at that time) one George Sterk. We had been married a year and a half. Our leisure time had been spent almost totally in sports car racing, with some skin diving thrown in. We had joined a diving club and they fabricated dry-suits for Sarge Allen, George Sterk, Barbara and I. The diving on the southern coast of California was wonderful. The *seeing* (visibility) was very clear. The most striking of the sea- life was the California Garibaldi. It is a large orange-gold fish that was protected from sport fishing by the Fish & Game Department. We took lobster, scallops and abalone. We never did any spear fishing.

George Sterk was out of the service, wanting to start his civilian life, job, kids, picket fence, etc. I think Barbara was attracted to that, whereas I was still 'playing race car' and had no desire to settle down.

And believe me, the sports car thing was a different matter.

# THIRTEEN     SPORT CAR RACING

**M**y first exposure to 'sports car' road racing occurred in 1950 at a race in Vanport Oregon and then later at Golden Gate Park in San Francisco. But now here I was with a 1951 MG-TD sports car and anxious to race. As I have mentioned, my first squadron commanding officer was Lt. Colonel Rick Hey. He drove and raced a Jaguar XK-120 in SCCA and Cal Club events in the greater Southern California area.

The summer 1955 Torrey Pines race, one marred by the death of a woman driver in the Morgensen Special (--later to become known as "Ol' Yaller"), found Colonel Hey driving against John César Critchlow. Colonel Hey was beaten by Critchlow, placing fourth against Critchlow's Third Place. Colonel Hey filed a 'protest' based on the fact that Critchlow's Jag had louvers punched in the bonnet, modifying the bonnet. The protest was accepted, robbing Critchlow of his well-earned 'podium'. Ces Critchlow *never* violated any "production" rules, earning his many trophies the hard way; by driving better than others. The louvers would have to be taped over in later races in order to avoid that type of rules conflict.

Lt. Colonel Hey was my Commanding Officer, but John César Critchlow later became one of my closest friends and remains so to this day.

I had planned on entering that race but my car was still being race prepped. The engine was apart for balancing and other tricks of the trade that one could barely get away with in those days of 'production-car'

116

racing.   Going through tech inspection and entry procedures, I was dismayed at how MG owners were treated like 'second-class' citizens.   For many, that car was the entry-level sports car and entitled to be raced. The sport had changed from the comradery of early days of the sport.  Now mind you, this was "amateur" racing. The rewards were a trophy and a name in the record book.

**1951 MG-TD**

In 1950 I had attended the Vanport race with a friend that owned an MG-TC.  We intended merely to spectate, however my friend was encouraged to enter his car.  Folks helped install a seat belt and someone loaned him a helmet and that was it.  He was a race driver, driving his first sports car race. I also had a chance to try my hand at it. That's what the early days were all about. But now, only five years later, the sport had changed.

Two major Sport Car Clubs controlled all racing in Southern California.  They were the SCCA (Sports Car Club of America) and the Cal Club (California Sports Car Club).  The SCCA was national and a bit on the 'uppity' side. I chose to join Cal Club. The races put on by both of those large clubs were pretty elaborate in the mid Fifties. It could be a bit intimidating for a novice.

I decided to start a race-club intended for novices, to help break into the game. My friend, Tom Norman and his wife Nancy, plus my wife Barbara, set out to do just that. We elected Tom to become the first President. I was Vice President and General Manager; Nancy was Secretary, and Barbara was the Treasurer.

We heard of a small race-track that had been built in Colton, California and decided to check it out. The owner and track builder was Herschel McGraw. We told him our plans and he said that we were crazy. The Cal Club and/or the local SCCA chapter would put us out of business. He suggested that we make it a *race-training* organization and we would probably draw support from the two big time clubs. It was the birth of the Road Race Training Association (RRTA).

To introduce the club to other sports car clubs in the greater Los Angeles area, we obtained a list and meeting times and proceeded to visit each of the clubs, one at a time, and present the RRTA plan. We were very well received.

We had decided on hosting Time Trials at various Southern California road courses. Trophies, for the Time Trials, would be awarded in the various classes and non-trophy races held for experience. The events would be closed to the general public. This format kept the liability insurance within reasonable parameters.

The response was beyond expectations.

We also visited The Cal Club and the Los Angeles Chapter of the Sports Car Club of America (SCCA). Our prime purpose at those two venues was to enlist coaching help from some of the better-known drivers of the period. Most were very enthusiastic and thought that the RRTA had a real purpose in life. Instructors included such luminaries as Phil Hill, Richie

Ginther, Ken Miles, Bob Oker, Bill Kinner and Ces Critchlow.

Our first event was at McGraw's track in Colton. The track was too small for races but okay for Time Trials.

The next two events were at Mile Square in Santa Ana. It was a triangular airport that the Marine Corps used for "off-Base" helicopter training operations. Being a fellow Marine Aviator helped acquire the use of the site for a weekend activity. I arranged to borrow a zillion red road-construction cones to layout a road course, from the City of Santa Ana Road Maintenance Department. Rented an ambulance and, fortunately one of our RRTA members was a Doctor, satisfying that requirement. Our entry fees actually covered the weekend expense, including the trophies for the Time Trials.

McGraw had left for Saudi Arabia on a one-year drilling contract. He hadn't participated in the founding and development of the club beyond suggesting the format, but later took credit for it in a ROAD & TRACK article.

Later in 1956 I went through my divorce to Barbara, Tom and Nancy had their first child, and the RRTA was slowing down. McGraw returned from his Arabian contract and offered to take over the club. We were happy to pass the baton to him.

McGraw put on RRTA events at Willow Springs, Pomona, and Hour Glass Field, doing a fine job. Later the club was to undergo a change from its non-profit standing, becoming the Road Race Training School.

Shortly after turning the RRTA over to McGraw I sold my MG-TD and bought Ces Critchlow's XK-120

Jaguar. Ces had purchased Jack Douglas's C-Type Jaguar (XKC-023) Sports Racer, after Jack had purchased a Jaguar D-Type Sports Racer. Douglas took delivery in New York and drove it across the United States. He mentioned that he had picked up a few moving violations. (What a story *that* would make!)

Ces's XK-120 had been a very successful racecar; one season picking up fourteen straight podiums (1st, 2nd, or 3rd). Looking for more low-end performance Ces changed the rear end ratio. He put in a Ford pick-up truck set of gears (4:11 ??). This resulted in a top speed of only 120 mph @ 6,000 rpm. The original gear ratio from the factory was 'too tall' for the shorter American tracks. The change provided more torque in 2nd and 3rd gears. As previously stated, this was not in violation of production rules. I found that I had to be careful not to exceed the 6,000 rpm red line, having to feather the throttle on longer straight-aways.

**Ces Critchlow in his Jaguar XK-120M at Torrey Pines –in the hay!**

John César Critchlow was named after César Franck (1822–1890) Belgium composer. "Ces" was of medium build, wore glasses and was very droll in attitude and speech. Ces helped me make my transition from the MG to the 120. It was a giant step for me. The acceleration in all of the gears was head snapping.

In flight training I had the opportunity to fly the Grumman F6F Hellcat for 35 hours. The Hellcat had a Pratt & Whitney R-2800 engine. This powerful engine *slammed* the pilot back into the seat upon application of take-off power. The jet fighter that I was flying at the time didn't even come close, not having afterburners. The Jag certainly covered that missing experience.

*(It was as if being in my first Fighter Squadron wasn't enough. But I had achieved my life goal! I'm writing this in 2015-2016 and looking, back examining this period in my life. Was it a time...place thing, I think not. Racing was a developing passion that needed to be fed. –either that or I was becoming an adrenalin junkie!)*

Ces worked with me on selected isolated road sections, in and around Laguna Beach, that were not heavily traveled. The "drift" was an important element to learn. It allowed carrying energy into a turn and thus able to exit the turn at high speed rates. This helped, but now I wanted to race the car. I learned that the RRTA had rented the Willow Springs racecourse for an event. Ces and I both entered. Ces needed track time to further sort out his newly acquired C-Type. He trailered the car to the track; I drove the XK120 up to Pasadena and then over the mountains to Rosemond and Willow Springs. That drive, in itself, was worth the weekend.

After observing various cars in practice I determined that my main competition would be Scooter Patrick, driving a Mercedes-Benz 300 SL. (Scooter would later go on to drive internationally for Alfa Romeo.)

121

During practice Ces let me have some laps in the C-Type. My Gawd! What an experience! Here I was driving a *real* racecar! As memory serves me (--and THAT's a laugh! Memory, that is.) the car presented no surprises. It was fast, very fast. It handled through corners like it was on rails leaving me almost breathless. It's one thing to drive a car fast, it's a totally different thing to drive a *fast car!*

Jaguar C-Type factory race car – Ces at Santa Barbara

Words escape me to adequately describe the weekend Jaguar driving-racing experience. For me, it was also the first time that I *thought* behind the wheel during a race, rather than *reacting* to the racing factors.

Scooter had won the Time Trials, leaving 2nd Place to me.

But now it was race time. We were soon both in the front of the pack. I would lead on the short sections, and then Scooter would pass me on the straights. This went on. I had to do something different. I fell back about ten to fifteen car lengths and let him get complacent. On the last lap, as he went into the sweeping right hand curve onto the straight-away and finish line, effectively hiding me from his mirrors, I closed the two or three car length gaps. Coming into the 90-degree right hand turn onto the straightaway I passed him *on the outside* in third gear and beat him to the finish line by barely a half car length.

It was a perfect day!

I was thrilled about having a car capable of putting me on the podium. Sadly, one of the few times that I drove the car on the road a woman ran a stop sign and I "T-boned" her car, killing her and injuring a couple of her kids. It could have been a real disaster. Here I was, a Marine pilot, driving a hot racecar, etc. Fortunately, behind her was an entourage, consisting of a Navy Chaplain, a Marine Commanding Officer and others on their way to tell a wife that her husband had been killed in an airplane crash. They attested to the fact that the woman didn't even slow down for the stop sign. Additionally, two civilians, attracted by the sound and sight of the Jaguar's somewhat 'open exhaust', attested that I was, surprisingly, doing less than 40 mph in a 55 mph zone. They were surprised I was driving so sedately.

We won the lawsuit. However, it was a sad ending to a great car.

I had been working part-time for John Horvath's Foreign Auto Rebuild in Costa Mesa. It was where I had met John César Critchlow, in fact. I had learned, when I started racing, to align myself with a good shop.

It was about this time that Ces moved in with me. I had had a couple of room-mates but Ces was the most fun. We did a lot of partying and double dating. He ended up getting drafted. On the day that he had to report I drove him up to Santa Ana, to the train station. I was in my Marine Officer's uniform and when we were in close proximity to the Army Sergeant that was in charge, I shook Ces's hand and said, "The General is proud of you, Mr. Critchlow…of the way that you're doing this without his help".

The Sergeant heard this, of course…. put Ces in charge of the group forming up, and also made notes in his file. (It followed Ces over his two-year Army obligation.)

Horvath was working with a Swiss gentleman importing interesting sports and racecars into the United States. They initially traded only in Ferraris', but later expanded to Maserati and Alfa Romeo's. One of Horvath's early sales was to Loren Castleman, a young, very wealthy gentleman from Riverside, California. His estate was what was left from one of the large Spanish Land Grants. (It was rumored that March AFB was built on a "99-year lease" to the Government.)

The car was a Ferrari 166 MM Barchetta. The car was one of thirty-nine Touring-bodied factory racecars built in 1949. A sister-ship took 4th Place in the 1950 Mille Miglia and also distinguished itself at Le Mans that year. It was a car designed to race and win.

It had a 1,995cc 60-degree V12 with twin cam overhead valves that put 140 horses on the ground, operating continuously up to 7,000 RPM. Three twin-choke downdraft Weber 32 DCF carburetors fed the engine. The gearbox was not synchromesh. Revs had to be perfectly matched changing up or down the box with double clutching. But it was a wonder to drive, augmented by the wonderful smell of Castrol-R Racing Oil. –ooh! And, it was a Ferrari! --body by 'Touring' and it was red.

Castleman decided to have the car raced and asked Horvath who he recommended as a driver. Ces had been drafted so John recommended me.

**Ferrari 166MM Barchetta**

One evening Loren showed up at my front door. I was still living in my little house on Laguna Canyon Road. He hadn't called, just showed up. I had seen him at the shop, been introduced, but really didn't know him. He asked if I wanted to go for a drive in the 166.

He told me to drive. We left the house, driving up Laguna Canyon Road and took the fork that leads up to the little hamlet of El Toro. The Union Pacific railroad tracks are on the outskirts of the town. It has a berm up to and over the tracks. Loren was calling out route and speed issues. I hit the berm at a high rate of speed, getting airborne for a period of time, managing to keep from over-revving the engine. –t'was indeed a bit of a thrill.

Loren said that we would take the over-mountain (Saddleback) route to Corona. It was paved for a bit of the way, then essentially forestry roads. Again, Loren knew the road pretty well and was calling out warnings and encouragement. It was one hellava drive, turning

125

darker.  The road had many twists and turns (and no escape areas).  A bad mistake could prove very hazardous to one's health.  Again, a bit of a thrill.

We made it to Corona in one piece.  Loren offered me the driving position, which I accepted.

I raced at several tracks in Southern California.  This was a very exciting time in my life.  –what great memories!  The smells (especially the smell of Castrol R racing oil), the sounds of racing engines revving up or running down a straight-away at close to 10,000 RPM, standing in line at a Porta-Potty for that last nervous pee before a race and the hot, dusty ambience of Southern California.

Sports car racing changed from "amateur" to "professional" in 1957.  It was no longer a gentleman's sporting event but something out of gasoline alley.  It resulted in many of the wealthy stable owners getting out of the sport.  Loren Castleman was one of those.  He sold the Ferrari and I was out of a ride.

I had purchased a 1955 Porsche Speedster, *as is*. (without an engine) It had been originally licensed as a Carrera, and the engine was disassembled and in a fruit basket.  A true "basket case".  The Carrera was a twin-cam design with a roller-bearing crankshaft and 1500cc engine displacement.  I was working part time for John Horvath and borrowed a VW engine to install in it.  It became my daily driver.  (Horvath had exchange VW engines and courtesy engines in stock.)

A kid, that used to hang around the shop, just *had* to have the Carrera engine.  Mind you, the damaged crankshaft was over $750 dealer cost.  In 1957, that was all the money in town.  He offered me a 1500cc stock Porsche engine and some money for the basket case.  I accepted.

Castleman had pre-paid the entry fee for the SCCA national event at Santa Barbara. I got the stock engine installed in the Speedster in time to make the event.

I only raced the Speedster three times. SCCA Santa Barbara, Cal-Club Paramount Ranch and the Inaugural International Riverside Raceways event, September 21$^{st}$ & 22$^{nd}$ 1957 sponsored by the California Car Club.

As to be expected, the car didn't do very well. It ran against Porsche Super and Carrera models. Maybe I should have kept and rebuilt the hot Carrera engine, but at the time I had been driving for Castleman and the Speedster was being used strictly as a street machine. It was the only car that I had to put on a track.

I had met "H. McKay Frasier" through Ces. Mac was also a racer. His father was in the Diplomatic Corps and Mac had gone to England with his family and was driving in international events. He had written to Ces encouraging him to come over. I was sorta invited as well. Just before I was scheduled to get off Active Duty Mac Frasier was killed at Spa, in France, driving for Lotus Works.

I didn't get any other offers to drive, my Speedster wasn't competitive so it was time to hang up the helmet and goggles. I wasn't going to Europe.

It was the end of my racing career.

**Riverside Raceways inaugural event – 1957**

# FOURTEEN     THE CIVILIAN SECTOR

**I** had extended my military obligation six months, in order to apply for a Regular Commission. After being turned down for the third time, I opted to get out. It was September 1957. Just prior to my release from Active Duty I applied for and received orders to a Jet Fighter Retraining Program. The training was conducted in the F9F-8T Cougar. The swept wing fighter was capable of supersonic flight.

I applied for a slot in a Marine Reserve "Weekend Warrior" squadron based at NAS Los Alamitos. I was informed that there was a two-year waiting list to get into a Reserve squadron. I did put my name on the list, however.

It was a ball getting back into a fighter. As part of the course I went super-sonic and *boomed* out over the Pacific Ocean. We also did a quick air-to-air refueling hop...my first and last experience of both of those aviation tasks.

And then it was over. I was a civilian.

-o-

I really didn't know what to do with myself. I was okay financially what with un-used Leave and Mustering-Out Pay. I kinda bummed around Laguna Beach, taking it easy. Having a few beers with a friend, Ron 'something', that I had done a little diving with, asked me if I would 'tend' for him. It seems that the California Fish & Game had opened the 'coast' for commercial abalone diving-fishing. However, it wouldn't allow free-scuba diving. It had to be with tethered shallow-water diving gear. Ron had decided that there was some serious bucks to be made and scrounged up a boat, and equipped it with a compressor, "Desco" Mask and weight belt, all tied together with a quick single release clamp. An air hose served as the 'tether' required by the Fish & Game Department.

His boat wasn't much more than a rowboat with an outboard motor. He had opted to dive off of Laguna Beach, since he was familiar with the area and work his way to the north. As his tender it was my job to haul up the basket with the abalone, measure them and throw the under-size ones back into the ocean. This action created another problem. The Abalone is a single-shelled marine creature. The open side was a suction-foot that allowed it to attach to a rock face. Throwing back the under-sized ones attracted Moray Eels. Abalone was a real treat to them. We had to devise another way.

We marked the Abalone knife with the correct legal dimensions in order to replace the undersized ones back where they had been attached. It helped.

I soon tired of just sitting in the boat so decided that I wanted to 'jump' in with my friend. We rigged another air hose and "Desco" Mask to the compressor. We were soon able to double our catch.

Another problem arose. When the ocean got a bit choppy, waves would break over the boat, shorting out the compressor. It didn't take very long, with both of us pulling air out of the compressor tank, to empty it. The only warning we had was the obvious difficulty in breathing.

Most of our diving was approximately 80 to 100 feet. This meant that one had to bail-out of the gear and make a 'free' ascent to the surface, being sure to exhale all the way up to prevent embolisms from forming. It

130

soon became almost second nature, having to bail out of the gear at least once a trip if not more.

The accumulation of nitrogen in your system was almost like being drunk. Walking around in town people avoided us thinking we were drunk.

We made some money then had a whole load spoil when we didn't make it to the processor in time.

That was enough for me. So, *'there I was'* on the beach.

I went back to working part time for John Horvath's Foreign Auto Service, for something to do. I was going Nuts!

Back when I was on Active Duty and after Barbara and I divorced, I returned to Seattle on leave. My friend, Tom Roselli, was out of the Navy and working for Boeing as an engineer. He fixed me up for a date with one of his wife's girlfriends. Her name was Alice Miller. She was from Kalispell, Montana and on her way to Japan as a civilian employee. We had a nice date and I promised to look her up on one of my Japan flights. Once again, merely a nice date. That changed and we got serious. I told her that when her contract was up to come to California and she could stay with me until she got settled.... or we could get more serious.

When I was working for John Horvath Alice wrote advising of her ETA at Travis AFB, up near the bay area. I drove my Porsche Speedster and picked her up at the base. We returned to Laguna and I moved her in. It wasn't a platonic relationship anymore. I was thinking marriage. A month later she advised me that she was pregnant. By then I didn't want to marry. She had a strange quirk. She would be very nice to me when we were alone but then, when we were around my friends;

she would start putting me down.  The 'put downs' were probably in my imagination.  In those days I had an ego the size of King Kong's and couldn't handle anything in the negative.  And I was still carrying way too much baggage from Barbara.  We decided on an abortion.

The cost was $400.  I didn't have it and borrowed the money from Loren Castleman.  I was able to repay it rather promptly.  Then Alice turned up pregnant again!  Back up to LA and the $400 doctor.  I was afraid to shake hands with her after that.  I finally got her settled into her own place in Santa Ana.  I was disgusted with myself and the two abortions were not something to be proud of, regardless of our not getting along.  That action haunted me for many years after.  It just wasn't right.  I had become Pro-Life.  I felt that sometime in the future I was going to be standing in front of 'The Man' and face responsibility for those actions.  I still feel that way.

I answered an ad in the Los Angeles Times for a pilot, and was the successful applicant.  My job was to select an airplane suitable for flying around the entire United States for extended periods of time.  It sounded like something to do.

In 1957 there wasn't much to choose from in the used aircraft market.  The light twin choice was either a Piper Apache or Cessna 310, both of which were very expensive.  I decided on a used Cessna 195.  It is a large five-place airplane with a single radial engine that was fast for its time.  We paid $6,500 for it.

It was going to be like flying Bud's CH-300 Bellanca out to an Eskimo village with the serum!

**Cessna 195**    *--round power and large cabin*

The check pilot, calling himself "Captain something," who checked me out, insisted on wheel landings. The Cessna 195 had a spring-steel landing gear and also crosswind landing gear, that was a bit hard to get used to. I finally told the check pilot to go screw himself and made full stall landings. He had no choice but to sign me off. Wheel landings are fine, look good, but can use up one hellava lot of landing turf.

The company was Time Tool Company. My boss, and Vice-President of the company was Ken Ferraie. Our first destination was Washington D.C. Departing Los Angeles, I planned my first refuel stop in Tucumcari, NM. It was there that I decided to pin up that damn crosswind landing gear. I told the mechanic at the Fixed Base Operation, (FBO, what they call an aviation gas station, service station, etc.) where we refueled to "weld that damn gear up!" --he said it would be easier to just pin 'em.

I had picked up Radio Facility charts and Approach Plates for the entire United States from my old transport squadron at El Toro. They worked well for the trip. When I was approaching Washington D.C. the weather had turned really bad. The D.C. area had gone down to minimums and I was having difficulty controlling the airplane, reading the chart and fighting the turbulence. No auto-pilot or co-pilot. I finally asked Approach Control for some help and they came through with a Precision Approach, similar to a military GCA. We survived. Ken told me he would be busy for a couple of days and to leave word with the FBO facility where I could be reached. I decided to just hang around the airport and fuss with the airplane. I added some instrument lighting to the panel.

Our next stop was New York. It was a clear, sunny day and upon arrival I flew around the city taking in the Statue of Liberty, Empire State Building and Manhattan Island. It was fun! (You sure can't do that type of thing now! --or even before 9/11.) I landed at Newark, NJ. It was the same drill; Ken would be gone for a couple of days. I hung around the airport. –lunch was the usual candy-bar and Coke, typical 'pilot-fare'.

Next stop was Chicago. I landed at Meigs Field, located on the shore and jutting out into Lake Michigan. It had a single 3,900-foot runway. After landing, you were in downtown Chicago. It was really convenient. Some years later Chicago "Daley politics" kicked in and Mayor Daley ordered X's plowed in the runway surface stranding sixteen aircraft.... all without warning. The sixteen aircraft were eventually allowed to depart using the taxiway for take-off...

"The signature act of Richard Daley's 22 years in office was the midnight bulldozing of Meigs Field," according to *Chicago Tribune* columnist Eric Zorn.[20] "He ruined Meigs because he wanted to, because he

134

could," columnist John Kass wrote of Daley in the *Chicago Tribune*.[21]

Gone, but not forgotten.

My boss, Ken, was starting to run short of traveling funds so I offered to put the airplane fuel on my Shell Oil credit card, to be reimbursed upon our return to LAX. That turned out to be a mistake.

We spent time in the Great Lakes region with side trips to Kenosha, Green Bay, Olathe, Dayton and some others, whose name I can't recall. We finally departed for LAX. I dropped Ken off and took the airplane down to Orange County Airport for maintenance.

Ken called the next day to say that the President of the company had folded the tent and stolen away, taking all the assets of the company, except the wall-paper, with him.

We were out our expense money. I promptly put a lien on the airplane. It was later sold, but I was still on the Title. (It took a couple of years to get the new owners to take me off of the Title and reimburse me.)

I told Shell what had happened, turned in my Credit Card and made arrangements to make payments on the approximately $ 2,500 owed. (In 1957, that was a lot of money. As a matter of note, when I made the last payment Shell sent me a new credit card.)

Once again, *'there I was'* back on the beach.

Okay, I've tried 'corporate aviation', now what. In the fall of 1957, when I came off of Active Duty, there was a bit of a depression in the country. Jobs were scarce. An aerospace company called Flexonics Corporation, headquartered in the greater Chicago area, built a new plant in Santa Ana to service the aerospace industry in

Southern California. When they advertised for help the lines went around the block.

I interviewed for a position as a Junior Engineer, having been a draftsman at Boeing one year. The personnel Manager, Bill Fortner, assumed that I was a college graduate since I had been a Commissioned Officer and Marine Aviator. I was told that I wouldn't report for work for two weeks, or so, since the plant was still being finished and manufacturing equipment moved in.

Bill was the only person interviewing people lined up for the various job openings. He was pretty hassled. I told him that I didn't have anything else to do and was tired of lying around on the beach so would come by in the morning and give him a hand. I don't think he even heard me, but the next morning at zero-dark-thirty I was there. I told him that I had had some personnel experience in the Marine Corps and would give him a hand. He was surprised but realized that he did indeed need some assistance so offered me a "Kelly Girl-type" temporary four-week contract. Since there wouldn't be any benefits, it paid me more than the $500 per month that I would be earning as a Junior Engineer. I set to work.

Initial screening of applicants included some discussion of wage levels. To assist me, Bill gave me a large, thick binder containing an 'area survey' of the area. It included area wages, union activity, railheads, utilities etc. It was very complete. Naturally I turned to the engineering section and there I was; *Jr. Engineer, $500 per month.* I turned the next page and there was the Sales Department. A Junior *Sales* Engineer started at $650 per month and was provided with a company car!

And THAT, dear reader, was how I got started in sales work.

136

My primary sales responsibility was Convair, in San Diego, and support of the Senior Sales Engineers that were dealing with Douglas, North American and Lockheed Aircraft companies. This support work usually involved going up to the designated facility and re-marking some parts, or delivering some expedited parts, etc. All three of these major aerospace firms were located on airports. Driving in the Los Angeles traffic was very time consuming. I convinced my boss, George Derum, that I could purchase block-time from Martin Aviation at Orange County Airport, for a Cessna 180, drive over to the airport (less than 10 minutes) fly up to the designated company where I would be met by the company engineers who were delighted to receive the badly needed goods. The system really worked!

Flexonics didn't have a very good reputation in the aero-space companies in Southern California. The extra effort expediting critical parts was creating a whole new reputation with Buyers and Project Managers. I soon became a rising star in the Sales Department. I even had some success with Convair, that hadn't ever been done before. In fact, Flexonics had been almost barred from that company over some past dispute involving delivery time.

On one of my delivery trips to North American the engineer that met me asked if I would work up a quote for some flexible lines. Upon my return to the factory I told the account Sales Engineer about them. He said to go ahead and work the quote up, it would be my sale. I did and the quote was accepted. The lines were for the X-15. As a result, I was invited up to North American Aviation for the rollout of the X-15 and also had an opportunity to meet Scott Crossfield, who would be piloting the initial sub-space flights.

137

During my tenure as an Assistant Personnel Manager I became involved in an employee problem. I interfaced with the Personnel Manager at another company in Santa Ana, where the subject employee had worked before. The employee had quit to take a new job at Flexonics that didn't work out. I was able to get her old job back for her.

The receptionist at the other company sounded kinda cute. After many calls back and forth we finally met. Her name was Linda Grafton. A few months later we married (since she thought she was with child). Twenty-eight days later we weren't married when it turned out that she wasn't.

A year or so later, George Derum got into some kind of difficulty and was sent back to Elgin, IL. His replacement arrived and the first thing the replacement did was to throw the 'airplane program' out the door. We did not get along at all.

I had finally paid off Shell, didn't owe anybody anything, didn't have a mortgage, was single, so elected to quit. Southern California had awakened somewhat so I didn't feel anxious about finding a good job. I was hanging out at Orange County airport and picked up a couple of charters.

There was a bar in Laguna called the Blue Beet. It was near the post office where I maintained a P.O. Box. I used to go pick up my mail and then drop in for a beer or two. The bartender's name was Darlene. She was the niece of a Gunny Sergeant I had served with in the Marine Corps.

She needed a place to stay so I let her move in with me. We kept the relationship very platonic until one night when I returned from partying a bit. The relationship changed. We were soon married and expecting our first child.

The summer of 1959 I enrolled at Westlake College of Modern Music, to open my G.I. Bill. (It was known as the "Julliard of the West Coast".) I was working part-time at the Blue Beet as a bartender by this time. I played the Vibes in a couple of gigs there. (Up to that point all my 'pro' jazz gigs were on piano.)

I had been planning on returning to Seattle at the end of the school year.

My Stepfather, Art Weishart, had founded Bel-Kirk Motors, in Kirkland, WA. . The car agency was Volvo and Roots Group, an English car company.

Art asked me to attend a "Dealer-required" maintenance class, in Los Angeles, that was in support of a Roots Group new electric-magnetic automatic transmission. I was happy to oblige.

Besides working for John Horvath's Foreign Auto Repair I had gotten involved with a few fellows that formed a car agency in Laguna Beach called "The Autohaus". They had attempted to obtain a Volkswagen-Porsche dealership to no avail, but did become a Service Center for the two makes. I had been responsible for the installation of an inventory control system by Diebold. It really worked well. The Autohaus did very well with just doing service work. I learned the value of what a good service department could do for a dealership.

When I returned to Seattle I started working with Art at Bel-Kirk Motors. I had personal, hands-on experience with the service side of the automobile business and knew the money pit that it could be. At the Autohaus, when they couldn't get the dealership they concentrated on service work. It became very profitable. My Step-father wanted me to do sales, he

139

had a high school kid doing new car prep work. That was the extent of 'service work'.

I contacted the local Diebold representative and asked him to come out to Bel-Kirk Motors. I explained about the success I had experienced at the Autohaus. He was kind enough to leave a sample supply of Volvo cards and a cardholder. Art wasn't interested in purchasing a system, wasn't interested in expanding the service department and wanted me to concentrate on sales, etc. It became obvious that our working together wasn't going to pan out.

My first-born, a daughter arrived March 29$^{th}$, 1960. She was named Katherine Dale McEniry. Her birth was not an easy one for Darlene. Due to some complications, she had to be delivered via a Caesarian Section at the last minute. (and no insurance.)

With the help of a friend, whom I had flown with on active duty (Ric Novak), I was able to get into a Marine Reserve squadron at NAS Seattle (Sand Point). The squadron was flying the Douglas AD-5 Skyraider, later designated the A1E by the Department of Defense. It was a large, single-engine dive-bomber, powered by the Wright R-3350 radial engine. (The second largest engine built, the P & W R-4360 being the largest, eight of which powered the Spruce Goose.

I was obligated to one weekend a month and two weeks Active Duty in the summer. Retirement points could be earned and if 60 points per year were acquired for 20 satisfactory years, a handsome retirement fund could be realized upon reaching age 60. It was a pretty good deal. Good company, fun airplanes, cheap booze at the club and earning retirement monies. However, there was also a chance that one could be activated in times of National Emergency. Oh well, WTFOver. One just ignored that factor. The 'fellowship' was what it was all about, and of course sharing drinks at the Officer's Club.

Douglas AD-5 Skyraider, designated A1E in Viet Nam

Note the racks…. this bird could take 10,000 pounds of ordnance a decent range and stick around for a couple of hours! Quite effective when covering a downed pilot until the chopper comes in. She became known as a "Spad" for her ancient status as a propeller-driven, slow and lumbering air-bird.

In fact, one weekend I was surprised to meet Gregory "Pappy" Boyington of Guadalcanal's "Black Sheep Squadron. (VMR-214) He had flown in China with the Flying Tigers before the United States entered the war. In April of 1942 he left China to re-join the Marine Corps. His accomplishments on the "Canal" are a part of history now.

Pappy was in Seattle doing something or other at the University of Washington. He was staying at the Officer's Club and quite a few of my squadron mates and I had a drink with him. It was a real honor.

Since it had become obvious that Art and I were not on the same page, it seemed that the prudent thing to do was to move on. I checked in the Seattle 'Yellow Pages' for a Flexonics branch and discovered that they used a distributor for their aerospace work with Boeing. In the telephone book I found another company called U.S. Flexible Metallic Tubing Company, when I had been looking up Flexonics.. I put my executive resume in shape and called for an appointment. It was granted.

The Seattle Branch manager was Chuck Clayton. He was impressed with my background at Flexonics and sought approval from the Los Angeles home office to make me an offer. He did and I accepted.

Darlene, the baby and I had been living in Kirkland. Chuck Clayton's secretary told me of an apartment that was available on Queen Anne hill. It had eight rooms, two full size bedrooms and a smaller one suitable for use as a nursery. It also had a magnificent view. It looked straight down on Pier 91 and to the south, Seattle's waterfront.

I started calling on Boeing and came across a new technology gaining increasing use. Boeing was moving into the space age. The new technology was called Cryogenics. The term is applied to the study of low temperature media, primarily liquid oxygen, liquid nitrogen and liquid hydrogen. The latter two require well-insulated containers or insulated lines to prevent the media from gassing off. In the case of the insulated flexible lines this would require twice as many flexible metal bellows, one inside of the other. I recognized it as a wonderful sales opportunity.

The only source of design information I could find was a book titled "Cryogenic Engineering", by a Dr. Thomas Flynn. Dr. Flynn was a professor at the University of Washington. After reading his book and realizing that I would be in need of a great deal of help, I

142

decided to call on him. I requested some samples from the home office, in stainless steel and of various sizes. They sent me some bellows that were absolute jewels. They were beautiful.

I made arrangements to call on Dr. Flynn. It was difficult getting past his secretary, but I finally succeeded. The Doctor was very impressed but said that he couldn't afford to buy them. I made it clear that they were a gift along with any others that he would need for lab work. He asked what he could do for me and I told him to just be available on the other end of the telephone. It was the beginning of a beautiful relationship. I would be exposed to a Boeing requirement and when running into problems would call Dr. Flynn. He found it fascinating and really helped me.

I ended up with a Boeing 'Consultant' badge along with an "EX" parking permit, normally issued only to Boeing executives. The badge gave me almost unlimited access to the various Boeing plants. It was wonderful and a lot of fun.

My most noteworthy accomplishment was the four-inch liquid hydrogen lines installed on the gantry of the Saturn launch vehicle. All of the test work was done out at the Tulalip Indian Reservation. I had done the actual design work for the inner and outer bellows assembly that would provide a vacuum jacket drawn down to 'ten-to-the minus-nine'. A hard vacuum.

When Boeing released the RFQ (Request for Quote) I found that Flexonics would also be quoting. In fact, they were the successful bidder. I knew that the Boeing delivery requirement was critical and also knew that Flexonics always quoted shipping as "Six Weeks After Receipt Of Order". They never made the quoted six weeks and always went in asking for extensions. I suggested to my home office that we go ahead and build the initial order.

I was right. Flexonics failed and asked for four weeks' extension. I was called in by Boeing Purchasing and asked what we could do. I told them that we could ship that day. The Buyer was stunned. I mentioned that I had worked for Flexonics and knew their techniques.

U.S. Flex was granted the order and became "sole source". Boeing continued to purchase those same assemblies throughout the Saturn era, long after I had left the company.

I had been working with Boeing Aerospace Division for all of their cryogenic applications. One day I got a call from the Transport Division asking me to come and look over a bellows requirement.

It was for the middle engine intake for the Boeing 727. The middle engine was buried in the fuselage, shock mounted and connected to the rear. It required a very large diameter but short live-length flexible connection. U.S. Flex came up with a sample of exactly what they needed. It was a thirty-six inch inside diameter and a four-inch live length. I was pleased to receive the Purchase Order.

When I sent the order down to the home office in Los Angeles, Frank McDonald (The sole owner of U.S. Flexible Metallic Tubing Company) sent it back, refusing the order. I was shocked!

I told my boss, Chuck Clayton, that I was going down to Los Angeles. He said that he couldn't approve of the trip, not having any budget for that sort of thing. I told him to never mind, I would use a Marine Corps airplane.

As I said, I was a member of the Organized Reserve, stationed at NAS Seattle (Sand Point). We were

144

encouraged to do more than our required one weekend a month. Night flying was available during the week and also cross-country flights, limited to one RON. (*R*emain *O*ver *N*ight) After checking with the Marine Detachment for aircraft availability I called the home office, spoke with the Chief Engineer and made arrangements for him to pick me up at MCAS El Toro, down near Santa Ana.

I was able to make my ETA at El Toro and my ride was there on time. Without even changing out of my flight suit we headed for Los Angeles. He took me directly to the Jonathan Club in downtown Los Angeles, where I was registered as a guest of Mr. F.A. McDonald. I was glad that I had brought along a blazer, shirt, slacks and tie. The Jonathan Club was very upscale, a bit stuffy, a gathering point for well to do folk. I had a couple of drinks followed by an impressive dinner. I retired for the night. Tomorrow would begin with an early start.

The Chief engineer picked me up at the appointed time. We went to the plant where he showed me around and introduced me to various people that I'd had occasion to work with from Seattle. At a time, that only he was aware of, we headed up to Mr. McDonald's office. His secretary greeted us. She was rather plain in appearance, hair in a bun but obviously efficient. She said that Mr. McDonald was expecting us and opened the door into his office. She stood back, allowing me to enter and then quietly closed the door. I was surprised that I would be left alone with the man.

Frank McDonald's office was quite large, carpeted with an expensive oriental rug. His oversize desk appeared to be made of a type of burl-wood. The desktop was relatively clear.

I marched smartly up to within eighteen inches of the edge of his desk and it took all of my effort not to bark out, *"Lieutenant McEniry reporting as ordered, Sir!"* It would not have been appropriate since I hadn't been ordered to appear before him and he was not a senior military officer.

Before I said anything, Frank stood with his hand out and after a firm handshake motioned for me to sit in a somewhat elegant chair near his desk.

After a brief exchange of pleasantries, I got immediately to the point. "Why?"

There was no question in anybody's mind the subject of my meaning. Chuck Clayton would have called telling him of my intentions. And, of course, the arrangements at the Jonathan Club didn't just happen.

Frank took his time responding as if to be absolutely clear with his response.

"An assembly aboard an FAA Certified airplane must in its turn be certified. This would put Boeing Inspection and Engineering personnel in our plant. Our method of multi-ply bellows assembly fabrication cannot be patent protected. Boeing has a reputation in the industry for stealing proprietary processes. I cannot allow that to happen."

"Then why did you let me go ahead with the sample and proposal?" I said.

"I didn't think that you would get the order and I didn't want to discourage your efforts. Congratulations, by the way." (The Saturn Cryogenic joints were not FAA 'certified' so didn't come under any "on-site" inspection issues.)

U.S. Flex had been primarily an industrial products firm. They had done very little in the aerospace field until I joined the company. I had always hoped to establish an Aerospace Division at the plant in Los Angeles and that I would head it up. This was now, obviously, out of the question. I told Frank McDonald that I would probably be moving on. He was disappointed with my remark but seemed to understand where I was coming from.

We had a nice lunch at the Jonathan Club and then I was handed back to the Chief Engineer who drove me back down to El Toro. Nothing more was said about my quitting.

My consulting activity also exposed me to other interesting projects at Boeing. One involved the Hotshot Wind Tunnel. It was there that I met an engineer that helped me *acquire* my college degree.

Over the period of the wind tunnel project we had lunch together a few times. During one lunch I commented that I wanted to apply for a job with Texaco as a pilot salesman flying around the west coast in a Cessna 310 selling Texaco aviation products. We both agreed that it would be a fun job. The only catch was that Texaco demanded a technical college degree. My engineer friend was astounded that I didn't have one. He had assumed that with my knowledge of bellows and flexible tubing that I had an engineering degree. I replied in the negative but went on to say that I had a lot of product knowledge but no degree. He said that he could remedy the college degree problem quickly.

We drove over to his apartment on Magnolia Bluff. He went in and returned shortly with a blank college degree from Louisiana Technical Institute. It was already signed and dated. The dates would work with my background. All that was left for me to do was to find a calligrapher and write in my name and selected technical degree. I chose Mechanical Engineering.

With a copy of my degree inserted into my resume I contacted Texaco only to find out that the position of Aviation Products Pilot salesman had been put on indefinite hold.

Watching the ads in "The Seattle Times" I saw one for a Pilot-Salesman, Aviation Products. I responded and it was the Seattle branch of Pacific Airmotive Corporation. I applied for the position and was accepted from about fifteen applicants. It was spring of 1962.

# FIFTEEN       PACIFIC AIRMOTIVE

The Seattle Branch Sales Manager and Chief Pilot was Fred J. Costello, who, until recently had been flying C-119's with the U.S. Air Force Reserve out of Paine Field, Everett Washington.

It was an interesting job, selling aviation products in the states of Washington, Oregon, Idaho, Montana and Alaska. The latter would be covered by commercial air carrier and the lower forty-eight (CONUS) with a Beechcraft Debonair.

The aviation products were anything and everything for any airplane with the exception of engine parts and radios. Such things as tires, wheels, batteries, spark plugs, light bulbs, anti-icing systems, magnetos, cable and just about anything air-motive.

The Debonair is a wonderful four place airplane; low wing, retractable landing gear, variable pitch propeller and a respectable range. She was powered by a Continental six cylinder, opposed IO-470, generating 225 hp. At 65% she would cruise at 145 knots (168 mph) and could make Seattle to San Francisco, four hours, non-stop on a clear day. That was the edge of her 'legal' fuel range.

Each of the four states was covered by a schedule of one week on the road, home on the weekend, another week on the road and then a week in town, covering 'local' accounts, including sea-plane operations like Kurtzer.

The travel schedule was a little hard on one's family but a wonderful job for someone that liked to fly.

149

Pacific Airmotive Corporation was a major aircraft parts distributor. It was similar to TBA in the automotive industry; tires, batteries, accessories. The latter included several of the Bendix Corporation product lines. We didn't have an engine line or avionics (until my last year with the company).

Fred Costello had pioneered the acquisition of the Seattle Branch Debonair. Prior to having his own airplane, he had to rent from a local Fix Base Operator. This created many problems like scheduling, aircraft discrepancies and samples. With our own airplane many of the products sold could be installed and displayed on it.

Our first sales trip together was an Eastern Washington trip and the first stop would be Yakima. It was a clear day and I apparently didn't know how to enter the civilian traffic pattern. I was used to either a military-break approach or an instrument approach. Fred had a bit of sport with my education including caustic comments about how the Navy needed a cable and hook to pull one down out of the sky. It was all in good fun. Fred was a delight to work for and he taught me many things about our product lines and the best way to present them to a customer.

Fred had worked up a beautiful sales approach. He said that we should never go into an account to sell something, but go into an account with something new to talk about; a new test procedure, helpful product, etc. We discovered a need for a 'low-stick' paint masking tape that wouldn't pull off the paint when removed. We had contacted various tape manufacturers with the request. Tuck Tape came through with a good product and their development engineer came out and traveled the territory demonstrating the product. We ended up selling a carload of tape!

150

1960 Beech Debonair BE-33

Together we worked up many innovative approaches to sales. We opted for a uniform instead of slacks and sport coat. Out in the boonies a suit or sport coat and tie was considered "city slicker" attire. A uniform was neutral. Even one that included a necktie. We developed counter displays, inventory control systems and other successful ideas. It was a lot of fun.

In 1965 Darlene gave birth to our son, Scott Michael McEniry. He was the first "man-child" born into the family. My sister had produced two girls. We had a lot of fun kidding Hal Love, my brother-in-law, about that fact. Our daughter, Kathy, being a whole five years older, took it upon herself to become "Mommy" and took great delight in taking care of Scotty.

Scott and Kathy became very close. Scott used to follow her around our ten room apartment on Queen Anne Hill…. calling out, "Batay, Batay…where was you tichen?" It was a real hoot to watch them play.

151

On my Montana trips I used to save my expense money for a steak dinner in Butte. Half way into town from the airport was the "Red Rooster". Their steaks could damn near be cut with a fork. Awesome. Usually the FBO at Butte had a 'courtesy car' for customer use. One would put a few dollars in the glove compartment for gas and such. It was fairly common in those days. Probably liability insurance issues have since gotten in the way these days.

On this one trip the car was gone, taken by someone that had arrived before me. I would have to take a cab. This posed a problem since my expense account didn't justify a cab into town, back out to the restaurant, then into town and out to the airport the next morning. Across the street from the Red Rooster was an old motor court, probably built in the 20's (before motels). A cabin, then covered carport, cabin, etc. I mean *old*, but it would solve the cab problem and I'd still get a great meal.

I arrived at the office of this derelict motel, went in and signed the register that was lying open on the counter. An old gentleman, fairly husky with reddish-gray hair came out. He walked up to the counter, turned the register around to see what I had written.... looked up at me and said. "Ah, ya must be Jimmy Mac-In-ary's boy. Come on in back and I'll be pouring ya a bit of a drink." (You could cut through his heavy Irish accent with a knife!) We quickly determined that he was talking about my Father.

We went into his back living quarters and he did pour me drinks or two, or three or four. Making a long story short I didn't ever get across the street. O'Brien was his name and he proceeded to tell me about my Father.

He started this wonderful yarn, *"Ya know, I was a bar tender in this speakeasy in Butte. T'was a tough town in those days, with the miners and all. Well, ya 'Da' came in, dressed to the nines and with his derby set at a jaunty angle. A couple of lads suggested that he remove his hat. Your Da, he commented that anyone was welcome to try to remove his hat. Well a couple of the lads chose to accept his offer and proceeded to beat the bejeezus out of him. But your Da...he kept getting oop! Okay, who's next? --and so it went on. Ya know, he sold stock...probably not worth the paper t'was printed on, but the lads took a liking to him. –he kept getting oop!" He mused.*

It was a wonderful evening and I got very drunk that night with Mr. O'Brien. The following morning was hell to pay but I survived. A couple of trips to Montana later I dropped in but was told that he had passed on. He left me with a great memory of my father, although he had probably embellished it a bit.... *Don-cha know!*

In 1966 I purchased my very first NEW car. It was a 1966 1300 "Beetle" Volkswagen. When the salesman handed me the keys at the curb, I asked him to please wait right where he was, that I'd be right back. I drove around the block, pulled up, rolled the window down and asked him, "How much money have I lost."

He laughed, pulled out his blue book, looked up the car and said, "You have lost exactly $185."

We were both still laughing as I pulled away.

I met wonderful people in this "General Aviation" market, one of the most outstanding was Richard E. "Bud" Rude. He was the General Manager of a Beech sub-dealership in Tacoma. In my attempt to make him an Associate Distributer I had to convince him to become an AC Spark Plug Stocking Dealer. Bud, having spent most

153

of his life in Alaska was a 'died in the wool' Champion Spark Plug believer…at the foot-of-the-cross believer!

Through persistent effort, charm and good looks I convinced him to at least give me a chance to prove that the AC plug was at least equal to the Champion. I let him pick the engine…. he chose the Lycoming 0-360 and first pick of bottom row left side, top row right side. I took the remaining with AC plugs.

Well, of course, the test showed equal plug wear or life…they were both good spark plugs. We were back in the office, the contract lay open on the desk between us, I took out my pen and lay it on the contract. Then I 'sealed' my lips, sat back and waited.

No one said a word.

It was quiet for some time.

Finally, Bud picked up the pen and signed while saying, "I don't even like this product…I don't know why I'm doing this."

We became very close friends and our paths would cross many times in the coming years.

Another was Bruce McCaw, later a room-mate, boat partner and business partner. More later.

After a couple of years Fred was promoted and transferred to Burbank. He later was transferred to Denver Colorado to take over the branch there. I became the Seattle Branch Chief Pilot and Sales Manager.

Now it was my turn to seek out and hire a pilot-salesman.

My sales success with PAC almost doubled each year. It was a wonderful job, but like I said earlier, hard on the family. My daughter, Kathy, would start to cry when she saw me walking down the hall with a suitcase in my hand. On Friday nights, if I would be returning at a

154

decent hour she would be standing at the window in the nursery watching for me to drive up. It was heart rending.

During this period the U.S. Air Force came and stole our A1E Skyraiders for service in Viet Nam. They would be put to use for the "Sandy" missions; flying over a downed pilot and keeping the bad guys away until a helicopter could get in and extract the pilot.

The AD, being a propeller-equipped aircraft, had a lot longer loiter capability than a jet, plus it could carry a 10,000-pound *external* ordinance load. It was perfect for that mission.

NAS Seattle only had a 5,000-foot runway, since it was built on land jutting out into Lake Washington, so we wouldn't be able to get jet fighters. We were hoping for the A4D Skyhawk, but not a chance. We got the Fairchild C-119 Flying Boxcar instead.

The C-119 was a twin-engine combat support transport. She had the cubic capacity of a railroad boxcar, hence the name. An ugly bird, squatty twin-boom and very noisy due to the pair of Wright R-3350 power plants.

At least it was still flying. Several of the pilots also flew for the airlines. We transitioned into it without many problems. My earlier military transport experience served me well. I became an Aircraft Commander early in the game, along with a "Special" Instrument Rating. (The rating allows one to sign his own flight clearance.)

With extensive travel time at PAC and coupled with Reserve activity I needed some relief. I was given authority by home office to hire another pilot-salesman.

Following is a short story that I wrote describing that effort.

155

# SIXTEEN        DEBONAIR, a short story

It was a little after two in the afternoon when Carson stuck his head in my office. This was a bit different. Jim spent most of his time trying to avoid me. Since the instrument flight check, things had been a bit strained between us. But here he was.

"Mike, do you have a couple of minutes?" he managed to get out.

"Sure Jim, come on in."

I had hired Jim Carson after hiring and firing a pilot-salesmen before him. It wasn't that I was hard to work for.... or at least I didn't think I was, it was the job requirements. This job required a special kind of guy.

I was Chief Pilot and Sales Manager for the Seattle Branch of Pacific Airmotive Corporation, Products Division. What a joke; beautiful, fancy titles. I got them instead of a raise! Oh, they were real enough. I was the only pilot in the Seattle Branch. I guess that alone made me Chief Pilot, and I was the only outside salesman in the Seattle Branch. --but the title was bestowed upon me when my predecessor, Fred Costello, got promoted and transferred to the home office down in Burbank. He had been the former Chief Pilot and Sales Manager...had hired me so there would be two pilots in the branch.

Yeah, the titles were a joke, but what a job. You couldn't ask for a better job-- if you were a pilot, liked to fly, sort of liked people, and loved aviation. The job called for selling aviation products in the states of Washington, Oregon, Idaho, Montana and Alaska. The position was salaried (if you wanted to call it that--it wasn't much of a

156

salary), and instead of a company car, you got an airplane; a Beechcraft Debonair.

Now a Beech Debonair is one of the sweetest airplanes to be spawned by the factory in Wichita. It was affectionately referred to as a "Debbie", or sometimes just a "Deb". The factory had intended it to be the utility model of their single-engine product line. Their Bonanza had established itself as the "Cadillac" of single-engine airplanes in the industry. She was all-metal, low wing, retractable tricycle landing gear, four place (including the pilot) and fast. Its "V" tail distinguished the Bonanza. There were lots of pros and cons about the "V" tail, but that's the way it was.

The Debonair looked just like the Bonanza, as well as it should have. It was probably built on the same tools and jigs. The fuselage, wing, landing gear was all the same...the airframe differing only in that it had a conventional tail configuration.

At the time of the Debonair model introduction, the Continental IO-470 engine powered both aircraft. The "I" designated the fact that the engine was fuel injected...the "O", an opposed flat-six cylinder layout and the "470"; the cubic inch displacement. Compression ratios and tuning factors created various models of the engine with power outputs of 225 hp to 285 hp. The Debonair had the 225 hp and the Bonanza had gone up the horsepower ladder to the 285 hp configuration.

The Bonanza had gotten fancier over its production life with richer materials for the interior, curtains on the windows, wood grain on portions of the instrument and side panels and other appointments that didn't have much to do with performance but a lot with the price. The factory kept the Debonair rather "Spartan" and priced her accordingly.

157

At sixty-five per-cent power settings, the Debonair cruised at 145 knots (168 mph) and burned twelve gallons an hour in the process. She had a range from Seattle to San Francisco. One hellava an airplane. In short, she was considered the best damn airplane that Beech ever built, and it had to have been an accident! They couldn't have done it on purpose.

Like I said, "What a job!"

An airplane has to stay in the air to justify its expense, existence, or just the plain reason for having one. It had taken my predecessor a year of hard work selling corporate on the fact that the Seattle Branch needed its own airplane. He had spent a year, and the year before that, renting an airplane for each sales trip--not a good deal. Sometimes the airplane wouldn't be available, sometimes the person who had rented or used it before hadn't told anybody something wasn't working just right...one just didn't have the right control over it.

But now the Seattle Branch had this beautiful airplane. And, it had to be used. The magic number was three hundred hours a year. Doesn't sound like such a difficult thing to do, but simple arithmetic puts it at twenty-five hours a month. Then you have to allow for maintenance, holidays, and the personal things that pop up. Well, it wasn't easy for one person to do, so the thing was to build up the sales enough in the territory to justify hiring a second person. Fred Costello had done just that, doubling sales each year. I had kept the trend going as well. This made it a lot easier to justify the airplane, and easier to satisfy some kind of a home life; wife, kids and that sort of thing.

Fred was gone, promoted, and I had been going through pilot-salesmen at an alarming rate.

158

Like I said, this job called for a special kind of guy. He had to first be a salesman. That's what he was hired to do. That was his job. That's what he did. After all, the airplane was merely a company car, a way to get from one account to another.

Seattle is in the Northwest. The Northwest gets lots of weather. It rains a lot. If it were any better, every nut in California would be moving up here. They (meaning the rest of the world) know of Washington as the "Evergreen State". Yeah, the Evergreen State....it stays green because it rains a lot. Now rain, in itself, isn't such a bad deal. But with rain, comes clouds. And when you fly in the clouds you can't see out...can't see the horizon, and if it wasn't for the instruments, you wouldn't know if you were right side up or upside down. For this situation, the folks who govern flying, the FAA, have what they call an Instrument Rating. This is a license to "fly in the clouds". They call it "IFR", which means "Instrument Flight Rules"; the rules and regulations that govern instrument flight.

There's another catch to the Evergreen State thing. --the rain and clouds thing. Except for a few months in the summer, we have "freezing levels" that are anywhere from the ground to ten or twelve thousand feet. For the most part, the freezing level stays around four to eight thousand feet, except in the colder part of the wintertime...and then it's on the ground. When the freezing level gets down to a thousand feet or lower, rain becomes snow. Sort of the way it works. I bet you knew that.

Well, getting back to my story, to keep an airplane in the air twenty-five hours a month, and the better part of twelve months out of the year, there is going to be some instrument flying. And this factor requires a pilot with an Instrument Rating....Oh, and he has to be able to sell.

159

As I said earlier, I had gone through one lad who couldn't sell and couldn't fly very well. His paperwork said one thing but he couldn't live up to it. Anyway, he's gone.

I had hired Jim Carson on the strength of his resume, his Pilot's Flight Log Book, his attitude and his demeanor. He was picked from about seventeen applicants.

(When you put an ad in the paper mentioning the word "pilot", the phone starts ringing off the hook. Try it sometime. You'll meet some very interesting people.)

Carson's resume said that he had sold a lot of things and his FAA Pilot Certificate said "SINGLE & MULTI-ENGINE LAND plus INSTRUMENT". I even called his flight instructor. He said Jim could fly instruments. What the hell else could he have said since he had given him the rating.

I had given Carson plenty of time to get acquainted with the "Deb". He had a lot of dual-flight time (with me in the cockpit with him) and had several solo hours as well. We had done sales trips together. This included both actual and simulated instrument work so he could experience what the conditions would be like and what was expected of him. I had told him he would get an instrument check in about a month...and told him just what, exactly, the instrument check-ride would consist of.

We would take-off from Boeing field, filing our flight plan direct to Tacoma Industrial Airport's ADF Approach fix, shoot an ADF approach there to a 'missed approach', (a missed approach is the designated altitude published on the approach plate, telling the pilot to abort the approach if the field is not in-sight.) then direct to the Olympia VOR and do the Omni Approach, again to a missed approach, then the airway Victor Twenty-Three to Seattle, filing for a Precision Approach (a civilian GCA-type radar approach) into Sea-Tac International Airport, to

160

a missed approach, proceeding to the Boeing Field Outer Marker and a standard ILS approach into Boeing Field.

No big deal, no tricks...no simulated emergencies, or anything like that. This was merely an expeditious way for him to demonstrate his ability to fly each of the types of instrument approaches that he would be expected to use in the course of doing his job...to be a salesman. After all, the airplane was simply a company car.

Being April, the worst part of the winter flying was behind us. But spring weather in the Northwest can get pretty changeable pretty quick, so this was intended to demonstrate his basic ability and, or for that matter, point up any areas that might need a bit of polishing up.

Jim had transitioned to the Debbie okay. It was obvious he liked the airplane and had learned to fly it pretty well. He still had to work at it a bit, but seemed to enjoy the process; which is more than half the battle. I didn't think he would have any problems.

One morning in mid-April I awoke to one of those rainy, overcast, drizzly days, which Seattle is so famous for. It seemed like just the right conditions for an instrument check. --A low freezing level being a possible problem. As I drove to my office on Boeing Field I noticed the ceiling was down to about eight hundred feet. Upon reaching my office a quick telephone check with Seattle Flight Service weather briefing, determined that the freezing level was holding pretty consistent at about six thousand feet. Our flight wouldn't require us to climb to over four thousand feet. The conditions were just right for a good *actual* instrument check.

After hanging up from talking to Seattle Flight Service, I called Carson into my office.

"Jim, I want you to go file the instrument check routing that I gave you a couple of weeks ago; direct

161

Tacoma, direct Olympia, victor Twenty-Three Seattle, direct Boeing. Request in the Remarks Section an approach at each to a missed approach. OK?"

He looked a bit confused. Filing that kind of a flight plan did have a few quirks in it. I was in the Marine Corps Reserve, flying C-119 Boxcars (--lovely airplane, and another story) and was one of the squadron Instrument Check Pilots. We did this sort of thing all of the time. I shouldn't have been surprised that he would have had a problem with it; at least doing it the first time. I decided to help him out.

"Come on Jim, let's walk over to Flight Service and I'll give you a hand."

The Seattle Flight Service Station was two buildings away on the same side of the ramp as the PAC offices and warehouse. We walked in.

Hank Layton had been with the FAA for about fifteen years or so, was a former Naval Aviator and a neat guy. When we got there he was just putting the latest Winds Aloft Sequence Report in the folder on the briefing counter. He glanced up as we came in.

"Hey Mike, go'in avi-atin?"

"Sort of, Hank...we're going to do an instrument flight check."

"--Great day for it. We're at minimums and so is most of the local area. Will you be staying on this side of the rocks?"

"Yeah, I thought that we'd hit Tacoma, Olympia, Seattle for a Precision, and back here for an ILS."

"Sounds good. You sure as hell won't need a hood."

Hank was alluding to the hood that a student wears when practicing instrument flight on a nice clear day. It is designed to confine the student's view to the aircraft

162

instruments, but not see out of the cockpit and not see the horizon.

I grabbed a Flight Plan form and motioned for Jim to watch closely how I was doing it. We didn't say anything; there wasn't any need to. All you really had to do was tell the FAA what you wanted to do, in what order, and how you planned to go about it. But, this was not a standard flight plan...and I didn't hold it against Carson for being reluctant to do it. He seemed to understand the use of the Remarks section.

"We're going to roll out the bird now, Hank, so you can go ahead and file this, if you would.

"Sure thing...don't scare yourself too badly."

Jim and I walked back to the office. I told him to go ahead and drive down to the hangar, pre-flight the bird and taxi up here and pick me up.

I went into the office, picked up my messages, told Pat Holly, the branch secretary, that Carson and I would be out for an hour or so. I stuck my head into the Branch Manager's office and told George that I was going to give Jim Carson an instrument check.

"In this weather?", he said with a startled look on his face, "You can't see anything."

"Yeah, I know, this way we won't have to use an Instrument Hood."

"Oh."

George wasn't a pilot.


I was returning my last call when Jim taxied up outside my office window. I wrapped up the call, grabbed my jacket and headed out the door.

Jim saw me coming and throttled back so that I wouldn't get blown off the wing. I jumped in, secured the door and nodded for him to go ahead. He called Ground Control.

"BOEING GROUND, DEBONAIR ZERO THREE VICTOR, P-A-C, FOR TAXI CLEARANCE, IFR ROUND ROBIN SEATTLE BOEING."

"ROGER ZERO THREE VICTOR, CLEARED TO RUNWAY THREE ONE, CALL WHEN READY TO COPY YOUR CLEARANCE."

"ZERO THREE VICTOR, ROGER RUNWAY THREE ONE."

I noticed that Jim was getting his radio procedures down. They don't do a very good job of teaching this in the civilian sector and I was sort of fussy about it. There's a time for chatty remarks to whoever is controlling you, but they have their place. Plus, I had introduced Jim to wearing a headset so he could hear his own voice in the side-tone and modulate it like some thirty-thousand-hour airline dude. It's almost a game, especially around a general aviation airport like Boeing where there is a lot of student flight activity.

We taxied out and all the way down to the far end of the long, ten-thousand-foot runway. While taxiing Jim ran through several of the Pre-Take-Off Check items, got to the run up area, set the brake and finished the check list. He looked over at me to confirm. I acknowledged with a nod. Jim picked up the microphone and called Ground Control.

"BOEING GROUND, DEBONAIR ZERO THREE VICTOR, STANDING BY FOR CLEARANCE."

Carson did a good job of copying the clearance and reading it back. He switched to tower frequency and called. We were cleared for take-off. Jim Carson appeared fairly calm, maybe a little anxious, but nothing outwardly unusual.

164

Jim taxied into position, set the brakes, re-set the directional gyro with the magnetic compass and set the clock...all good procedures that are in the book, but not all instructors insist on them. I was one who did.

The take-off was smooth; Jim selected "Gear Up", went to first power reduction, and then when the gear indicated UP, set climb power and quickly completed the Climb Check List. About that time we entered the base of the eight hundred foot overcast. It was right where the briefing said it would be.

I couldn't believe what was happening! --the transition in Carson. He appeared frozen. Sweat was breaking out all over him, running down into his eyes, which had grown the size of saucers...both of his hands were on the yoke, his knuckles white...his grip was about to bend something...and in less time than it takes to tell about it, a severe case of vertigo had set in and he was losing control of the aircraft. It was like he hadn't ever been in the soup before. He was starting to stall and spin! We had managed to climb to about twelve hundred feet. I let the airplane go through a half turn of a spin and then reached over, and knocking Carson's hands off of the yoke, flopped it over to my side, and told him, "I have it!"

He had the good sense to let everything go and not get in the way. I recovered the airplane, picked up the microphone and asked Seattle Departure Control for clearance to return to Boeing Field. They cleared us to change frequency to Seattle Approach Control, who then cleared us to the Boeing Field Outer Marker and for the ILS Approach back to the field. We were soon on the ground.

Nothing was said during the recovery, the ILS approach, the landing and taxi back to the office. I climbed

165

out and told Jim to put the bird away and to come see me when he was finished.

When he came in I told him I liked to give instrument checks under actual instrument conditions as opposed to having him fly under the hood. I went on to say that it looked like we should spend some time doing weather flying. I probably gave some indication that I wasn't overjoyed with his performance. I don't think I chewed on him, though. Maybe I did, maybe I didn't. Like I said, he was the second guy I was trying to get on board, and doing what he was being paid to do. What the Hell, he hadn't flunked *selling* yet. He hadn't done much selling, but folks still seemed to listen to him and place a few orders.

And so, for the next week or so, Jim had been trying to stay out of my way. And now, here he was.

He had a funny way of talking. It was sort of like his jaws were wired shut. He clenched his teeth. I always wondered how he did that. He had been talking for some time and I don't think I had heard a word. I asked him to repeat his last statement.

He said Alaska Airlines had accepted him for a Flight Engineer position and that he would like to be able to give just one week's notice instead of two. He had a chance to get into a class right away or he would have to wait about five weeks for the next one.

He mumbled, but went on, "—it's not like I'm leaving you in the lurch, 'cause I have this friend of mine who's a good salesman, kinda low-time pilot...but a good salesman."

I couldn't think of anything to say for the moment. It was always fascinating to watch him talk through clenched teeth, though a tad bit distracting. I guessed that he was quitting...and wanted to leave in a week.

166

Jim was still talking, "--he's also a former Marine. I know you'd get along well with him and you could teach him your way of flying...since he is kinda low time."

What the Hell. What could I lose? There wasn't any way in the world that I would be able to change Jim Carson's mind about leaving the company. The airlines had been his goal all along. I'm sure his job with PAC had a lot to do with building more flight time. Pilot flight hours were the criteria with the airlines. That plus age, Stanine Tests, and the like. And how could you argue with his choice? In five to eight years Jim would be making over fifty thousand dollars a year and working about eighteen to twenty days a month. It had been a hard financial road for Carson, the financial investment of getting to the minimum flight time and the additional ratings; Multi-Engine, Commercial, and about two hundred and fifty hours. And probably at an average cost of twenty-five bucks an hour, considering the dual instructor time along with the solo hours. Hell, that's over six thousand dollars alone, plus the minimum of two years of college. Yeah, you could say that Jim Carson had made a major investment in getting this job with Alaska Airlines.

Damn! I should have applied myself. But, I was an old man at thirty and nearly all of the airlines were holding the age thing at twenty-eight...as I recall. And besides, I had decided long ago that I didn't want to fly 'airlines'. Maybe it was twenty-five. Anyway, it sure wasn't thirty! Maybe this Marine friend of Carson's was worth a look.

"What's his name, Jim?"

"Clem Bentley."

"--Clem?"

"Well, actually its Wallace Clemens Bentley, the Second."

167

"--you're kidding me, Jim....Clem?" I chewed on this for a few moments, "Well, have Clem give me call. And uh, sure you can give a short notice. I wish you the best with Alaska; I think they're a good outfit. --at least they don't have a domicile in Cleveland or Detroit!"

About nine o'clock the next morning, Clem called. We arranged to meet at my apartment in Seattle that evening. It turned out Clem was working and living in Longview, Washington...down near Portland. It would be about a two and a half hour drive for him up to Seattle. And the same back. If hired, he'd have to relocate to the Seattle area.

Whatever. I was looking forward to meeting this friend of Carson's'.

## *Chapter II*

The doorbell rang. I glanced at my watch. This Clem person was on time. Maybe it was going to be all right. At least he's off to a good start. He had to come all the way from Longview...down by Portland...and then find his way to my apartment on Queen Anne Hill. Not bad.

I opened the door and looked him over. The dark blue blazer and old school tie were the first things that caught my eye. Light blue, oxford cloth, button-down collared shirt and gray slacks finished the image. Wallace Clemens Bentley, the Second had either read a good book on how to dress, or he had some good training. Whatever the case, I was suitably impressed.

"Hi, I'm Clem Bentley, and you must be Mike McEniry. I hope that I'm on time." He said this with his hand outstretched and all the time looking me straight in the eye.

His handshake was firm and demeanor confident.

"Come on in Clem, would you like a cup of coffee? --I assume you take it black, not being some kind of pogie-bait Marine."

He muttered something like "--that sounds just fine."

I didn't know it at the time, but until that moment, Wallace Clemens Bentley the Second had always drank his coffee with cream and lots of sugar. He had taken a lot of crap about it when he was serving on active duty with the Marines. But from that moment on...it was, and still is...black and hot.

Clem was about five foot, ten inches tall, medium to slight build, ready smile, short hair...probably a carryover from the Marine Corps... poised and yet there was something you couldn't quite put your finger on. An image of Tony Randall came to mind. But a Tony Randall that could stand in your living room with his hand carelessly dangling in your fish aquarium and mention that '--it seems a bit damp in here.'

It was just a passing thought.

"Grab a chair, Clem, I'll get the coffee and be right with you. Did you bring your paperwork?" I said this last over my shoulder as I ducked into the kitchen to get the coffee.

Clem called out to me from the living room, "Yes Sir, I did. Carson didn't give me much time, but he had mentioned that he might be able to arrange an interview, so I put some material together."

I had poured his cup, refilled my own and walked back into the living room. He was still standing where I had left him, not quite sure what the seating arrangements would be. I motioned him to a chair, handed him his cup and took the material that he had removed from his briefcase. From the looks of it, Jim Carson had told him

169

about arranging this meeting six months ago; it was a very well prepared, bound, resume.

The resume was divided into tabbed sections; work history, business references, personal references, military service and on the last page, his aviation data. This data consisted of photocopies of his FAA Private Pilot's License, Third Class Medical Certificate and Third Class FCC Radio Operator's License. All of these cards were copied onto one piece of paper and bound into his resume. The binding was the curly plastic GBC type, with hard covers front and back. He had gone to a lot of trouble and expense. Here was a man who wanted this job!

That was just my first impression...I hadn't read any of it yet.

"Relax a bit and let me give this a quick read, Clem, then we can chat about your qualifications. I haven't placed an ad in the paper to replace Carson yet...this is all moving rather quickly."

"I understand, Sir."

"Give me a couple of minutes...you go by Clem? --I'd like to look this over for a minute or two."

He had nodded in the affirmative at the 'Clem', but didn't say anything.

A couple of things in the resume caught my eye.

"You were in the Allied Stores Management Training program. What was the main thrust of the program?"

"Essentially Sir, it was sales techniques, communication and, of course, personnel management. -- but really, the emphasis was on selling, selling and more selling."

"And now you're with this Longview newspaper, why is that?"

"Well Sir, I've always thought of the newspaper business as being rather exciting. And since getting out of the Marine Corps, things have been a bit tame. I had a chance to go to MarCad...you know, the Marine Aviation Cadet Program, but I was due to get out...and like a damn fool, didn't go into the flight cadet program. As you know, I've been taking flying lessons and have my license, but it sure isn't the same as flying fighters in the Marine Corps. Carson mentioned to me that you were a Marine pilot."

"That's true, I was...and still am, flying now in the Reserve. I went through NavCad; the Naval Aviation Cadet Program. They didn't have MarCad until later. When I was in the Training Command you had to compete for a chance to apply to the Marine Corps for a Second Lieutenant's commission, otherwise you end up a damn Ensign in the Navy!"

I returned to his resume. The past experience, education and various types of jobs indicated strong sales activity, and that's what I was looking for. I turned to his aviation experience.

"It says here that you have your Private Single-Engine Land license, but you haven't listed your total flight time. How many hours do you have, Clem?"

There was a moment of silence.

"--uh, about forty-three point two, Sir."

"Total? --forty-three point two TOTAL hours?"

"Yes Sir."

"DAMNATION! SHIT! Didn't Carson tell you anything about this job?"

"Well Sir, yes he did. He said that I would be a little light on time but that with my sales experience and the fact that I'm now working on my Commercial and Instrument Ratings that maybe you would....uh, ...you

171

know...give me a shot at this. You wouldn't be sorry...I'd do one hellava job for you, Sir."

"--a *little* light on hours!...hell and damnation!" I still couldn't believe it.

"Jim told me that you had some very straight forward procedures that makes it a lot easier...that you do a lot of instrument and night work...but that you really know how to teach, and that it is understandable...I would really like to study under you, Sir!"

"Clem, I'm not an FAA Certified Instrument Flight Instructor. I do a lot of training in the Reserve, I'm a member of the Instrument Review Board...neither factor recognized by the FAA...you would have to do your dual work with an instructor who can legally sign you off."

It was quiet for a moment.

"Does this mean that you would consider taking me on, Sir?"

"Clem, I didn't say that. I respect your dedication. But frankly, I don't even know if our insurance would cover you. There are a lot of things to consider. I'll have to get back to you."

"I understand, Sir."

"Quit calling me 'SIR' with every other breath, Clem."

"Sorry Si..uh...well, it's force of habit. And you *are* an officer and I was an enlisted man."

"That may be, Clem, but what's more important is that we're both Marines."

"You got that right Sir, once a Marine, ALWAYS a Marine! --yes Sir!"

That was pretty much it. We talked on for another hour. Clem had a long drive back to Longview; he had to be back at work the next morning. --Since he didn't have the job with PAC as yet.

I had some thinking to do, and if I decided in his favor, then I was going to have some selling to corporate to do myself. Frankly, I liked him. I liked the idea of his apparent selling ability and his technical acumen. --but JEE-ZUS, forty-three hours! Hell, it takes at least forty hours minimum to qualify for your Private License. Here was this very green, barely qualified pilot with three, damn point two hours over '*Private*' and I was going to put him into a low-wing, retractable gear, constant-speed, propeller driven, fast airplane and turn him loose in the four Northwestern states! --Holy jumpin' muthers! What in hell was I thinking about?

On the other hand, it was almost the first of May. He would have to give notice, move to Seattle, study products for at least a week or two...the four territories took a week each to cover...with a week local between two weekly road trips.

Let's see that's at least eight weeks, or ten if he gives two weeks' notice. The four weeks of flying in the territory would be fifty hours of dual instruction, not to mention evening training periods while on the road instead of sitting in the bar in some motel. --that would account for another ten or fifteen hours...and we'd be crowding August and the kid would have himself about an even hundred hours, sixty of which would be "in-type". The weather will hold in the Northwest through September, and that will give him another thirty hours. And with some outside help, maybe I can get somebody to "sign him off" to take his FAA Instrument Check Ride.

This just might work.

I remember the thoughts that had gone through my head as if it was yesterday...

Let's see, who the Hell owes me some favors and has an Instrument Instructor's Rating? I was going to have to think about that. Wait a minute, how about Doug Black down at Flightcraft? He had me talk to that student of his at lunch that day...we were talking about my giving his student a "pre-FAA" check ride. Doug seemed to feel that if he (the student) could pass <u>my</u> check ride, the FAA ride would be a piece of cake.

In the morning...make a list; ...let's see:

1. Call down to corporate and find out minimum flight hours for insurance.
2. If questioned, remind them that we need salesmen who can fly, not professional pilots who would only *try* to sell!
3. Stress the Allied Stores Management Program and technical acumen. (I wondered if anybody at corporate would know what that meant.)
4. Call Doug Black at Flightcraft and feel him out about the use of his Parker 51 pen.
5. Do I really want to do all of this? (--answer in the morning AFTER the second cup of coffee!) I think it'll work....

And yes, it did work. Doug Black even agreed to sign off on some of the hours, saving Clem some bucks. Doug knew the kind of flying that we did and respected my knowledge.

Clem found a house in West Seattle, not too far from Boeing Field. Margie, his wife and two young boys seemed to like the idea and Clem's new job. They were all looking forward to some flying.

We didn't get out of the office Monday afternoon like I wanted. George's Monday-morning Branch Meeting

174

ran into early afternoon. I don't even remember what it was all about, but I did know that the Eastern Washington sales trip, to do it right, took the better part of four and a half days.

By the time Clem and I sorted out what the trip feature would be, arranged the samples, stuffed the Customer Contact Folders, and worked out the flight plan, it was too late to leave Monday night. I told Clem to be at the hangar at 0700, ready to go.

God! --it was a beautiful morning! The sun was still below the horizon at 0615 when I got in my car for the drive to Boeing Field. The western sky was golden, and the Cascades were etched so clear they appeared to be a cutout stage prop twenty feet away. There was a bit of crispness in the air. This was going to be a good trip.

I was satisfied with Clem's progress in product knowledge. He had needed a good understanding of our major product lines; AC Spark Plugs, Exide Batteries, B.F. Goodrich Tires and Bendix Scintilla magnetos. He seemed to have the basics of these four major products down pretty well. We sold many other products, but these were the primary items that one needed to be totally familiar with.

We had been working on transitional orientation into flying the Debonair. I hadn't soloed him yet, but I hadn't made it that type of thing either. I kept it in the 'familiarization' mode. Once Clem felt comfortable landing and taking-off, we would trade seats each flight leg. We operated the airplane as if it was a transport-category bird...the 'right' seat handled the radio and Check Lists and the 'Left' seat flew the airplane. And Clem did well. He was becoming more familiar with power settings, applying them to the complexity of manifold pressure and controllable-pitch prop. Retractable landing gear can be a snake ready to bite you at any time. The best way to avoid that terrible crunching sound of landing "wheels up" is full use of check lists each and every time. I was a stickler for check lists anyway.

Another problem with a wheels up landing; it really takes a lot of power to taxi...not to mention filling out all of the paperwork for the insurance company, your Chief Pilot and your boss. It really ruins your whole day!

But now it was time to get into the instrument-training phase.

I remembered my introduction to instrument flight. The Navy spent a great deal of time and money developing training techniques to accomplish this in the most economical time frame possible. I felt that it would be smart to do the same.

This took some digging around, not only in my memory but also in some boxes of flight material that I had at home. Yeah, I'm one of those people who don't throw *anything* away...especially flight things. I found what I had been looking for; a book called "Flight Through Instruments". It was the most concise, clearly put and easy to understand explanation of instrument flight and how to do it that I had ever seen. It clearly explained the mysteries of scan-patterns or what instrument, or instruments, to watch for any flight configuration or maneuver.

One of the basics of instrument flight is to *never watch a moving instrument*. Oh, you monitor the moving instrument in order to check your progress. For example, if you wanted to descend a thousand feet you wouldn't want to watch just your altimeter...but you would check, or monitor, it from time to time to note your progress toward the altitude selected for level off.

Clem was at the hangar and had the Debbie rolled out and was in the process of doing the pre-flight inspection. I pulled my car into the hangar and parked beside his car. I grabbed my suitcase and clothing bag and walked over to the airplane.

"Good morning, Clem. It looks like a beautiful day to go fly around and sell something."

"Sure does Boss. Would you come over and take a look at the oil level?"

I put my gear in the baggage compartment and walked around to the front of the Debonair. Clem had the cowl open and was standing with the dipstick in his hand. I took it and checked. It was about a quart down.

"This is about right, Clem. I like to keep it about a quart low since it seems to blow out the top quart. Remember, this engine has an oil capacity of twelve quarts."

"OK, I've completed the pre-flight, unless you want to take another look," he said as he was buttoning the cowl back down.

"No, let's get going. Have you filed?"

"No I didn't. I wasn't sure if you wanted to go IFR or VFR and since I thought you said last night that we'd be going to Wenatchee first...I wasn't sure how you wanted to do it."

"That's fine, we'll file in the air... direct VFR. It will be the fastest and it doesn't look like there will be a cloud in the sky."

So, we were ready to go. We had everything we needed for our Eastern Washington trip; account folders, stuffed with product brochures and 'spec' sheets for the products that we were going to be selling, expense advance monies and the book Clem was going to be introduced to on this trip.

In the back of the "Flight Through Instruments" book were flight patterns to be practiced. We would be starting with simple flight patterns. The first was the OBOE PATTERN. Very simple; fly straight and level for two minutes, then climb one thousand feet (another two minutes) while executing a 360 degree turn to the left (which also takes two minutes), level out straight and level for two minutes and then descend one thousand feet while turning to the right 360 degrees, level out for another two minutes ...and you're finished. Sounds easy? Not on your life! The climbs and descents are done at 500 feet per minute, which is FAA *standard* for non-pressurized aircraft, especially with passengers. Otherwise you blow their eardrums out. So the 'standard' is applied to all instrument exercises. *Standard Rate Turn* is 3 degrees per second. This translates to: 30 seconds to do a 90 degree turn, one minute to do a 180 degree turn and, two minutes to do a 360 degree turn.

All of these exercise patterns were done by including the Clock in your *scan pattern* when looking at the instruments. The Navy taught us to LEAD the second hand of the clock by 3 seconds prior to initiating a maneuver.

*So, it went something like this...start the exercise/pattern when the "clock is UP" (second hand on 12:00) and a heading of North (000 degrees), straight and level until 3 seconds before the two minutes are up...Apply climb power and start your climbing turn to the left...when the second hand is on 12:15 you should have turned 45 degrees (a heading of 315 degrees) and 125 feet higher, at second hand at 12:30 you should now have climbed 250 feet and be just passing a heading of 270 degrees, and so on and so on, but the clock runs and you have to be at a certain place at each position of the second hand until the ten minutes of the Oboe Pattern are completed. The instructor is carefully observing your corrections to accomplish that criteria...essentially every 15 seconds. --and God help you if you haven't attempted to correct!*

And, like I said, the Oboe Pattern is the easiest. You progress to the Baker Pattern, which is your graduation from 'pattern flying'. --it is a bastard! Roughly shaped like a square with four, two minute straight legs...in the corners are 270 degree turns and 450 degree turns, climbing and descending...one of the two minute straight legs is done in "slow cruise" one in "normal cruise" and one in "fast cruise". It is a very complicated pattern, incorporating all modes and attitudes of flight. It requires a great deal of concentration and precision by the pilot.

By this time, you have gained the skills needed to be a smooth instrument pilot. And you're ready to go on into learning the different type of instrument approaches that you will be called upon to do for the FAA Instrument Check Ride, but also what you will have to do when using your Instrument Rating and flying around the country in various weather conditions. These approaches consist of ADF, VOR, ILS, DME GCA and ILS/Precision approaches. The nomenclature determines the avionic equipment both on the ground transmitting, and in the aircraft receiving, what equipment will be used for the approach. They vary in complexity and, more importantly, the minimum height above the ground that the clouds and subsequent visibility allows for the approach, at your destination.

For example, a GCA is a *talk-down* approach capable of bringing an airplane into a landing with virtually zero visibility and zero ceiling. You would probably refer to this as a "thick fog". This is truly the finest example of the symbiotic relationship between the controller on the ground and the pilot in the airplane, and the skills displayed by both. (I have had the good fortune to experience a true "zero-zero" approach once. It was easy, kind of fun and extremely satisfying. (--not to mention the fact that I didn't have any place else to go.) The GCA is military and the ILS/Precision is a civilian version of talk-down, like the GCA, and also incorporates the ILS instrumentation in the cockpit. All of the other approaches are done with instrumentation in the cockpit and a published Approach Plate showing the pattern that must be flown to avoid contact with granite-type rocks and/or the ground.

Clem and I had a loo-o-ng way to go. But I'll say this for him; he applied himself, studied hard and was ready for each phase of his training.

Our standard procedure was to go on a sales trip, trading flight legs as pilot and co-pilot. We divided the cockpit as if the Debonair was a multi-engine transport; the pilot (left seat) flew the airplane and the co-pilot did power settings and handled the radio communications. This gave Clem an opportunity to phase into the routines in a practical fashion. --I think I already said this.

Then, at the end of the sales day we would have an early dinner and brief on the evening flight syllabus and then go fly for an hour or so doing patterns, approaches, night landings or whatever needed work. It was summertime so there wasn't much night work initially...most of the air work being under the hood.

My original schedule was working out. By the time I was ready to turn Clem loose in the field solo, he had accumulated a lot of good experience and had over 100 hours, satisfying the insurance folks. And, well on his way to getting his FAA Instrument Rating.

*       *       *

There was one memorable training session never to be forgotten by either Clem or myself.

It was an Eastern Washington sales trip. The first sales call was a helicopter operation based at a tiny airfield on Lake Chelan, then on to an operation based in Wenatchee, finally getting to Spokane in time for one sales call. We would be staying the night in Spokane due to the number of accounts who had to be called upon in the Spokane area.

We had an early dinner and planned to start "Baker Patterns". Clem was ready for it; having studied hard and essentially memorized the pattern plate.

We took off from Geiger Field, the main commercial airport in Spokane, and climbed out to the north to an area well away from any air traffic. Clem was about half way through the first pattern when I noticed a very broad line of thunderstorms approaching from the South. --Well South. There wasn't as much cloud activity as there was lightning. It was a wall of lightning from horizon to horizon. I told Clem to pop his hood and pointed out the phenomenon.

He hadn't ever seen anything like this before (neither had I) and exclaimed, "Jeezus! --what'll we do?"

"Head back to Geiger," I replied. And in the time it takes to describe, the lightning was up to and around us. It was really moving fast!

Lightning strikes were going by us the size, in thickness, of telephone poles. Clem was obviously scared, anybody in his or her right mind would be! He managed to yell out, "What'll I do? --aren't you scared?"

"Sure I'm scared, Clem...but fly the fuck'in airplane! --That's what you have to do. We fly it until it doesn't fly anymore!"

181

(Bob Hoover, the noted Air Show pilot, once said, "When crashing, *fly all the way into the crash until you stop!"*)

It was getting dusk but I noticed the runway lights were not on at Geiger. Plus, it took a long time for them to answer my radio requests for landing instructions. They finally came up on frequency and said that all of their power had been knocked out, and they were using emergency power to transmit...and we could land on any runway, or taxi way, --for that matter-- that we could get to.

We were still surrounded by lightning going by all around us but Clem had settled down once he realized that I was scared also, and made a pretty decent landing.

We were through for the night except to make our way to the nearest bar and have a couple, if not several, drinks to steady our nerves. Like I said, "...never to be forgotten!"

The following morning, we flew from Geiger Field over to Felts Field, which is on the other side of Spokane. Felts Field hosts the majority of general aviation aircraft and services in the area. And we had three major accounts to call on there.

Our first, and primary account, was Western Aircraft, owned and operated by Harley Pry. He was always glad to see us and we went to the coffee shop for some coffee and discussion about the exciting storm the night before. Sometime later Harley asked a favor. He had a customer, a retired Air Force Colonel who was having major maintenance done on his Bonanza. He needed a ride back to his home field...could we drop him off. The field was about eighty miles South of Spokane and would be on our way to Pullman-Moscow. (Harley knew our general itinerary.) I thought of a better plan.

182

I told him, "Sure, we'll be happy to do it. Clem can fly him down while you and I are conducting our business, Harley. What's his field like?"

"It's a grass strip, about fifteen hundred feet long; no sweat for your Debonair."

This was quite a bit shorter than anything Clem had experienced up to now. But, I felt he had demonstrated good, precise control of the airplane in instrument training and it would all relate to a "visual" application. I wasn't worried.

I could see a slow flush coming over Clem, but chose to ignore it. It was about time he earned his spurs.

The Colonel arrived about a half hour later, Harley introduced us and he and Clem proceeded out to the Debonair.

Harley and I watched them take-off. It was done by the numbers, and the gear came up crisply after rotation. As we turned to go back into the hangar where we had been going over his inventory I mentioned that this was Clem's solo. Harley turned and looked at me for a moment and then laughingly asked if we should be worried. I told him I thought not. --if Clem couldn't land there, the Colonel certainly could. The Debonair wasn't that much different from his Bonanza. We went on with our business.

A couple of hours later, Clem flew back into Felts. I watched him taxi in, park and get out of the airplane. He looked ten feet tall. He headed for the cafe, thinking (and rightly so) that I would probably be there. For some reason his walk somehow reminded me of John Wayne.

He joined Harley and me at our table.

"How'd it go," Harley asked.

"Piece of cake," came the quick reply.

We finished our business at Felts Field and got into the Debonair for our flight South to Pullman-Moscow.

Once we were airborne I turned to Clem and asked him how it had *really* gone.

"Well, the landing went OK. I was maybe a little faster than I should have been for a short field and for the grass. I hadn't taken into consideration what little braking action I would have on the grass so all in all I used up ALL of the strip and was still braking hard at the end of the runway. --The Colonel didn't say anything."

"Hmmpf! We'd better do some short fieldwork tonight. I know just the spot. --anything else?"

"Yeah, sort of...my take-off went OK, but I raised the gear too soon...it was hot and dry...and the airplane sort of settled back down. I cleared the fence OK but I chopped some wheat for a while until the airspeed built up. I hope the Colonel didn't see it."

"Clem, I've told you that when you retract the gear other parts of the wheel fairings open up to allow the gear to fold into the under belly...all of this occurs at the part of the wing that is where the majority of the lift is taking place. That 'hole' opening up couldn't be at a worst place. You lose lift, especially at lower speeds!"

"I know, Boss, I know. And my take-off proved all of those words to be correct. It won't happen again." Clem could be profound.

The rest of the trip was relatively uneventful.

Clem and I had arranged to take our wives out to dinner Saturday night, and then leaving them at my house, Clem and I went out to NAS Seattle (Sand Point Naval Air Station). I had arranged to use the basic multi-engine flight simulator in the Link Trainer Building. The Navy had watch-standers there all night anyway, so it wasn't hard to arrange. It made their watch more interesting. This way I was able to get Clem some real down to earth training.

You can do a lot more in a Link Trainer-Simulator than you can in the real airplane. --like CRASH, for instance.

My favorite trick was to run him out of fuel during instrument approaches...he would be so wrapped up in the approach that he wouldn't monitor his engine instruments (--they weren't primary to his scan, but should be checked once in a while) He wouldn't catch the loss of fuel...a simulated fuel leak...and usually one engine would run out of gas first. He would have to go through a shut-down, set up for single engine operation...while flying the instrument approach and about then the second engine would quit. He would turn and look and say "--what now?"

I would answer, "--we crash and burn!"

### EPILOGU:

Clem's skill as a salesman exceeded my expectations, and his skills as a pilot became quite something else! He would have made a great fighter pilot, or a caring, skilled airline pilot! The bottom line, --he was good.

Jim Carson did make it through Flight Engineer's school for Alaska Airlines. Sad to say, he was the Flight Engineer on the Boeing 727 crash in Juneau, Alaska that held the record for the number of people killed until the jumbos started crashing.

Clem died the 30th of November 1993 of a heart attack, while taking a shower. His companionship both in, and out of a cockpit, is sorely missed.

--as the noted novelist, Ernie Gann said, *"Fate Is The Hunter"*.

# SEVENTEEN GENERAL AVIATION
## And a couple of War Stories

I was attracted to the job at Pacific Airmotive for the flying that it would entail. I have since learned about this industry called "General Aviation" (it is everything other than military and airline). It is the world of Flight Instruction, crop dusting, forestry fire-bombing, air charter, package freight, and the FBO (Fixed Base Operations), the core of this industry...usually barely scratching a living out of it. This is "grass roots" aviation. I love it.

Fire Tanker Pilots. Now there's a group of ballsy folk! It's like being around a bunch of fighter pilots. Maybe they weren't being shot at, but the *fires* wanted to eat 'em alive! It's difficult, and very hazardous flying.

FBO's (Fixed Base Operations), trying to make a living selling gas and maintenance. Some were big enough to provide flight instruction and maybe air charter. I would try to save refueling along the way to give a smaller FBO a 'full tank'.

Then there's 'corporate'. Ah yes, the Learjet, King Air's, Citations and the Gulf Stars, Falcons and even some like John Travolta's Boeing 707. Big, beautiful "Gods of Tin", as James Salter wrote about.

And the up-graders, modifiers and builders that enrich the industry. However, it is said that if you wish to make a little money in aviation, start with a lot!

None of them pay all that well. –ya just gotta love it! And the people that you did business with you usually did so with a hand shake. It really was that way...once.

Aviation, a mystical calling.

One PAC customer, who became a very close friend, was Richard "Bud" Rude. He was General Manager of a Beech Sub-Dealership at Tacoma Industrial Airport. I sold him AC Spark Plugs, among other things. You have no idea what that entailed. Bud was a former Alaska Bush pilot. And let me tell you, that's "Champion Spark Plug" country!

Making a long story short, it involved cross-plugging his 'worst-on-plugs' engine. He picked a Lycoming O-360, four cylinder opposed engine. He chose right side, upper row with Champions and lower row, left side with Champs..

I got the lower side and upper side left with my AC plugs. The deal was if my AC plugs were equal to the Champs.....he'd sign the Stocking Dealer contract. Well the time came to check the results. I was not only equal but a tad bit better than the Champs. We went into his office. I pulled out the contract, turned it around and placed my open pen on top of it and '*sealed my lips*'. We sat there. Bud just sorta looked around...kinda hummed a bit. I didn't say a word. After what seemed like an hour Bud picked up the pen and saying, "I don't know why I'm doing this, I really don't like the product..." and signed the contract.

We were friends for life. (Bud Rude, an Alaska "Legend", --check him out.)

For young people the path today is self-funding all the way through the ratings of Multi-Engine, Instrument and Commercial FAA ratings. Plus, in some cases adding Instructor Rating to help build time. That is a lot of dollars. It's all about building hours. Some will find their way into flight instruction, and then there's night package freight, --another link to building more hours to qualify for a major airline.

It really takes money, passion and commitment.

And there's the story about the mechanic, working for an airline, who's main job was 'servicing' the lavatory "holding tanks". He contracted a painful rash from the contaminants, and when the doctor told him he's have to go get another job, exclaimed, *"What? --and get out of aviation!"*

As wonderful an airplane as the Beechcraft Debonair was, it did have one drawback. It was not equipped with anti-ice or de-ice equipment, other than a heated Pitot-Tube. (The Pitot-Tube takes in air and pressure to provide inputs to the airspeed and altimeter instruments.)

As I mentioned, we had to put three hundred hours a year on the airplane to justify keeping it and this would mean a lot of night flying plus instrument flying, due to the weather patterns in the northwest. Instrument flying in the northwest in the fall, winter and spring seasons exposes one to various degrees of icing.

Icing affects the entire airplane, especially aerodynamic surfaces. The most visible are the wing and tail leading edges. However, the propeller blades also ice up, turning the airscrew into a baseball bat. The loss of power causes the aircraft to slow, and if one is trying to maintain an altitude, forces the nose up exposing the belly of the aircraft to icing. So losing power, aerodynamic lift and adding weight to the airframe can be disastrous.

I had always wanted to install a "hot prop" system on the airplane. There was an aftermarket Supplemental Type Certificated system available for the engine-propeller combination of the Debonair. It wouldn't be the complete answer to the potential problem but keeping the prop clear of ice would allow you to maintain power and perhaps be able to climb out of the icing environment.

There were two experiences that will remain forever in my mind relating to icing problems in my five years with Pacific Airmotive Corporation.

The worst was trying to get out of Butte, Montana.

There was an Arctic frontal system occluding with a Pacific system. All weather reports included heavy icing, freezing rain and snow from western Montana to eastern Washington. I had been stuck in Butte for two days.

I would go over to the FAA Flight Service Station and hang around watching the reports come in. One night, while at the station I heard a Log-Air flight report in to Butte Radio that he was on-top at 12,000 feet. The Log-Air flight was a C-46 transport. 'On-top' means clear of the clouds. Icing occurs in "visible moisture" conditions. A cloud is visible moisture. At the same time there was a large, clear hole over Butte. I would be able to climb to on-top, staying clear of the clouds and the icing conditions. I decided to give it a shot. As it turned out, it wasn't a very good decision.

The climb out was uneventful and I was able to get on-top of the cloud layers. I had filed an Instrument Flight Plan with Butte so upon reaching altitude was handed off to Great Falls Center. It wasn't long before I ran into more cloud and I requested a higher altitude clearance. There was very little traffic that night so Great Falls cleared me to try a higher altitude and report reaching. I was climbing in the clouds and began icing up rapidly. It didn't take very long to be unable to climb higher and in fact I started losing altitude. I reported this to Great Falls and when asked my intentions told them that I requested an instrument approach into Missoula. Current weather in Missoula was ceiling of 800 feet, half mile of visibility and snow, mixed with freezing rain. It would be tight.

I was unable to maintain altitude and trouble keeping airspeed. It would be disastrous stalling and then spinning in. Great Falls Center was good about vectoring me clear of the higher rocks since I had descended below the "minimum enroute altitude" in the area east of Missoula. I was really in the glue and freezing rain, picking up a real load of ice. I made it to the VOR station and descended in an abbreviated approach pattern, breaking out of the clouds at 800 feet, and able to land.

The following morning, I pushed the Debbie into the Johnson Flying Service's hangar to thaw the ice off. The crew that helped me were amazed at the thickness of the wing ice…six inches thick in some places. It certainly wasn't an airplane anymore, but more like a brick.

The second experience, (although this same thing happened more than once), occurred on the leg from Ellensburg to Seattle. Flight time, at cruise power settings, was thirty minutes. Published IFR Minimum Enroute Altitude on that leg was 8,000 ft. Usually upon reaching Ellensburg westbound one could 'see' clear conditions for a ways. I figured that it looked like about ten minutes of flight, then into the clouds (and probably icing) for another ten minutes before Seattle Center starts you downhill toward the initial approach altitude for the ILS approach into Boeing Field.

Knowing that I would probably be picking up a lot of ice and not wanting to be losing altitude down into this busy corridor I would file my IFR flight plan for the 8,000 foot Minimum Enroute Altitude.

What would "usually" (it happened twice) happen is that the ten-minute middle section of the thirty minute leg would be enough to really ice up the airplane, causing a loss of altitude and I would report to Seattle Center, "Seattle, this is Debonair 603 Victor unable to maintain 8,000."

"Roger, Zero Three Victor, expect lower altitude shortly, contact Seattle Approach Control on 119 decimal 5."

"Seattle Approach, Zero Three Victor, over."

"Zero Three Victor descend to 5,000 ft., report reaching, over."

"Roger Seattle, Zero Three Victor passing through 4,500, over."

"Okay Zero Three Victor we'll try to vector you around some of the rocks...turn right to 280 degrees, expect lower.)

And so it would go. More time than naught I would finally catch up with an altitude assignment at the 2200-foot Initial Approach Altitude for the ILS into Boeing.

And that's a General Aviation "icing story". If you keep flying in the Northwest long enough, you'll create your own. Now the following is a rare "war" story, due to today's technology and regulations.

On a trip, coming out of Montana on a Friday night, I had filed IFR since Seattle was socked in and expecting fog. I used Yakima for my IFR "Alternate". By the time that I got to Seattle Boeing Field, Sea-Tac and Paine Field were all "below minimums". Yakima and all of Eastern Washington were also fogged in behind me. The Seattle Approach Control asked my intentions and I requested a GCA into NAS Seattle (Sand Point).

I had long since made arrangements to land at a military base by filing a Hold Harmless Agreement with the Navy so that I could legally land at Sand Point on a drill weekend. I knew that the GCA Minimums were a lot lower than any other instrument approaches in the greater Seattle area.

Seattle Approach Control didn't hesitate, or ask any questions, merely gave me a VHF frequency for Navy GCA. When I switched over to the Navy controller I detected that he was pretty nervous. He advised me that NAS Seattle was below GCA minimums…was "zero-zero" in fact. (Zero feet *overcast*, zero feet *visibility*.) I told him that I didn't have any place to go.

The GCA operators go through a scripted routine. When he got to the section for the pilot's name and unit, I responded, "Lt. McEniry, VMA-216.", --he was very obviously relieved and commented, "O-kay! --let's get this thing done."

The rest of the approach went smoothly. Doing a GCA with the Debonair was really a piece of cake. Kinda funny, though, when the operator gets his 'customer' to the point of the GCA Minimums, he says, "You are at GCA minimums, take over visually and land your aircraft, GCA standing by for your comments."

Well when he got to that point he said the scripted words very rapidly, and then went on to say, "—picking up a slight drift to the right expect touchdown in 5 seconds, drift stopped…GCA notes touchdown….keep it straight….keep it straight….GCA notes that you have stopped."

It was a wonderful approach and a true "zero-zero" approach. GCA had to *radar-vector* the Follow-Me truck out to me!

-o-

Dear reader, please understand I'm not trying to make myself out to be some kind of 'Hero-driver' or 'risk-taker'. It was a matter of keeping three hundred hours a

192

year on the airplane. Plus, I was very current with instrument flying skills from the Reserve flying and learning about the changing weather encountered in the Northwest. In the five-year period working for Pacific Airmotive, I only lost two days due to heavy weather. I should have lost four or five, hence the 'war stories'. They are usually born when you do something that you really should not have done!

One of our major product lines was B.F. Goodrich, not just tires but also anti-ice and de-ice systems. One of my corporate customers was Gene Wing, who flew a Grumman Mallard amphibian for Lincoln Federal Savings Bank.. (I believe I mentioned him earlier in this narrative, when talking about "smooth pilots".)

The Grumman Mallard was designed for the tropics and didn't have any wing-tail de-ice boots or 'hot props'. Gene wanted to install 'hot props' to enable him to fly out of more icing than he wanted to deal with, and for the obvious safety reasons.

I was able to provide an after-market kit that would require a STC (Supplemental Type Certificate) and some flight testing. Flying with Gene was an eye-opening experience. The needles didn't move! Flying as co-pilot, I once reached up, and with palms of both hands hit the shock-mounted instrument panel.

"What the Hell.....why did you do that?" Gene exclaimed.

"I wanted to see if the instruments were all frozen."
Gene just smiled.

It was great having the use of one's own airplane. One of the perks was weekend use under the pretext of having to dry it off after washing it. Kathy and Scott loved to fly, but Darlene wasn't ever very comfortable in the air. Being a good sport she put up with it, though.

I think what I'm trying to say is that General Aviation has become my "core".

# EIGHTEEN   MARINE CORPS RESERVE

Life as a "Weekend Warrior" was great.  Good companionship, cheap drinks at the bar, fun flying and a wonderful change away from the hassles of corporate life.

Marine Attack Squadron VMA-216 was flying the Douglas AD-5 Skyraider.  She was a very large, carrier-based attack bomber initially built in the closing days of War2.  The AD-5, later designated as the A-1E, was used in the Korean conflict and saw service in Viet Nam in the role of the "Sandy Mission".  Its job in that role was to circle a downed pilot, keeping the gooks away until the Jolly Green Giant rescue helicopter arrived.  The AD-5 was well suited for that role.  Being prop-driven she could stay on site for a very long time and carried enough ordnance to accomplish its mission.  In fact, the Spad, as she became known, (due to being a "propeller-driven" airplane in the world of jets) carried 10,000 pounds of bombs, rockets, napalm and combinations there-of.  For the sake of comparison, 10,000 pounds was the average bomb-load of the B-17 in War2.

Powered by the Wright R-3350, producing 2700 hp, the Spad had a cruise speed of 200 mph and maximum speed of 311 mph.  She could climb to 26,000 ft. at a rate of 2,300 ft. per minute.  Not bad for a bomber!

I've mentioned some of this earlier.

The AD was a delight to fly.  Agile, and an exceptionally stable gun platform.  It was easy for a pilot to deliver his selected ordnance with a high degree of accuracy.

The Weekend Warrior routine was Saturday morning muster at 0800, followed by a pilot's meeting.  Squadron business was discussed, flight schedule posted and if not scheduled to fly one took care of assigned collateral duties. The flying part was the best, of course. The weekend drill continued thru 1700 Sunday.

During the course of the Fiscal Year we had to complete an annual syllabus that included formation flying; Division (4 a/c) and Section (2 a/c) maneuvers, instrument, night formation, cross-country, gunnery and all of the range of ordnance that included Napalm, bombs, and 5 inch HVAR rockets. This was all "dumb" ordnance from War2, Korea and Viet Nam. Most of our live ordnance was conducted during our annual two week (AcDuTra) Active Duty for Training period usually held in the summer.

The aircraft were available for 'extra drill' sessions. It was a good way to get the required night flying in and also cross-country. A typical session was to leave work, head out to the base, suit-up and fly down to Eugene, shoot a couple of instrument approaches, land and eat dinner then fly back to NAS Seattle. Long cross country flying was available subject to the Detachment's approval. I used the bird for a trip down to Los Angeles on company business. Reserve life was fun and it paid well.

The pay was good especially if supplemented with "extra drills". It was enough to allow my wife to stay home with the kids instead of her working and then having to pay for child care.

The two-week summer drill periods were hard on the family since that was my company summer vacation. One had to schedule mini-vacations with the family to make up for it.

And then came the retirement benefits. It took me 26 years to get the full 20-year 'point' requirements for retirement. The benefits didn't kick in until reaching age 60. If the Reservist died before reaching age 60 no benefits would be forthcoming to the surviving spouse. However, after receiving the first check the Reservist could die and the spouse would receive Survivor Benefits unless or until she remarries.

I retired as a Major and receive about $1,000/month. This doesn't come close to what it would be if I had full active-duty for 20 years. But still, a grand is still a grand. After hitting age 65, I came under 'Medicare'. Medicare pays 80% of the medical expenses then Marine Corps "TriCare For Life" (Military medical benefit) picks up the remaining 20%. Most drugs are furnished with a nominal co-pay of $9 or less.

Like I said, Reserve flying was a lot of fun. We trained in various phases of formation flying, dive-bombing, rockets, strafing and lots of instrument work. Cross country flying was encouraged as well as night flying. A quick call to the Marine Operations Detachment out at NAS Sand Point requesting an airplane and I was set. I could come home from work, change clothes and head out to the base and go fly for a couple of hours. –hellava deal.

We were required to attend eleven Weekend Drills and a two-week active-duty summer period annually. The two-week period was usually spent down at MCAS El Toro, in Southern California. For me, it was back to my first base and near Laguna Beach where I had lived and still had many friends.

I had been promoted to First Lieutenant when I was still on active duty. I had expected to get promoted to Captain when in the Reserve squadron but it hadn't happened. I kept getting "passed over". This happened twice and if it happened a third time I would be forced out of the Reserve. The following is how I managed to stay in the Reserve and make it to retirement.

# NINETEEN    PROMOTION TO CAPTAIN

**I**t was the summer of 1966. My Marine Reserve squadron, VMA-216, was preparing for our annual AcDuTra. It would consist of a two week deployment to MCAS El Toro, California. I had been a Weekend Warrior since 1960, after waiting for close to three years to get into a squadron. The waiting-list was long. It was really a good deal; one drill weekend a month and two weeks active duty in the summer. And, on top of that you get paid good money to fly airplanes. Plus, if you earn enough 'points' for twenty 'good' years (60 points /year) you get a pension and awesome medical benefits! (I'm beginning to sound like a "Peddler".)

The Douglas AD Skyraider was developed in the closing years of War2, as a dive-bomber and close air support weapons delivery aircraft. The Curtis-Wright R-3350, the second largest reciprocating engine built, powered her. (The largest was the Pratt & Whitney R-4360, developed to power the B-36 SAC bomber, and eight of 'em powered Howard Hughes' Spruce Goose.) --and that's a whole lot of "Round Power"!

The AD could carry 10,000 lbs. of ordnance *external*, equal to the *internal* bomb load of the Boeing B-17 Flying Fortress    There had been at least six model variations of the AD; most were single-seat, fighter-type configurations. There was a hunter-killer model that had the large "guppy" bubble under the wing and one with a Sonar sensor. Our squadron model AD-5 was a varied mission model, side-by-side cockpit, and large greenhouse area behind the cockpit. The area could take four passenger seats or four litters and had tie-downs for freight or removable in-flight ECM equipment.  The model was used by the Air Force in Viet Nam for the "Sandy" missions; go out to where a downed pilot was transmitting a distress signal, orbit and suppress Viet-Cong activity until the Jolly Green Giant large rescue helicopter could arrive on the scene.

Being a reciprocating engine aircraft, (not a jet) coupled with high ordnance load capability the 'dash five' was perfect for the Sandy Mission.  She could loiter on site for much longer than a jet-powered aircraft and carried enough weapons to discourage the VC from going after a downed airman.  Many a pilot owed their lives to the bird.

We didn't know it at the time but this would be our last AcDuTra with the AD since the Air Force would be around soon to collect 'em.  When the word came down that we would be losing them our hopes rose and rumors flew, about getting the little Douglas A4D Skyhawk.  Then, we were told that due to the limited runway length of NAS Seattle (Sandpoint) we would not be getting a jet fighter replacement.   No, instead we got the Fairchild C-119 Flying Boxcar, changing our squadron designation from "Attack" (VM*A*) to "Transport" (VM*R*). --but, that comes later.

This would be a major AcDuTra, taking place at MCAS El Toro, California.  It would encompass all Marine Reserve units, land, sea and air, from around the country. Its title was Operation MARLEX.   It would include amphibious landings at Camp Pendleton, and desert operations in the Bullion Mountains Marine Corps Training and Restricted area just north of Twenty-Nine Palms capped with a simulated nuclear attack in the desert.

Annual Reserve Active Duty is two weeks.  The first week would be spent in live ordnance training; bombs, rockets, napalm and strafing. The second week would start the actual MARLEX.

VMA-216 had a mix of fine aviators, some of which had served in War2 and then recalled for Korea. Close Air Support was well entrenched in their experience. They were skilled at passing this experience to the younger pilots in the squadron. As a result, our hit/score averages were high. The AD was an excellent weapons platform, which also helped a lot.

The reserve squadrons taking part in the MARLEX were from all over the country, consisting of jet fighters, helicopters, transports and our AD's (last of the props). The aggressors (bad guys) were an FJ-4 squadron (Navy/Marine version of the F-86) out of Dallas. A F9F-7 Cougar Squadron out of Spokane served as our high-fighter CAP (Combat Air Patrol), protecting the helicopters and us. The transports were only support aircraft, well out of any combat zone.

On the third day of the MARLEX we were hit with a surprise ORI (Operational Readiness Inspection). The Inspection Team arrived unannounced, and spread through various departments checking all aspects of squadron activities, from pilot training jackets, personnel files, maintenance records, etc.

I was on the flight schedule with "Tex" Ritter as my wingman. (All fighter pilots have 'handles'.... anybody with the last name of Ritter automatically get "Tex" added to it.) Now Tex was one of the *older* young pilots, a Boeing engineer, only flew as much as he had to, and generally kind of a fuddy-duddy. He was a Captain and also in the zone for Major, in fact might have already been selected. I just remember that he was still a Captain during this MARLEX.

On the other hand, I was the most senior First Lieutenant in the Marine Corps. There was one other almost as senior as me...and he was also a member of VMA-216; Al Parent, by name. I didn't ever know how or why he had not made the Captain's promotion list. I knew why I hadn't....been in a bit of trouble in past years. --but that's another story I may have already talked about.

During the MARLEX operations we were scheduled as flights of two aircraft instead of four. This was due to safety precautions in force in the training area; lessening congestion.

Tex was not a qualified "Division Leader" (Flight of four) so I was scheduled as the flight leader, even though it would be a Section Flight instead of a Division. Flight leads were not by rank unless the flight members were equally qualified.

Tex and I were in briefing when approached by a young Captain, all spiffed out in a semi-starched flight suit, neck kerchief and very squared away. I noticed that he wore "the ring" from one of the trade schools. --obviously *Regular Establishment.*

He informed us that he was a member of the ORI Team and would be flying with us. The squadron patch on his flight suit identified him as a member of the first F-4 Phantom squadron at El Toro. --a hot outfit.

Both Tex and I had been living in our already-oil-stained flight suits for over a week. The engine on the AD, the R-3350, did throw oil mist from the exhausts...it was pretty hard to stay clean n'spiffy. I wore a bright red, very non-regulation T-shirt under my flight suit and capped it off with a large plastic black bear, symbol of the "Oso Negros" Mexican gin & vodka beverages, fastened to my zipper. The Captain was clearly displeased with our appearance. I don't think the idea of flying with a *Weekend Warrior* in a dirty airplane thrilled him very much either.

The Captain accompanied me on my pre-flight, taking special interest in our very full bomb & rocket ordnance load. Our mission was live ordnance delivery into the impact area, well clear of, but adjacent to ground personnel.

He strapped into the right seat of the side-by-side cockpit. We started up and I called for taxi instructions for the flight of two. We were given clearance to the active prop runway, instead of the normal active. Maybe this is why Tex turned the wrong way when leaving the chocks. I noticed that the Captain was furiously making notes.

I requested a section take-off from the tower. This brought a disdainful look from my ORI man. On take-off Tex managed to stay with me pretty well, but once in the air he opened his formation position. When I saw him moving out I signaled for a loose formation, attempting to cover his actions. The Captain wasn't fooled, making more notes.

We climbed out to our assigned altitude of 12,000 feet and arriving at our check-in point (X-Ray) near Twenty-Nine Palms, attempted to check-in with Air Group Control. We had been instructed that no one could enter the Training Area without positive control. Group Control would usually hand us off to a Forward Air Controller (FAC) for mission assignment and coordination.

We hadn't been able to contact anyone when I received a distress call on "Guard Channel" (monitored simultaneously with any frequency) from 'Jolly Joe', a FAC. It seems that he was under attack by two FJ's. They were yo-yoing on him. I told him our type of aircraft and ordnance load. He was hoping that we were the fighter CAP. I told him we would do what we could.

202

Tex had been monitoring my radio transmissions and closed-up as we departed Point X-Ray.

As we approached Jolly Joe's position, from our high altitude position, I noticed the two FJ's. They were very low, in a vertical circular flight path making runs on the FAC's position, which was in a tight defilade in this mountainous, desert area. When one was on target the other was at the top of the looped flight path. I transmitted to Tex, "Let's go!" --another look from the Captain.

I rolled in and went straight down. The AD comes downhill pretty fast...especially with a full bomb load. I intercepted the top FJ closing enough to read the aircraft Bureau Number under his horizontal tail...the printing 2-3 inches high. As I was closing the ORI Captain was pretty excited...yelling, "You got him, this is a confirmed kill...he's history!"

I pulled off going for number two. As I pulled up it was obvious that I wouldn't be able to get inside of his flight path to pull enough lead for a kill.

Tex came on line, "Doc, I can get him!"

Tex had been in tight, but was on my right, inside of our flight path. I did a *'flight school formal lead pass'*, passing the lead to him. My ORI Captain was impressed as I fell into place on Tex's wing. Tex was in the right position and would have been able to kill, had this been actual combat. Our energy was rapidly bleeding off so we broke away.

The surprised FJ's tried to jockey on us but my ORI Captain transmitted on Guard Channel, "Don't bother, guys, you're both dead."

We were unable to contact the Air Group or any other FAC so we left the area and proceeded to our briefed destination at MCAS Yuma, where we were to RON (Remain Over Night).

Our live ordnance was removed. We spent a little time in the bar at the Officer's Club that night. The FJ's were staging out of Yuma and we had some drinks with our two victims. --they bought. The ORI Captain said that he was very impressed with Reserves, if we were any example of the ordinary. Even the FJ's, due to attempting an attack that they were hardly suited for...requiring them to be in the "low 'n slow" configuration that got them "killed". He had been led to believe that *Weekend Warriors* weren't very aggressive. We had managed to change his mind.

The following morning, we were assigned a mission of troop suppression with a simulated ordnance load of napalm and 20mm wing gun ammo.

Our section take-off and formation flight was pretty tight. Ol' Tex was standing ten feet tall! --very proud of himself as well he should have been!

My ORI Captain was pretty talkative on inter-com and had been since our experience of the day before. He was pretty happy with the way things had gone and not afraid to say so. I had always been impressed with 'trade-school' folks and this Annapolis man further solidified that feeling. The trade schools turn out some damn fine officers!

Our flight from Yuma was to be under radar, so we were on the deck. As we approached the Training Area we saw the atomic cloud shape of the simulated nuclear bomb, and followed by the 'aggressor attack'. We came into the area, not under Group Control but seeing the aggressor forces out in the open rushing to attack our friendly forces that had just been "nuked".

Golly, gee...there we were with simulated napalm and 20mm. My ORI said that we decimated the enemy forces. Group Control finally came on line to inform us that we had done the right thing and were now cleared to return to El Toro.

A hero's welcome awaited us. There was a staff car waiting to take us to see the General. It was General Robertshaw, Commanding Officer, Fourth Marine Air Wing. Our ORI's report had been filed from Yuma and that alone was enough to turn heads. It turned out that we had gotten the only two 'confirmed kills' in the entire operation! --aggressor or friendly! And with AD's, no less. Tex and I were invited to have dinner with the General that night. General Robertshaw felt that he had met me before.

Exploring possibilities revealed that when I was flying R5D's, when still on Active Duty, the name Major "Gene-The-Marine" Nelson came up as he was an Aircraft Commander. On a flight to Japan, with Gene the AC, we had met then Colonel Robertshaw at NAS Atsugi. He and Gene had served in Korea together. That night was a real party-on affair...I was the designated "keep 'em outta trouble" Lieutenant. I ended up earning my keep since Gene had initiated some problems at a club and I had managed to get them the hell outta there before the Gendarmes arrived. I hadn't remembered, but the General had. --this was to prove very valuable later.

The MARLEX was over; Friday was spent in final debriefing and evaluation. The General was extremely pleased with the results. The squadron was scheduled to depart MCAS El Toro for NAS Seattle Saturday morning.

## Promotion to Captain

I was scheduled to be the last to leave El Toro. I was flying the "hangar-queen" home. The hangar-queen had been our *routable spares inventory* for the two week AcDuTra. She had been cannibalized for parts, keeping the rest of the squadron flying. Spares had been ordered and arrived in time to get her in flying condition for the trip home.

Our recently acquired Detachment Operations Officer, Major Herb Valentine (Navy Cross, former helo pilot for President Eisenhower) and neat guy had asked me if I would transport a sealed box back to Seattle for him. I asked what the sealed box contained, since its shape and size identified it as containing booze. Herb's reply was "mouth wash". --good enough for me. An officer's word is his bond.

(Military Regulations clearly state that it is acceptable to carry sealed intoxicating beverages in Transport or Utility Category aircraft but illegal to transport them in Tactical aircraft…. the A1E was considered a "tactical" aircraft.)

My flight plan was Direct Bakersfield, Victor 23 Seattle. "Direct" Bakersfield would put my route of flight over Lancaster and Palmdale.

The pre-flight was normal. I checked the Yellow Sheets (maintenance records) very closely due to the bird's recent status. Everything checked. There was a centerline drop tank installed for additional range, even though the AD could easily do the four-and-a-half-hour flight without additional fuel.

The take-off was normal and I started my climb to 10,000 feet, my assigned flight plan altitude. Upon reaching altitude I set my cruising power and was in the process of switching to the drop tank when there was a loud engine explosion, followed by heavy vibrations. I transmitted a "May-Day" and looked for a landing site. I could see the Palmdale airport and tried for it. The airplane had lost all power, shaking so bad the instruments couldn't

206

be read and coming down out of the sky like a *"turd from a tall cow's ass!"*

A military GCI site answered my "May-Day", asking me to "stand-by". I told them that I was unable to *stand-by*, that I was crashing. I really would have liked to abandon this falling safe, or brick, but there was the case of booze in the back and I wouldn't have time to get out of my parachute, climb in back, throw the booze overboard, climb back into the front, get back into my parachute and bail out. --no time, and what's more...it looked like I wouldn't be able to make the Palmdale airport so I gave it up and selected a farmer's field that appeared to have been recently plowed.

I remembered my Operating Handbook; *land with the rows*, not across and go in wheels up so as not to flip over on your back, trapping you in the cockpit while the full gas tank leaked onto the red-hot exhaust stacks and you explode and burn. --terrible way to end a day! (The AD is a tail-dragger.)

And, speaking of gas tanks, at about two hundred feet I happened to notice my shadow on the ground reminding me that I had a drop tank full of 115/145 high octane airplane gasoline still attached to the centerline hard point of the AD. I pulled the Center Line Manual Release Handle, dropped the nose, picking up another five knots of airspeed and skimmed the ground before impacting. It worked. The drop tank ended up a hundred yards behind the airplane...it didn't blow, the airplane didn't catch fire...I was alive and the crash didn't break a booze bottle.....and I was out and running before the dust cleared.

The Government was paying the farmer, that owned the dirt, "not to grow" anything. He arrived in his air-conditioned Cadillac and seeing that I wasn't injured thanked me for destroying the crop that he was being paid

207

not to grow. (--I'm sure that a claim of some sort went in to that effect.)

A helicopter from Edwards AFB arrived with Air Police on board to cordon off the crash site and then to transport me to the base for medical evaluation.

I was examined by an Air Force Flight Surgeon and being pronounced fit, I requested my two ounces of brandy. He had never heard of such a thing. Being an 'eight-and-a-half' year First Lieutenant, I was not impressed or intimidated by a Lieutenant Colonel Flight Surgeon and insisted that he comply with Naval Regulations and grant my request. I got away with it. He finally found some Medical Brandy and gave it to me, mumbling something about Marines that I didn't catch.

Another helicopter soon arrived, this one from MCAS El Toro. It was almost too much; two helicopter rides in one day! Against my better judgment I climbed in and was returned to the Marine Corps. I had found room in my parachute bag, that was my sole piece of luggage, for the case of Valentine's "mouth wash".

Meanwhile, the squadron arrived back at NAS Seattle. Upon opening the mail that had accumulated during the AcDuTra, there were orders transferring me to "Class Three" (civilian, non-military person) since I had failed promotion to Captain for the third time. The orders were to go into effect at midnight that night. --but, *there I was*...still in California...still on Active Duty...there would have to be an Aircraft Accident Review Board and only a few hours left before I became a reluctant Cinderella!

Some folk from the City of Palmdale called the squadron upon learning the identity of the airplane and wanted to commend the pilot for turning away from the city while on fire and coming down, etc. The Squadron Duty

Officer, knowing about the Class Three thing told the caller that perhaps a few telegrams to that effect would be in order. Several arrived later.

Somebody had to make a decision. It started up-line, finally getting all the way up to CG, 4$^{th}$ MAW.... General Robertshaw. His reply, I was later told, was that the obvious answer was to convene an emergency Captain's Promotion Board, promote me to Captain and then obviously Court Martial me for "willful and negligent destruction of Government Property". So he did just that. --the promotion thing, the rest would have to wait for the accident board's findings.

That night I was allowed leave base and went down to Laguna Beach to party with some friends. The following morning, I was rudely awakened by a Steward who informed me that there was a car waiting to take me over to Base Operations...that some senior Naval Officers were waiting for me.

I was hung over, needed a shave but the Steward said there was no time for any of that; I was to report immediately. I threw on my flight suit...the same oil-soaked, smelly flight suit that I had lived in for two weeks, grabbed my piss cutter (fore & aft cap) and followed the Steward out to the waiting car.

At Base Operations I was directed into a conference room where three Navy TAR (Temporary Active Reservists) Commanders (equal to Lieutenant Colonels) were sitting at a table. It seemed that the Palmdale area crash site was two miles closer to NAS Alamitos than to El Toro, so the Navy had been given the responsibility of conducting the Aircraft Accident Review Board.

The nearest Commander spoke the first words. "Why did you choose to land the airplane wheels-up?

I couldn't believe what I had heard. He repeated the question.

I replied, "Well, to start with, I've read the Pilot's Hand Book and you obviously haven't!". Things deteriorated from there.

At one point in the interrogation I said, "I refuse to answer any further questions without representation by civilian counsel."

Their reply was that this wasn't a Court Martial.

210

My answer to that was for them to cease conducting the review like one, then. It got nasty. The problem was that (1) I had no respect for TAR's, (2) not much more for Navy Commanders that were fat, needed haircuts, shoe shines and didn't know anything about the AD Skyraider, (3) I was an eight and a half year First Lieutenant, and (4) had a hangover...and some idiots were trying to pin "Pilot Error" on me for an engine blowing up! I was not impressed or intimidated, period. And I wasn't about to have some damn Squids blame me or my Maintenance people for the accident. It very nearly got out of hand.

It finally ended with them issuing several threats of various kinds and that I should perhaps find that civilian attorney to represent me in a General Court Martial.

I, quite frankly, didn't give a shit!

My good friend, Ric Novak arrived from Seattle in one of our AD's. He told me what had happened and that I was being promoted to Captain. We flew back to NAS Seattle.

After the Review Board findings were published, I was given a Letter Of Commendation (with the words that I could have been a bit more cooperative with our Navy Brothers) --there is a God! (And SHE has a hellava sense of humor!)

-o-

The war in Viet Nam was heating up and in the spring of 1967 we were told that the U.S. Air force would be taking our AD's for service in Viet Nam. They were to be used primarily for the "Sandy Mission" and for close air support.

We were hoping to get the little A4D Douglas Sky Hawk as a replacement, but the Gods didn't smile so we ended up getting the R4Q-2 Flying Boxcar, later designated the C-119. (One has to say "R4Q, two" fast, for the full effect.) Saying C-119 was a lot safer. –oh well.

We soon received our first two airplanes and the work of transitioning a group of fighter pilots into the mysteries of transport flying began. Those pilots that were also flying with the airlines were easier to transition. My former transport experience with the R5D (C-54) came in handy and I was soon qualified as a co-pilot and then later made "Aircraft Commander" once I had acquired the hours set forth in the regulations.

The C-119 Flying Boxcar got its name from the fact that the cargo area was almost equal in capacity as the standard railroad boxcar. Her primary mission was combat support of the ground troops. Delivering supplies and/or vehicles into a forward air base plus parachute troops, cargo airdrop and similar missions became our training goals.

The C-119 was designed for a crew of five; two pilots, a flight engineer/plane captain, and a radioman and cargo master. This gave our enlisted personnel an opportunity to acquire the necessary skills to become "Aircrew" and earn the extra flight-pay.

The airplane had a payload of about 10,000 pounds. She could carry sixty-two combat troops with full equipment, or thirty-five stretchers with attending medical personnel or any variations.

Her empty weight was approximately 40,000 pounds and we maxed out at 72,000 pounds that included crew personnel, fuel, and cargo or passengers. She was powered by two Curtis-Wright R-3350-85 Cyclone radial engines of 2,500 hp each.

The performance figures weren't too bad. She had a range of over 2200 miles, cruised at 180 knots and since she wasn't pressurized, lived in the 10-12,000 ft. altitude air space.

We did a lot of cross-country flying. The longest trip that I made was from NAS Seattle, over to Geiger AFB in Spokane and then across the United States and over the Gulf of Mexico to Guantanamo Bay. And then back. (I couldn't hear anything for a week.) It wasn't until the last year that we flew the C-119 that we were told to wear either "Mickey Mouse" headphones or a helmet that had built-in hearing protection. Better late than never...but the damage to my hearing had already happened.

Once we started flying the C-119 I found that I later missed being able to get upside down and stuff. I had gotten to know Major Herb Valentine, the Detachment Operations Officer, pretty well. (It was *his* case of 'mouthwash' that had been in the back of the Spad that I crashed without breaking a bottle!) Herb allowed me to check out in both of the air station's T-34 and T-28 trainers. I just had to be sure that I was up to 'numbers' on all of the transport training phases, including night and instrument. It was indeed a privilege to be able to fly those two aircraft.

The T-34 was almost identical to the Beech Debonair, that I had been flying for Pacific Airmotive, that Herb didn't even "check me out" but put it on the flight schedule and told me to go fly it. He did give me some dual in the T-28 however.

Both of them were loads of fun to fly.

Enclosed is a short story of my first C-119 flight as Aircraft Commander. (Pilot in command) I originally wrote this for a writer's contest some years ago. I felt that it deserved a place in this narrative.

213

C-119F (131694) VMGR-353
Taken at Westfield, MA - c.1961

Copyright Photo
Tom Hildreth

**Fairchild   C-119**

**Flying Boxcar**

# TWENTY     THE FLYING BOXCAR
### ...a short story

It was a typical Seattle fall day. Low overcast with an occasional light misting. It wasn't really raining, just trying to. Captain "Doc" McEniry, United States Marine Corps Reserve, was walking across the broad concrete ramp toward the squatting Fairchild C-119 Flying Boxcar. He couldn't help but admire the aging twin-boom transport. This was to be his first official flight as Aircraft Commander. He had received the designation after a complex, long and tiring flight check the previous drill weekend. The squadron was transitioning from an attack squadron to transports. It is a different world.

His good friend, Don Wohlers, had also received his TPC designation and would be flying as his co-pilot on this trip. Doc had won the toss, so to speak. Actually the Operations Officer had scheduled him as the Aircraft Commander for this trip. --No special reason, luck of the draw. They were both recently promoted Captains. Doc was slightly senior in date of rank, but that didn't usually have anything to do with anything in the Reserve.

Doc McEniry and Don Wohlers were members, in good standing, of that elite group of military known as "Weekend Warriors". The Reserve establishment is made up of men that happen to believe in the concept of *readiness*. Some of the enlisted men were under obligation to serve in the Reserve capacity for a given number of years, in return for a reduced active duty obligation.

Officers are commissioned in the Reserve unless they are graduates of one of the trade schools...Annapolis, West Point, the Air Force Academy or the Coast Guard

215

Academy. There were a couple of other schools that would insure a graduate of a regular commission, like Virginia Military Institute or The Citadel. A Reservist could *apply* for integration into the regular establishment. Not many were accepted.

For an aviator, the Reserve is wonderful. He is paid for attending one weekend drill a month, and two weeks' active duty during the summer. The purpose, of course, is to maintain some degree of currency in whatever type of aircraft his squadron is flying. The monthly check is a welcome addition to any family's budget and he gets to fly airplanes...stay up late, drink cheap booze, talk dirty and smoke cigars. --Hellava deal! And, if he can stick it out for twenty years, earn retirement monies. He receives the monthly checks starting on his sixtieth birthday. The catch is that he has to live to receive the first check then he can die and his wife will receive Survivor Benefits for her lifetime. If the Reservist dies before his sixtieth birthday nobody gets anything. Granted, a crap shoot, but he still had the good companionship, flight time and income for the twenty years. Yes indeed, a hellava deal.

On the other hand, the purpose of the Reserve is to have a force ready to augment the regular establishment during some national crisis. At such time as the President and/or the Congress determined the necessity, the reservist would be activated. This would mean twenty-four-hour notice to pack a bag and report to his unit for the duration of the crisis. His job must be held open and his wife isn't supposed to divorce him and the children are to be reminded that their father is off defending their country. This is sometimes a better paying situation than his civilian job salary.

McEniry believed in the reserve concept. Not for the money or retirement, but for the flying and the

216

companionship that he had grown to love. Warriors are a different breed of humanity. Perhaps it's an attitude. Whatever it was it was one of the three ingredients that made Doc's life good. He had a good wife, liked what he did with his company and enjoyed the Reserve life. The equipment they flew could be more exciting, the squadron previously flew AD-5's, now re-designated the A1-E Douglas Skyraider. The Air Force had taken them for use in Viet Nam. Now the squadron had these C-119's. The mission was different, being a transport squadron now. Lots of cross-country flying. At least it was flying and he was getting paid to do it.

And today would be his first flight as an Aircraft Commander. The mission was moving fifty-eight troops and two officers, plus some cargo, to Minneapolis. Doc was looking forward to the trip. He had a buddy living in the town, that he had gone through flight training with. He had often spoken to Wohlers about him. The three of them would probably end up staying up too late, having too much to drink and sharing war stories. What was it Don had told him the other day? --the difference between a fairy tale and a war story? Oh yeah. The fairy tale usually starts, "Once upon a time..." --and the war story most always starts, "Now, this is no shit..."

The flight planning for the mission had been interesting. The C-119 is rated at seventy-two thousand pounds' maximum gross take-off weight. The basic weight, which includes the airplane, oil, and five crew members is about forty-three thousand pounds. The sixty passengers, manifested at a hundred and eighty pounds each and the cargo, manifested at six thousand six hundred eighty pounds, came to a total of a little over sixty-one thousand pounds. This left eleven thousand pounds for fuel. (AvGas; 115/145 octane, weighs six pounds per

217

gallon.) Fuel gauge instruments and flight planning calculations are done in pounds instead of gallons.

Transport aircraft have complex formulas for their fuel burn calculations. As an example, the C-119 was equipped with eight heaters that not only supplied heat to the cargo and crew compartments but also heat to the leading edge of the wing and tail for anti-ice functions. And it was winter. Even if it wasn't winter, heat had to be provided to the crew and cargo compartments except in rare summer or tropical operations. It is cold at altitude. The heaters burned the same fuel as the engines, at a rate of a hundred and ninety-two pounds per hour. Calculations for an instrument departure, even fuel-burn data for taxi and engine run-up, are all part of the planning process.

The mission profile, Seattle to Minneapolis, was twelve hundred and five nautical miles and with the C-119 cruising at a hundred and eighty knots, flight time enroute would be six hours and forty-five minutes. After factoring in the various fuel consumption details, this would require about thirteen thousand pounds of fuel, placing the aircraft in an over-weight configuration.

As the scheduled co-pilot it had been Wohler's responsibility to compute the weight and balance and flight plan details. Being Doc's first flight as the MMWIC ('*main mutha what's in charge*') he stayed very close to the details so had been working with Don all the way through the planning process. They alerted Sergeant Alexander, their assigned crew chief, to put eleven thousand pounds of fuel on board. --Not enough to make Minneapolis so they would have to stop enroute and refuel.

Standard operating procedures dictated refueling be done at military bases unless authorized otherwise or an emergency. There was a difference in price between a military base and 'contract-fuel' at a civilian field. Don suggested Minot Air Force Base in North Dakota. It was nine hundred and twenty-two nautical miles from Seattle and would flight plan at a little over five hours. Fuel reserve requirements, and the help of a forecast tail wind, placed their planning right on the numbers.

Wohlers had gone out to the airplane to pre-flight and supervise loading. Doc remained back at Base Operations to file their flight plan and pick up a final check on the weather

As he approached the C-119 Sergeant Alexander came up to him, saluting and said, "I'm sorry Captain, but they over-fueled the airplane. I have tried to get a de-fueler truck but I've been told it'll be an hour or so."

"How much over-fill? Did you tell Captain Wohlers?"

"Yes sir. He went into the line shack and tried to get a de-fueler expedited but didn't get anywhere," Alexander said, then added, "They filled her all the way, Sir. Sixteen thousand eight hundred pounds."

"Well shit! We're running late now. If we wait much longer, we'll no sooner get to Minneapolis and we'll have to turn around and come back." They continued walking toward the airplane. "Is everything else ready to go, Sergeant?"

"Yes sir. The bird looks good, passengers and crew are all aboard and the cargo tied down. We'll be a bit heavy, but it looks good."

"Well the good news is that we won't have to stop in Minot and refuel. It's snowing there and colder than a well digger's ass. Hell, let's go to Minneapolis." Doc said. They were now at the airplane and Doc climbed aboard.

He noticed the six-centerline seats that had been installed down the middle of the cargo bay. The bucket seats on each side of the bay accommodated forty-two

219

passengers. Two officers were seated in the front seat and Doc noticed that NCO's occupied the others. He introduced himself to the senior officer.

"Good morning Major, I'm Captain McEniry, the Aircraft Commander. We thought that we might have to stop in Minot, North Dakota and refuel, but it looks now like we'll have enough to go non-stop to Minneapolis. Our flight time is estimated at six plus forty-five or better. There's a forecast tailwind. Minneapolis is forecast to be clear and cold. Should be a good trip. Any questions?"

"That's good to hear, Captain. The other pilot said that we might have to stop. I haven't lost a damn thing in Minot, and don't feel any need to go there." The Major said.

As was expected of him, Doc chuckled, turned and climbed up into the cockpit. He handed the flight plan to Don, who was already strapped in. Doc told the assistant crew chief to go ahead and start the APU (Auxiliary Power Unit) , climbed into the left seat and strapped in.

Turning to Don he said, "Alex told me that they over fueled the airplane. I guess we'll be pretty heavy out of here but I figure we won't have to stop in Minot. We can change our flight plan down the road."

Problems that happen in aircraft can usually be traced back to some minor little part failure or a decision that shouldn't have been made. Doc McEniry had made a bad decision that was about to drive home a very important lesson to be added to his growing and expanding aviation experiences. –the kind of 'experiences' that give birth to a "War Story".

He had been influenced by a couple of factors. He was anxious to get going in order to be able to spend some time with his friend in Minneapolis, he didn't want to take the time to off-load the passengers and de-fuel the airplane. Besides, what harm can there be to having too much fuel?

It has been said that the only time you have 'too much' fuel is when you're on fire! --well, it can cause another problem, as we'll see.

James Michael McEniry was soon to discover the answer to that question.

Naval Air Station Seattle is located on a bump, or piece of land, sticking out into Lake Washington called Sand Point. The lake is about twenty-five miles long and one to two miles wide. It forms the eastern border of the city of Seattle. The western border of Seattle is formed by Puget Sound. Lake Washington has two floating bridges, dividing the lake into thirds. The bridges connect the ever-growing east side suburbs to Seattle. Sand Point is located in the northern third of the lake.

The main runway at the Naval Air Station is built across the point, parallel to the shoreline...with water at each end. This fact limited the runway length to a little over five thousand feet.

Engine run-up complete, Wohlers called for take-off clearance. They were cleared into 'position and hold'. Doc briefed Don and Sergeant Alexander, emphasizing that they would all three agree on engine performance prior to brake release. He commented that they were a bit heavy. The tower cleared them.

"MARINE ONE THREE ONE SIX SIX NINER IS CLEARED FOR TAKE-OFF. CONTACT SEATTLE DEPARTURE TWO EIGHT FOUR DECIMAL SEVEN, AFTER TAKE-OFF, SQUAWK FOUR NINER ZERO ZERO, WINDS CALM, ALTIMETER TWO NINER EIGHT SEVEN, OVER."

Wohlers reached for his microphone hanging on a hook by the window as Doc slowly pushed the throttles up.

221

"ROGER, SEATTLE DEPARTURE TWO EIGHT FOUR DECIMAL SEVEN AND THE SQUAWK. SIX SIX NINER's ROLLING. OUT." He placed his hand on the throttles also. Engines looked good, all agreed and Doc released the brakes. The C-119 started to roll down the runway. And it rolled. And it rolled. And it rolled!

They knew they were heavy, but the very slow acceleration rate was disturbing. There was a slight bow in the runway and Doc attributed the lack of speed to the upgrade and their weight. He was half right. The airplane had passed the point of aborting the take-off. They were committed.

Doc had applied backpressure to the yoke when rudder control had been attained. This occurred at about forty knots. Easing the backpressure, the nose wheel broke free and Doc rotated to the normal take-off attitude; nose wheel just clear of the ground. The airplane was supposed to accelerate to around ninety to ninety-five knots and lift off. They hadn't reached ninety knots when they came to the end of the runway. The main landing gear was still on the ground.

"Gear up!" Doc called. Wohlers and Alexander looked sharply at him, then Don shrugged and complied with the order. He realized that the gear wasn't going to do them a bit of good out in the water and maybe the drag reduction would help.

The gear came up, the lights indicating that all three were up and locked. The airplane didn't gain or lose an inch of altitude. They were mushing through the air in "ground effect" at about eighty-five knots slowly, very slowly inching up in airspeed. The airplane was barely flying, but at least they weren't getting wet! Yet!

"Jee-zuz Skipper, we can only hold this power setting for five minutes. We're maxed out!" Sergeant

Alexander said in a low-key manner, not panicked, just stating facts.

"I know Alex, I know. Just keep the cylinder heads from melting off and I'll try to keep us out of the water," Doc replied.

Wohlers was getting ready to switch to Seattle Departure Control, as their flight clearance dictated, "Doc, do you want to tell Departure anything?" He asked

"Yeah. You can tell 'em to stand by, that we're having a problem."

"Roger that, will do." He reached for the microphone. "SEATTLE DEPARTURE, MARINE THREE ONE SIX SIX NINER WITH YOU ON TWO EIGHTY-FOUR POINT SEVEN. PLEASE STAND BY; WE'RE HAVING A PROBLEM. OVER."

"ROGER MARINE SIX SIX NINER. DEPARTURE STANDING BY." The controllers were astute enough to not bother a flight crew dealing with a problem.

The C-119 had staggered to about two hundred feet and ninety-five knots. Doc called for a slight power reduction. Sergeant Alexander slowly eased the power, carefully monitoring aircraft performance and his engine conditions. They were approaching the Evergreen Point Floating Bridge. Doc had held the two-hundred-foot altitude during the power reduction and had slowly gained another five knots. They were now indicating one hundred knots. The base of the cloud overcast was eight hundred feet. Doc kept the airplane flying down the lake, holding the two-hundred-foot altitude.

Don Wholers looked over at him and asked, "Do you want to go straight-in to Renton?" Renton Municipal Airport was at the extreme southern end of Lake Washington.

"Not yet, Don...not yet," Doc replied. He noticed a slight gain in airspeed. The airplane was now indicating a hundred and five knots. "Take a look at our airspeed, gentlemen."

In another moment, agonizingly slow, the airspeed climbed to a hundred and ten and then a hundred and fifteen and now had reached a hundred and twenty knots.

The Rate Of Climb instrument practically leaped to "five hundred feet per minute" climb. The C-119 was actually flying like a real airplane, not 'mushing' through the air. It came as a surprise to all three crewmembers.

It was a very relieved Aircraft Commander that turned to his co-pilot and said, "Give me Climb Power and you can tell Seattle that we're okay and proceeding enroute, Captain."

Doc held the nose down until they were indicating a hundred and forty knots, their standard climb speed, then eased the large, heavy airplane into the climb. "--and when you get a chance you can give me the Climb Check List."

They climbed out to their assigned cruise altitude of nine thousand feet without further incident. It was very quiet in the cockpit. The full impact of what had transpired had soaked in and each crewmember was lost in his own thoughts. When they settled into cruise Doc asked Don to work with Alexander and re-do the weight and balance.

It was a chagrined Captain Wohlers that came back with the facts.

"Doc, I think there's some kind of lesson here. First, the basic weight of this specific airplane is forty-three thousand eight hundred pounds...eight hundred pounds more." He held up his hand as Doc started to say something. "Next, we have fifty-eight passengers that have M-16's and sea-bags. They're supposed to be figured at two hundred fifty pounds each, not a hundred eighty. --The two officers can stay at a hundred eighty pounds.  The six centerline seats are two hundred pounds and last, but not least, we also have chutes aboard.  Sixty chutes weigh in at one thousand, three hundred and fifty pounds.  As near as we can tell the cargo weight was manifested properly.  But, this means that we weighed just under seventy thousand pounds *before* they over-fueled the airplane.  With full fuel load at sixteen thousand seven hundred and eighty-eight pounds, Alex and I figured that we're about eighty-four thousand pounds...*only* twelve thousand pounds over gross!"  Don let the number sink in for a minute, then added, "This piece of shit wasn't supposed to fly at all!"

Doc responded immediately to this last comment.  "Hey Captain, don't call this beautiful airplane a piece of shit.  It did fly, not well until we hit a hundred and twenty knots indicated, but then she quit mushing and flew.  I'm impressed."  He thought for a moment then added, "As much as I hate to air our stupidity, this is something we should talk about at the next pilot's meeting.  There's a real lesson here.  We learned it the hard way."

Doc turned back to the business at hand, getting the airplane, passengers and cargo to Minneapolis.

It stayed quiet in the cockpit for a long time.

# TWENTY-ONE    H & H ENGINEERING

**O**n the 3$^{rd}$ of May, 1965 I was blessed with the birth of a man-child, one Scott Michael McEniry. My Sister and her husband Hal, had three daughters and it was fun rubbing it in to Hal. Hal was a successful sales executive, a good father and a real gentleman. It wasn't often that I had a chance to rub anything in his face. However, the birth of a 'man-child' did bring some changes to the nursery. The door knob was painted Blue. The handles on the padded 'changing chest' were painted Blue. –the baby in this room was a **_Male._** –so stated. OVER. (I never got over it.)

In 1967 Fred Costello came up to Seattle to meet with me. We flew the Debonair over to Ocean Shores for lunch. Fred had left Pacific Airmotive Corporation and had gone to work as Sales Manager for H & H Engineering in Denver, Colorado. He was in Seattle to offer me a job as Western Regional Manager, and I would be based in Southern California.

Fred knew how much I was making at PAC and the corporate pay policies. His offer actually *doubled* my existing salary. I accepted the offer.

H & H Engineering manufactured precision tube bending tools for use on a McDonald-Douglas or Pines Tube Bending Machine. My primary mission was to get the Douglas and Lockheed jumbo jets tooling orders. This would be *long-term* selling, so I would also call on industrial, marine equipment companies and government facilities in Southern California and the Bay area.

I moved the family back down to Laguna Beach. I bought a new five-bedroom house in Blue Bird Canyon. It had an ocean view out of two bedroom windows. It had two lemon trees on the property. The back yard was very small, with high banking along the rear property line. The house was on a long street that ended in a cul-de-sac. The street sloped down about ten or maybe fifteen houses to the end.

The slope wasn't too steep, thank God, because very young Scott got on just about every piece of rolling-stock that he owned and would go for it. The problem, however, was that none of his vehicles were designed for much speed and the poor little guy would crash frequently. The older kids would bring him home.... bloody, but ready to try it again. The worst vehicle was a little play tractor that had large rear wheels and a tiny front wheel. It would get out of control and tumble end over end. Scott must have been all of two and a half at the time.

Laguna is half way between San Diego and Burbank. The location worked out pretty well. Fred offered me a company car or I could drive our 1966 Volkswagon beetle for twenty-five cents a mile. I opted for the latter. That "bug" was a real moneymaker! However, when Fred came out to work with me I rented a larger car with air conditioning, at his "suggestion".

-o-

Once back in California I became interested in racing again. One of my tooling customers in San Diego was building some "Formula Vee", single-seat race cars, a new "Racing Class" based on the VW engine and suspension. I thought that I could do a better job. I was wrong. You just couldn't really do anything to the suspension following the 'formula rules'. I had put my drafting skills to work and had done a couple of design approaches, but way too limited. Harry Morrow had pointed me in the 'Formula Ford' direction. That 'formula' allowed for greater design flexibility.

My friend, Bud Rude flew down in his Twin Beech 18, landing at Orange County Airport. (Now "John Wayne"). He brought his kids, Neil, Kathy and Donna, their ages meshing with my Kathy and Scott. The kids stayed at our house in Laguna...Darlene packing everybody off to the beach every day, while Bud and I examined the race-car thing going on in Southern California.

We looked at the Formula Vee cars in San Diego and when I told him about Formula Ford he got pretty excited.

I had gotten to know Harry Morrow, of "Autobooks" in Burbank during the RRTA days. Harry was the founder, leader, and mentor of the 500cc Formula 3 single-seat race-cars. It was the only 'formula class' at that time in the 'States'. Formula 2 or formula 1 hadn't made its way into amateur racing in California yet. Harry helped me with research and books for car design and discouraged me from going after the limited design Formula V, but told me to go for the new Formula Ford class that was just coming into the game. He told me that a good chassis design could also take a much hotter engine, and then run in Formula B as well. (Formula B was the closest thing to Europe's Formula 2, in this country.) I took his advice. Harry also said that there was an outfit using Formula Ford cars in a driving school up at Willow Springs. So, when Bud Rude was there and I had told him about the school, he enrolled us. We flew the twin Beech up to the desert race track and landed on the straight-away.

It was my first time driving an open-wheel race car. More importantly, the ten-year period since I had driven last, also marked the enormous gains in tire development.

228

Driving Willow Springs on real race tires was an eye-opening experience. The car felt like it was on rails. I was driving at what would have been the old "Lap record" and I wasn't even working hard at it. (You might recall my previous drive at Willow Springs in both my Jaguar XK-120 and Ces's C-Type Jaguar.)

Bud Rude later raced a Formula Ford in the Northwest races. His daughter Kathy started racing as well, ended up driving for Porsche until a serious crash ended her racing career.

The H & H Engineering expense money of twenty-five cents a mile (using my year-old 1966 VW) paid for the development of the Aries Race Engineering (ARE) Formula Ford, Formula B racecar. A new 'partner' in Riverside did build one chassis. I had gone into his shop to get a price on welding up the tubular chassis of the racecar He looked at my drawings and suggested that maybe he should build a 'few' cars, not charging me for mine. I thought that to be a wonderful idea. By this time, I had been transferred to Denver and was just coming back to Southern California for sales trips. That way I was able to see the chassis take shape. Eventually it was complete. I had called for Triumph front uprights and cast rear uprights in the design. My partner borrowed a pair of Lotus cast-uprights for the rear and arranged to borrow a Ford engine and Lotus body nosepiece for testing. I did get a chance to test-drive the Aires with all that borrowed equipment. He told me that he was going to build some large number, that he could get a contract for five or more, but that didn't ever happen. I told him that he could do with the design whatever. The one chassis that I hadn't paid anything for, got sold. I didn't ever find out to whom or for what…or for where, etc. I would sure like to find it now. It may have been a bad business experience, but it was fun doing the design work.

It took the better part of nine months to win the Douglas DC-10 tooling contract, followed shortly after for about 75% of the Lockheed L-1011 requirements.

The primary reason for H & H's success was our pioneering in "hot bending" of exotic metal tubing. We specialized in titanium, 19-9 DL and other equally difficult-to-bend metals.

Shortly after getting the Douglas purchase order (the largest single order in the history of H & H) Fred called me to complain about one of my expense reports. I remembered a joke that he had told me some years back and told him to "go fuck himself", and slammed the phone down.

The president of the company had walked into Fred's office during our telephone conversation and saw the surprised look on Fred's face. Responding to the President's question, Fred told him what had transpired. The President was irate and Fred told him to go ahead and call me. He did and I told the President to "go shit in his hat"! --and hung up on him.

By this time Fred smelled a rat and suggested that they both go and check to see if I had turned in any new orders. When they saw the Douglas order Fred turned to the President and said, "Hell, all you have to do is buy a new hat. I've got a *real* problem."

Fred had remembered the joke and understood. He then shared that information with the President and they both had a good laugh. I was given a substantial raise.

-o-

Shortly after moving back down to Laguna Beach I had gotten in touch with the U.S. Marine Corps Reserve

230

detachment at NAS Los Alamitos, up near Long Beach. I wanted to fly fighters again but there weren't any openings for a Major. I was offered the single billet in a Navy Transport squadron open to a field-grade Marine pilot. I accepted. At least it would be flying. The squadron was equipped with the military version of the Douglas DC-6A. It was a wonderful airplane. It was fast, cruising at 300 mph, it was pressurized, had R-2800 P & W engines ("Works Good & lasts a long time" engines) and had a microwave oven on board for unprepared rations. This meant that we didn't have to put up with Box Lunches. (A military device designed to totally cement up one's colon!)

Due to my former experience in the military version of the DC-4, and recent experience in the C-119, I quickly qualified as Co-Pilot and made Aircraft Commander about six months later. We did a lot of CONUS (Continental United States) flying and during our annual two-week Active Duty did a flight down to Panama. It was a wonderful tour and one that I enjoyed very much. The Navy really knows how to live.

The C-118, being pressurized, flew above most of the weather. The fast cruising speed really made for comfortable flight. I became spoiled very soon. Plus, it was fun being the "token Marine". I tried to teach them the Marine Corps way of working with the troops. Simple things like making sure that they were treated right upon getting to our destination…. food, decent billeting, etc. And insuring quick servicing of our airplane so that the crew would have time for play.

The squadron was scheduled to attend their annual Dress-Blues inspection. The skipper said that I could be excused, but I insisted on participating as a squadron member. I got out my Marine *Dress* Blues, cleaned and pressed etc. (Marine 'dress blues are a *higher dress* than

Navy Dress Blues, which is actually their winter working uniform. The Marine winter working uniform is olive drab.)

During the inspection the Senior Navy Inspector (a full Commander) said when he got to me, "I'm not sure I really know how to inspect a Marine".

When an inspecting officer addresses you in ranks it requires a response.

I responded with, "Well Sir, with all due respect, you could start by getting a haircut and maybe put a shine on your shoes."

My Commanding Officer was standing behind the Inspecting Officer and I thought that he would have apoplexy. The Commander recovered himself and chuckled saying, "You're probably right, Major."

It was talked about for some time in the squadron.

- o –

Fred Costello had convinced the company that we needed an airplane. It was decided to find a good Aero Commander 500B. We found the right one in Portland. It had been equipped and sold in the Northwest and had full de-icing; props, plus wing and tail de-icing. Exactly what we were looking for.

The 500B didn't have turbo-chargers. The previous owner had installed after-market RAJAY turbo-chargers. They were manually controlled from the instrument panel with two spring-loaded toggle switches. Upon reaching five or six thousand feet and having advanced throttle until hitting the maximum Manifold Pressure, you then toggled open the Turbo-Charger Waste-Gates, maintaining the 'climb' Manifold Pressure power setting. Now all you needed was oxygen as you climbed on up to eighteen thousand feet.

I only flew the airplane once, and since I wasn't going above ten thousand feet didn't need oxygen. But it was nice being able to maintain 'climb power' all the way up to ten thousand. The flight was from Orange County Airport to Boeing Field, in Seattle. I took my wife and both kids along so that they could visit with friends while Fred and I called on Boeing together. We wanted to repeat the success that we had enjoyed with Douglas's DC-10 Program for Boeing's 747 Program. We ended up with only about 50% of the Boeing tube bending tooling requirements.

We flew back to Orange County. Flying the Aero Commander was blissful. A great airplane. I loved the RAJAYs'…. they really work well.

In order to get higher usage out of the airplane Fred thought that if I was stationed in Denver with him we could be more efficient.

There was an east coast Regional Manager also, but he wasn't a pilot and had no intention of ever becoming one. It was decided to transfer me up to Denver. My wife was not pleased.

I made multiple trips to Denver in an attempt to find a house. Nothing was available. There was a severe shortage of housing in the greater Denver area and what little availability there, was owned by the home-builders. They would make available a rental if you agreed to build a new house. I had accumulated some equity in our house in Laguna Beach and was told that it would sell quickly…which it did. We moved into a little rental house south of Denver down near the Fair-grounds in Englewood, after agreeing to build a new home.

Our new house was actually in the township of Aurora, down near the Cherry Creek Lake & Dam. It was a two story Colonial with a full basement on a corner lot

233

in a new development. It was supposed to be $36,500 but when finished it ran closer to $45,000. The City of Aurora assigned a $4,500 per year tax on it.

I was enraged. I personally addressed the City Council and said that I had friends in Seattle on Lake Washington that didn't have to pay those kinds of taxes. They suggested that I might want to consider moving back to Seattle.

I had been assigned the Midwest Region as well as my Southern California responsibilities. Fred was *bogarting* the Aero Commander so I was stuck with commercial air travel.

When we had lived in Seattle the family had taken up ice-skating. I had been a skier in my youth but didn't feel that I would be able to go often enough to stay safe, without breaking a leg. Ice Skating could be something that the whole family could do. We took lessons. Due to my age (30 years old), my coach wanted to put me in a Dance Class. I told him 'no way' that I wanted to do "Free Style"; the jumps and stuff. He said okay.

The first jump that I learned was a Waltz Jump. Then I learned the Toe Loop followed by another single-rotation jump, the Sauchow. I was ready to start working on an Axel, which is a turn and a half.

On one occasion, when working on an Axel, I caught an edge in a rut in the ice and lost control. I was falling backwards, flailing my arms and legs. The heel of my right skate buried itself into my left shin bone. It was a real nasty, painful accident. It was treated like a broken leg and I was stuck on crutches for some time. I wouldn't be able to fly the Debonair for six weeks. It really pleased Fred, who was still in Seattle at that time and he

234

had to do what would have been my coverage of the territory.

We hadn't done any skating when living in California. In Englewood there was an ice rink close by. We started skating there and joined a club. Our daughter, Kathy, studied with Carlo Fassi (Peggy Fleming's 'Pro'), and his wife coached Scott.

The club put on an Ice Show every year. I was elected Musical Director and in addition, since I was one of the few adults that could do "free style" got some nice parts in the show. I was *Wicked Barnaby* in BABES IN TOYLAND, and *Billy the Kid* in Aaron Copeland's RODEO, plus some other smaller parts.

Actually this was not a good time in my life. Darlene was continuously ill. It turned out to be thymus gland related and she ended up having to have her goiter removed. The company was good about keeping me off the road during her ill periods…that wasn't the problem. We were strapped financially; I couldn't continue to coincide my California sales trips with the Reserve drills so had to give that up. There weren't any Reserve units in Denver that I could get into. The progress payments on the new house were killing me as well.

When we weren't skating the kids and I would drive up into the mountains around Denver and go exploring ghost towns. I had a Volkswagen bus that was equipped with a "Janitrol" aircraft gas heater. The air-cooled VW's of the day weren't much suited for cold weather operation. The Janitrol made it possible. We, the kids and I became interested in early Colorado railroads.

I had seen an ad in the paper for some HO model train stuff from an estate. For a very nominal sum I acquired two locomotives, several cars and some building models still in the box not built. The kids and I built up a

235

model railroad layout, doing the papier-mâché and scenery things. It was a fun project.

About this time the owners of H & H Engineering decided to sell the company to Pines Engineering, our largest competitor. The first thing Pines did was to sell the airplane. Fred was out of town. I was fed up and went into the President's office, who was still on board temporarily, and asked him how I went about quitting. He said to say, "I quit". So I said, "I quit." --it was the dumbest thing I've ever done!

I was in a strange town, didn't really know anybody and had no prospects for another job, and a gigantic mortgage.

My friend, Richard E. "Bud" Rude, came through Denver and called. I had met Bud when I was with Pacific Airmotive Corporation. He had been the General Manager of a Beechcraft Dealership in Tacoma. We had become very good friends.

"Mike-yal…what the hell are ya do'in?"

I told him I was "--starv'in to death…"

"Well hell, why not come starve with me back in Seattle…wanna sell bread?"

Bud asked me if I would be interested in taking over the Sales Manager slot of Rhodes Frozen Bread, at his plant in Auburn, Washington. He would handle the relocation expense. I quickly accepted

What's that old cliché, "A good friend will help ya move…a REAL friend will help ya move the body!"

Okay, it wasn't a body…. but it was *life-saving!*

(You can learn more about Richard "Bud" Rude by checking "Alaska Aviation Legends – Bud Rude.")

# TWENTY-TWO RETURN TO SEATTLE

**W**e still had all of our packing and moving supplies so preparing for the move was fairly easy. I went ahead again to find suitable housing in Seattle. I stayed with my sister and brother-in-law, Patsy and Hal, while looking around. Patsy helped me find a house. We found something suitable in Medina, a suburb of Bellevue. It was a small, two-bedroom house that would work until something else could be found.

Bud Rude provided a company semi-truck and trailer from Rhodes Frozen Bread. I drove the Volkswagon bus and we stuck our other car, the 1966 VW Beetle in the back of the semi. Darlene and the kids and the two cats flew up on an airline. It would be the second time that the cats flew. We had gotten them in Laguna Beach. One was named "Snoopy" and the other "Shivers".

I was able to get back into my Reserve Squadron at NAS Seattle. Thank Gawd! However, it was a bit of a come-down going back to the C-119 after flying the Navy's very luxurious C-118/DC-6! --it was back to a non-pressurized, very loud, slow, shaking airplane...but at least it was flying.

I commuted to Auburn to the Rhodes Frozen Bread plant. It was an unusual company, founded and staffed by members of the Seventh Day Adventist church. Their religion called for no working after sundown on Friday. Saturday was their holy day. I found them to be a bit strange but their work ethic was extremely high. One could literally eat off of the shop floor. The Adventist dietary restrictions are as confining as the Jewish religion, in

237

different ways. But, as a result, the ingredients in the frozen bread dough were of the highest order. The company purchased all of their ingredients on the 'futures market' to insure quality. It is a wonderful product and one that I would highly recommend to any and all. I still use it to this day. –and when you're baking bread it makes the house smell good! Most folk are very familiar with the Rhodes frozen dough biscuits but do try their bread.

My responsibility as Sales Manager was to work with the "Reps" that sold our products. I was more used to working with company salesmen and it took some getting used to. The "Reps" had to be catered to in order to achieve any results. It wasn't my style but I tried to make it work

The 'Factory Representatives' have a full line of products that they represent. The lines that they 'pushed' were the lines that paid them the most commission, either that or the line that was 'easy' to sell. By making sales calls with them, I was able to push the product line a bit. That was the way that industry works.

We had a couple of airplanes at our beck and call…a Mooney 20E and a Beechcraft S Model Bonanza. Bud made me "Chief Pilot" of Rhodes Frozen Bread Company. Then later, Bud bought an Enstrom helicopter and said that I had to get checked out also since he had registered the helo with Rhodes and said that I had to fly everything in the "fleet". (He just wanted to 'share' the humbling of transition from 'fixed-wing' to 'fling-wing'.)

Well, checking-out in helicopters was interesting but very humbling. My instructor, whose name I can't remember, took me out to the middle of a mile square field in the south Renton valley area. He said to try to hover. I said, "Where?" And he replied, "Just try to stay inside the field boundary." As it turned out, that wasn't an easy thing to do.

**Helicopters.** –my personal opinion.

Allow me to open the discussion with the fact that when I was on active duty, the Marine Corps was pushing hard for Helo drivers. It was said that once you got a Helo MOS (Military Occupational Specialty) you never got back to 'fixed wing'. It was something that I avoided.

It was in the Civilian Sector, where I encountered the need to get the rating. Therefore, I started training.

The only thing a "Fixed Wing" pilot brings to the 'Learning Table' is *air sense.* For example, *t*o take-off and climb in an "airplane", you ease back on the stick. To take-off in a helicopter, you reach down with your right hand and lift up a long bar of sorts…twisting the handle that is now your throttle…. your left hand is on the stick and as you "lift-off-the-skids", you push it *forward,* gathering speed then ease into a climb. Just a whole lot of things to do at the same time. You better not be chewing gum.

It was fun and pleasurable, as you integrate with the all-new way of things. As I said earlier, humbling, very humbling. Oh, and let's not forget "Auto-Rotation" …the helicopter's parachute. The way it works is that when an engine problem occurs you sorta disconnect the engine from the whirling blades up over your head…and then as you fall toward the earth the whirling blades slow you down and you 'whirl down' to safety. Right?

Umn…. not quite. What they don't talk about is the hundred feet or so that it takes for the 'whirling blades' to speed up. Until the 'speed-up' gets it up, the helicopter *hurtles……plummets*, toward earth bringing your ass-hole right up around your neck…choking you. (It leaves a 'brown' ring around your neck!)

239

When I left 'Rhodes' I had an hour or so to go for my Commercial Helicopter Rating and didn't go back and do it. I didn't want the Rating. What would I do with twenty-five hours or so, with folk coming outta 'Nam' with hundreds of hours. And besides, they're dangerous. My instructor was killed later trying to lift a large "Air-Makeup" unit at Bel-Square remodel...a tethered-load and engine problem. Too low to Auto-Rotate and high enough to rupture fuel cells upon impact and Boom. I lost another friend in that manner, only it was logging with a tethered-load. Very dangerous.

I really do not like helicopters.

The Adventists didn't believe in advertising, choosing rather to use "sampling" as the best way to present the product to new customers. Employees were encouraged to take home product and distribute it among their friends and neighbors. I ended up giving my friend, Clem Bentley, a full case. He owned a Mini Cooper at the time and put the case of frozen bread in the small storage area behind the rear seat and promptly forgot it.

Well, you know what happened. It was a hot summer day; Clem was driving down Westlake Avenue, in Seattle, toward Lake Union. Now frozen bread dough will rise when thawed. And when he looked up and saw, in his rear mirror, this blob that came bubbling up over the rear seat, he almost drove off of the road! It actually wasn't too difficult to clean up and we laughed about it for many years.

One of our plants on the east coast had to shut-down for plant maintenance and our Auburn plant was to provide product for the one-week period of shut-down. I discovered that there was no way that an air carrier could guarantee delivery of a frozen food product. Bread dough will start to rise when thawing. The air carrier people thought that they could deliver in the given time period if we packed the product in dry-ice. It would require a lot of dry-ice and also increase our air shipment weight. We could chance shipping without a lot of dry-ice packing and take a chance that the product would stay frozen It was what we did, but it was taking a chance.

I started to think about the use of a cryogen, such as liquid nitrogen in a special container just for frozen food products. I checked into FAA regulations and spoke with a couple of local air carriers. I took my idea to the new Plant Manager and he turned it down. We had not been getting along anyway and one thing led to another and I was either let go or quit.

I called Bud Rude, who was Corporate CEO, and told him what had happened. He was disgusted with the situation but didn't feel that he could do much about it since the Plant Manager had purchased himself a job by investing in the company. (It wasn't long after that when he was down the road in spite of his investment.)

I decided to continue with the concept and decided to start my own company. My sales administrator, Roger Benson, decided to throw his hat in my ring and we started developing the cryogenic product. The company was named "Freeze Flight". We bought a 747 Belly Box from Boeing Surplus and started insulating and developing the plumbing to handle the liquid nitrogen. We had hired a laid-off Boeing engineer that presumably knew something about cryogenics. (His pay was stock in Freeze Flight.)

Bud Rude stopped by my house (and Freeze Flight office) and asked if I had any free time. The engineer was doing all of the hardware work; Roger was developing a relationship with Pan American Airways so I was free at the moment.

241

Bud owned Flying Fireman, Ltd., which was operating Catalina's, in Victoria, B.C. Their primary function was forestry fire-fighting. He asked me if I could go down to Long Beach, California, at his expense, and purchase a couple of the surplus Navy Catalina's that were for sale. For some reason, Bud wanted to remain out of the direct purchase. I said sure, no problem since I could take care of a couple of other things for my company at the same time. The deal went through without any hitches. Bud arranged for them to be ferried up to Victoria, B.C. Canada. He had developed a water pick-up method of filling the airplane water tank on the Catalina's, while skimming across a body of water. The additional Catalina's would add to his operating fleet. (I had wanted to fly one of the PBY's ...they're such a piece of History...but Bud didn't want to take the time to have me checked out,

After the deal had settled Bud came by and handed me a check for $5,000. I hadn't expected any remuneration for that effort, feeling that I owed him for getting me back to Seattle and I did my own personal business at the same time. We certainly could use the money so I shut-up!

Bud knew that Powers & George, another active forestry fire-fighting company, wanted to purchase some Fairchild C-119's from the Canadian government. Bud had told them about the job that I had done for him and the fact that I was flying C-119's in the Reserve. He told me to call them, which I promptly did.

We made some more money with that effort and I suddenly found myself in the aircraft brokering business. Roger had finally quit Rhodes Frozen Bread and was working full time at Aries Engineering, the corporate umbrella over the Freeze Flight project.

One day Mr. 'Jeeb' Hallaby, President and Chairman of Pan American Airways, called in response to a telegram that we had sent requesting an around-the-world flight with our sample Freeze flight container. My young son Scott, age four, had answered the telephone. He was carrying on an extensive conversation when, walking by, I asked who he was talking to. Scott told me and I took the phone, apologizing profusely. Mr. Hallaby was very complimentary about Scott, asking his age and amazed at his adult-like presence.

Roger and I got wrapped up in the aircraft business, the engineer had finally found a real job and our interest in Freeze Flight was put on the back burner.

We made a lot of money in a short period of time and then I lost it all due to my own stupidity. We had been working a deal with the government of Peru for a package from Aerlingus, the Irish National airline. The package was for six, four-engine, turbo-prop DeHavilland Viscounts, one of which had an executive interior. I let one of our 'associates' handle the final transaction and it went bad. The whole thing came tumbling down like a house of cards. I couldn't believe how quickly it all fell apart. My banker pleaded with me to take bankruptcy (in order to get him off of the papers) and, not knowing any better, I did.

I lost everything. –and the beginning of the break-up of wife and family.

# TWENTY-THREE THE RAISBECK SAGA

**I**t was 1970 and The Boeing Company had recently dumped over 55,000 engineers out on the street. You needed an Aeronautical Engineering degree to drive Yellow Cab! A few engineers, who had a sense of humor, rented an outdoor signboard. They had it printed, *"WILL THE LAST PERSON LEAVING SEATTLE - TURN OFF THE LIGHTS".* –it made TIME magazine.

We were living near the Bellevue airport at the time. I remembered a company at that airport where I had sold airplane parts when I was with Pacific Airmotive. It was Robertson STOL. Jim Robertson had designed a series of aerodynamic modifications for the Cessna family of single engine airplanes. The after-market modification had been quite successful. Not only that but I remembered him as a pretty neat guy that loved aviation. I decided to go talk to him.

I drove out to the airfield, parked and walked in. There was a different receptionist than I remembered at the front desk. I asked for Jim Robertson. She informed me that he had died and that Jim Raisbeck was now the president of the company.

Behind the receptionist was an open door where a meeting of some kind was taking place. I heard a voice call out, "Send that person in, Ruth." She motioned for me to go on in.

"Well, who are you and what do you want?"

I replied, "I'm Mike McEniry and I used to sell aircraft stuff to this outfit. Quite frankly, I'm looking for a job and I have several ideas that I believe are ripe for marketing in General Aviation."

The curly-headed guy that I later learned was Jim Raisbeck said, "Oh really. And what do you think is your best idea?"

I thought for a moment before answering. "I think an 'aileron trim' system for single-engine birds would be a winner."

"Are you a pilot?"

"Yeah, I'm a pilot. Single, Multi-Engine Land with Instrument, a DC-4 Type Rating and about four thousand hours. But I like to think that I'm a pretty good salesman."

And that was it. I was hired. The pay wasn't all that great but better than drawing unemployment, and it was Aviation!

Henry McKay was the Chief Pilot and company Test Pilot. He didn't have an Instrument Rating. But he didn't need one for the type of flying that he did for the company. He checked me out in the company Cessna 182 as to the best way to demonstrate the STOL performance. The major features of the modification were a new leading edge cuff and the ailerons would come part way down with the flaps. The result was a 'full-span' flap system. This made "slow-flight" easy. One could fly around all day long at 60 miles per hour indicated, with an extra margin of safety.

For example, a standard FAA runway is 200 feet wide. I used to demonstrate taking off *across* the width, getting airborne in the 200 feet then staying in 'ground effect' and climbing out as speed permitted. It made a believer out of me anyway. I was familiar with the slow flight envelope, due to military aircraft carrier approach work, but this was easy. The term STOL stood for "Short

Take-off or Landing". The Robertson modification accomplished that in spades.

McKay showed me how <u>he</u> demonstrates the STOL package. I felt that it did the job quite well, and without radical maneuvers. –he suggested that I develop my own dialogue however.

My job was to arrange demonstrations around the country by telephone-qualifying potential customers. Accumulating enough potential customers to justify setting up an itinerary, that made some kind of sense and heading out for a week or so. Hey! --we're talking "grass-roots" aviation here! I just wasn't landing in farmer's fields, but it was still "barn-storming"!

Most of the potential customers were professional people, doctors or lawyers. Their reasons usually were wanting to go into their favorite field that was short or had other hazards where a STOL-equipped aircraft provided that "extra margin of safety", which was the company slogan.

My first sales trip was two weeks long, covering about six states and doing about 15-20 flight demos. Even after careful qualifying I wasn't able to close anyone. I had stirred up a lot of enthusiasm, and promises but no signed sales. I finally figured out what was happening. The doctor, or potential customer, wanted to discuss it with his Cessna Dealer, where he was probably also an investor. I'm certain that the dealer would say something like, "if the system was so good, why isn't Cessna doing it?"

I shared my feelings in my report to Jim Raisbeck. I told him that we should make the fixed base operator and or the dealer a "Robertson Associate Distributor". A very simple matter of an additional 10% to the dealer would put him on 'our side'.

Raisbeck thought that was a crazy idea and if I couldn't sell the system he would do the selling. I would be put to work ferrying airplanes and training new owners. Fall and winter-type weather was approaching fast and I was the only Instrument Pilot in the company.

The customer airplanes would have to be modified at the Bellevue Airport facility. I would be given an airline ticket; a Pilot's Operating Handbook, for a given airplane, like a Piper Cherokee 6, and sent on my way, reading the 'book' about the Cherokee 6 that I was going to pick up and fly out to Bellevue Washington.

Once completed I would deliver the airplane to a customer, train him, then get on a commercial flight to pick up the next airplane to be flown back to the plant....

It was kind of fun flying different airplanes from reading the handbooks. At the time the Robertson STOL kits were available for the Cessna 172, 180, 182, 210 and the *push me-pull me* twin. The Piper family included the Twin Comanche, Cherokee's 140, 180, 235 and the Cherokee 6.

The Twin Comanche program came about after a few crashes occurring during, or shortly after, take-off. Pug Piper flew out to Bellevue to interest Raisbeck into taking on the program. It seems that the "Blue Line" (slowest airspeed where the aircraft was controllable with one engine out and the 'dead' engine-prop wind-milling) was close to 100 indicated. Since the airplane rotated at about 70 this left a real hole that had caught a few airplanes with engine failures in that 'dead zone', resulting in a snap-roll close to the ground, killing all on board.

Raisbeck did a wonderful job bringing the Blue Line down to controlling numbers... (I don't recall the numbers...but it was that sort of scenario.)

247

I was impressed with this "Aerodynamicist". I learned that he did a major part of the design work on the B-727 "blow-down" Flap System. It made the 727 almost a STOL-performance transport, able to get into and out of short runways in the International market place. I thought Raisbeck a genius…and still do to this day!

Winter was gone, another pilot came aboard and I decided to look around since my skills were not in demand. Jim Raisbeck and I didn't get along all that well so it was probably time to move on.

One day I ran into Bob Florence, one of my competitors from the Pacific Airmotive days. We brought each other up to date in this wonderful world of aviation.

Bob Florence had sold his prior company and now had a new one called Airmarc Corporation. The major product lines were aircraft & marine radios and some related avionics.

The FCC had recently changed the marine radio spectrum from low-frequency double-side band AM, to VHF/FM (for use up to 25 miles) and Single Side-band (SSB) for offshore, over-the-horizon applications. Florence, ever the entrepreneur, had decided to take advantage of this newly created market.

When asked what I was doing I told him that I was about through with Robertson STOL and ready to move on. He said why don't I come and starve with him until Airmarc got off the ground. The other folks in the company were taking just enough money for bare necessities; food and rent, etc. He offered me the position of Sales Manager with stock options and credits for the initial efforts. –it was better than unemployment and an interesting industry. And, it was still in aviation.

He did have an aircraft avionics product available, a switch panel with a built-in three-light marker beacon

248

receiver. There was also a small three-light marker beacon receiver and also a switch panel without the built in device. The products were very competitively priced. I still had good contacts in the general aviation market and was able to successfully move enough products to stay ahead of our production rate. (It's always more fun to be in the position to sell 'lead time' instead of the 'product'.)

We eventually had a working model of the FM Marine ship-to-shore radio and established a good niche in the market. The single side-band was another story.

One of the best sales trips I ever had was with Airmarc. We did the New York Boat Show, and then I rented a car and drove down the Atlantic seaboard to Miami, calling on marine electronic dealers, and arriving in time for the Miami Boat Show.

I'm sort of a history buff and it seemed that there was a History Marker every mile. I've always wanted to go back and do that trip again, taking the time to investigate much of the historical sites.

The Miami Boat Show was a huge success and really kicked off our Marine FM product line. Florence developed a wonderful sales approach for setting up dealers. He had acquired a copy of the Bendix Marine Radio Dealers list. Bob then composed a short letter with a questionnaire and freshly-minted two-dollar bills, ordered from our bank. The letter said that the two-dollar bill was to buy a portion of the dealer's time to take the trouble to fill out the questionnaire, the substance of which was "what did they want in a "dealer network". Our return mail was phenomenal! --something like 65% return. Florence wanted to know what the dealer wanted from the manufacturer as far as policy, etc. Then, of course, he established our dealer program accordingly.

And the interesting thing was that when I arrived at a dealership that hadn't sent the questionnaire back…they were apologetic and would point out that it was right there, still in their IN basket.

To save money I was coming home for lunch every day. One day my wife, Darlene, told me that if I would go get a job that paid *real money* she would "stay with me". I was a bit surprised and wanted clarification. I told her that I wanted to really understand what it was that she wanted. (1) I was to go get a job that *she* approved of, (2) making the money that *she approved of* and then she would consider "staying with me".

She said that was correct.

And that moment in time was the end of our marriage.

It took some time to work out the details. I moved downstairs to a basement bedroom. Darlene had earlier obtained a job as a bartender to help with finances. She was making more money than I was. I worked days, she worked nights. We didn't have to see each other and in that way the kids were taken care of.

I paid for her to go through Bank Teller Training so that she wouldn't have to tend bar the rest of her life…and also had some dental work done for her... We worked out the financial part of the divorce stuff.

Then I had to find someplace to live.

# TWENTY-FOUR   A NEW LIFE

**I** was talking to my friend Clem Bentley, bringing him up to date on my current tribulations. Since I was looking for a place to live he suggested that I contact Bruce McCaw, one of our former PAC customers. Bruce was single and both Clem and I had enjoyed his company during those PAC days. Clem told me that Bruce had recently purchased a house in Bellevue. It seems that his tax attorney had told him to either get married or buy a house. He chose the latter.

I got hold of him and asked if he wanted a roommate. He offered the unfinished basement saying that I could do whatever I wanted with it. I walled off a corner and set up a nice little area.

One morning I was sitting at the kitchen table, hung over and happened to notice the woman next door, bending over feeding her dog. It was the first time that I saw anybody next door and I had been living with Bruce for the better part of a month. She was beautiful! I think I fell in lust immediately. I just had a quick glimpse of her face but her body was great!

Bruce didn't have a washer or dryer and Darlene decided to sell hers (ours?). I bought them. (–there's nothing quite like buying some of that stuff twice.) I had a large pile of dirty clothes and wanted to get started washing. I decided to go next door and borrow a cup of laundry soap before heading up to the store to get washing supplies.

I went to the "gorgeous neighbor's" front door with measuring cup in hand and rang the bell.

The lovely neighbor lady opened the door.

251

I was stunned. I couldn't speak. I think I just stood there with my mouth working but nothing coming out.

She looked down seeing the cup in my hand and asked, "Sugar?"

I nodded 'No'. Then she asked, "Martini?"

That got my attention and I snapped out of it long enough to ask for laundry soap and then proceeded to tell her my life story.

Bruce's house had stood empty since being built. The neighbor, whose name I learned was Peggy, had gone on an extensive trip. Upon her return she found the house occupied and strange doings going on. She was curious so asked me in, while she took the cup and filled it with laundry soap. She politely asked some questions to satisfy her curiosity.

It was the start of my new life.

**Peggy Lou Robinson & her neighbor** (me)

Peggy became the "girl next door" that I had been searching for all of my life. I guess that I had just been looking in the wrong places. Well, by virtue of the try and try again I finally found the right one. For that matter, it's a good thing that I didn't find her sooner since she had been happily married and the mother of three wonderful children. Her husband of nineteen years, Kearney Robinson, had passed away rather suddenly from a heart attack. Peggy was still recovering from that grievous loss and not anxious to move into anything quickly.

Airmarc had sold a few SSB radios, unfortunately. There were still problems with the Single Side-band units. One was to a gentleman that had a large sport fishing boat out of Miami. One day, while several miles off shore, he suffered a heart attack and his wife couldn't make the SSB radio work. He died and she sued. The company was back to being broke. I offered to take a leave of absence.

It was during this time that the U.S. Air Force Lockheed C-141 jet transports had developed wing cracks. The entire C-141 fleet was grounded. All transport squadrons, both Active Duty and Reserve, had to pick up the requirements. Our Fairchild C-119 Flying Boxcar transport squadron was offered all of the flight time that we wanted. Each pilot normally had a few extra drills, which we were paid to perform and when they ran out we were offered Active Duty "Man Days" at full per-diem. The pay structure for Man Days was quite a bit different and very substantial. I started living the life of an airline pilot, flying over twenty days a month. –it was fun.

Bruce had another roommate, one Jim England.

Jim England was very wealthy (on paper) but didn't have any cash flow. On the other hand, I was bankrupt, broke but had a substantial cash flow. (–thanks to the Marine Corps Reserve.)

In fact, arriving at McCaw's doorstep I owned twenty-eight boxes of books, the clothes on my back, a VW Bus with a blown engine and the baby grand piano that I had bought while still in high school. (The piano was still

253

with Darlene, since my daughter Kathy played, but 'owned' by me.)

Both Jim and Bruce were members of the Seattle Yacht Club. Bruce didn't have a boat, at the time, but Jim had a forty-five foot tri-cabin Chriscraft. He offered me a partnership in the boat. When I asked him how that would work he said to just pay the moorage and insurance and he would work out the details later.

He invited Peggy and me to an overnight cruise that was what power boaters call a "Predicted Log Race". (--about as interesting as watching paint dry.) It was time-distance calculations that the winning condition was whoever came closest to their planning. There would be a Race Official on-board to observe.

The race started from just outside of the Seattle locks, over to Bremerton for an RON and then up through Agate Pass and back to the locks the following day. It was fun being on the water and heavy duty partying at Bremerton.

Once inside the locks Jim pulled over to a gas dock and put about a hundred dollars' worth of gasoline aboard. (The price of gas at that time was about thirty-five cents a gallon!)

I told England that I couldn't afford 'hundred dollar weekends' so I wouldn't become a partner in his boat. I took a heavy interest in sailing.

I smoked KOOL cigarettes at the time. They had a promotion going on. For the end off of a KOOL cigarette carton and $88 they would send you a SNARK sailboat.

The SNARK was made of Styrofoam, eight feet long and with a beam of three and a half feet. It had a centerboard, rudder and sail that was a "lanteen rig" of forty-five square foot sail area.

I asked Peggy if I could have it sent to her address since I was gone so much. She accepted. It arrived while I was on a trip to Washington, D.C. Upon my return we assembled it on her living room floor. The following day I tied it to the top of my car and we drove down to Meydenbauer Bay to put it in the water for the first time.

During the drive Peggy was reading the Instruction Manual to me. It was full of nautical terms, some of which I understood and some that I didn't. I asked her what happens when the wind hits the sail. She said, "I'm getting to that, this next section is about capsizing!"

We put it in the water and I went through the suggested points of sail, outlined in the Instruction Manual, and then asked Peggy to get in. I didn't know at the time that she was very uncomfortable in water that was over her head. At any rate we managed to do a quick sail even though a smart-ass in a ski boat came by very close. When we got back to the dock I noticed that Peggy had left hand indentations in the coaming of the Styrofoam hull.

Peggy was a good sport about the Snark but it was not one of her favorite things.

The Seattle Yacht Club decided to replace their Penguin fleet with C-Larks and offered the Penguins to members at a ridiculous price. England had a house on Yarrow Bay that would eventually be sold to satisfy his divorce settlement. I purchased a Penguin (--thru Jim) and he did also. This gave us two Penguins at his house.

It was a fun summer with lots of beach parties and sailing. Peggy's two older kids (Debi 19 and Woody 18) along with my daughter Kathy (age 13) took to sailing quickly. Scott, age 8 and Erik, age 6 would get into sailing later, as they grew.

The Penguin was ten feet in length, five-foot beam and carried about eighty square feet of sail area. She was still a centerboard vessel and subject to capsizing. Again, Peggy was not comfortable in this one either. –but we were moving up in size!

One day Peggy asked me, if she helped me with a boat loan could we get something that wouldn't tip over and maybe had a cabin of some sort? We could be partners.

A boat loan was out of the question for me due to my recent bankruptcy. Peggy's financial rating was pristine. I could easily afford my half of the payments but it would be a loan in her name. I agreed reluctantly.

We started researching and looking for something suitable. It took close to six months of looking to decide on a model. We elected to go with a Coronado 25. Then it took another six months to find the right Coronado 25. We had even gone to San Francisco to check one out. We ended up finding one locally and buying from a fellow in Everett that, as it turned out, used to work with Kearney, Peggy's first husband. It was in beautiful condition, and fully equipped, including an electric-start outboard motor. We paid $6,500 for it. Interestingly enough, with the "truth in lending" the total ten-year loan came to $8,800. We had gone from the Snark, at $88, to this new acquisition at ten times the price, in a couple of years.

Moorage was found at Yarrow Bay Marina. Woody became my early sailing buddy. We were trying to find out just how the Coronado would handle inclement weather. When the winter storms blew in we'd head out onto Lake Washington and hang on. We did that a lot! We soon learned that the boat could take a hellava lot more than we wanted to take. But, we learned.

**Coronado 25**

We made many friends at Yarrow Bay Marina. Sail boaters tend to help each other with various maintenance problems or just hang out together. This evolved to my starting a Friday night racing event. We decided to go from the mouth of Yarrow Bay over to the last buoy in the Montlake channel and then on to Kirkland. It usually took about an hour and a half for that route. I printed up some 'Flyers' and distributed to sailboats in our marina as well as those in Kirkland. The response was surprising. We soon had a pretty good fleet.

And, surprise, surprise who should turn up at Yarrow Bay Marina in his newly acquired Coronado 23, but my old room-mate from NavCad days Dr. Benjamin King. He was now a professor at the University of Washington. Ben had taken up the Recorder and I was learning how to play the flute. We would get together a few times and play Flute Duets. He hadn't lost his touch. His playing was soulful as always.

One of the competitors, Bill Mathieson (--a well-known NW metal sculptor) asked me if I minded if he tried to get Anthony's Home Port Restaurant interested in sponsoring our Friday night "beer-can" races. Bill was successful but it cost him, in that he was to make the beer-can trophies for the various classes. The course was altered. It now was to start at Kirkland, abeam the restaurant.... south to Hunt's point, where there would be a real race buoy...then a spinnaker run north to Sand Point, around another buoy and back to Kirkland. The fleet had grown, drawing boats from as far away as Lake Union and Leshi. Bill and I became the "founders". –an honor that netted us zilch, but we had a lot of fun. Bill has since taken up residence in La Conner, an art colony up in the Skagit Valley where he has his own studio.

And, the race series still run now...these many years later.

-o-

One day I got a call from Darlene saying that she wanted to meet, having something of importance to discuss. We met and the subject turned out to be Kathy and Scott. Darlene felt that it would be better for the kids to have the

258

structured environment that living with Peggy and I would provide. (Peggy was a 'stay-at-home' Mom.)

There was one small problem. Peggy and I were not married. We had discussed it, but there was still a large disparity in our financial status. Peggy wasn't in any hurry to make that transition. I told Darlene that I would get back to her that I had to discuss this with Peggy. I was a little surprised at Peggy's reaction, she had grown fond of my two kids and thought Scott was good for Erik, --and it was good for Scott to have a 'little brother', instead of him being the 'little brother'.

One afternoon Peggy and I were watching Erik and Katherine Gaiser playing in the backyard. Katherine had apparently done something that led Erik to say, "You better not do that, I'll tell my Dad."

Katherine's replay was, "Oh, has your Mother married Michael?"

Of course, Erik's reply was negative. Peggy and I saw this take place. I turned to Peggy and said that I thought that maybe it was time. She agreed.

Early in our courtship Peggy and I spent a lot of time watching TV. One day the movie "The Bad & The Beautiful" was on. There was a scene where Gloria Graham said to Dick Powell, whose movie name was James David something or other, "James David, you have a very naughty mind…. I'm happy to say!"

From that time on Peggy would frequently call me "James Michael" and I, in return would call her, "Peggy Lou". (Her real middle name.) It stuck  From that time on she became "Peggy Lou"...and remains so to this day to close friends.

We decided to drive down to Reno to marry. At the time, my folks, Momma-Boo and Poppa-Boo (so named by Patsy's first born, Robin) were retired and living in Carson

City. Peggy and I were married at the courthouse on August 16th, 1973. Art Weishart (Poppa-Boo) was my Best Man and Betty Braga-McEniry-Weishart (Momma-Boo), Matron of Honor.

During this period Airmarc was back in business and I had been scheduled for an international sales trip, starting in Vigo, Spain then on to Zurich, Athens and Istanbul. The company trip had been planned before our marriage. So the way it turned out, I moved my kids into Peggy's house and then left on our honeymoon by myself. –what a great way to start our marriage. It's a wonder that it survived but it did.

While I was in Europe Kathy got busted shop-lifting at Nordstrom's. Scott (age 8) made the transition pretty well, enjoying having a younger brother Erik (age 6) but Kathy, at the age of thirteen, brought a lot of baggage with her. With Debi, Woody, Erik, Scott and Kathy we had our own "Brady Bunch".

When Peggy Lou and I married the partnership on the Coronado became "one". I wasn't really looking for another partner but Jim England said that he had a friend that was looking to get into a sailboat. He made arrangements for us to meet. The chap was Dennis Martin, who owned a company, called 'Monitor' that did computerized freight-payment billing. We struck a deal.

Dennis had a few problems with boat handling not being used to inclement weather that can come up rapidly. When that happened in one case he was out on the lake…a storm blew up…he couldn't get the sails down or the outboard motor started. He ended up getting blown down the lake to Kirkland where the Wawona was moored and struck her. The Wawona was not damaged, but our boat was.

Dennis took care of it. In the process we had the hull painted with a new-age paint that had been developed for the Boeing 747. It withstood the extreme temperature range and the expansion and contraction of the fuselage that the jumbo experienced. In addition, we added an ironwood rub strip to the sides. It worked out pretty well. –but Dennis didn't ever live down the fact that he had tried to sink the historical vessel!

Things at Airmarc took a turn for the worse and it became time to move on. Dennis and I had planned on entering a Saturday morning sailboat race. I couldn't get a hold of him so went ahead and met him at our boat. I told him that I had to work on my resume and wouldn't be able to join him for the race.

Dennis was amazed. He thought that I owned Airmarc. Anyway, he said that he had been looking for a National Sales Manager for his company and would I be interested. We talked about it and cut a deal that would include a used Cadillac, I had seen and thought it pretty neat. He said to go find one, he didn't care…just tell him where to send the check!

I ended up with a 1968 "triple blue Cadillac Brougham". The family really enjoyed that car and she became known as "Bro-jam".

We had offices in Los Angeles, New York, Cleveland and Seattle, of course.

Monitor had the first IBM System 3 in Seattle. The company got into trouble when a glitch in the IBM hardware caused the system to print 'duplicate' freight payments. It was all recoverable but things came apart very quickly and the company was forced into bankruptcy. Dennis was sued by several of our customers and I was also named in the suit. I was innocent and proved so in court…but I had to hire the 'Robinson' family attorney to

261

do so. I was out of a job again and Dennis couldn't afford the boat payments. Bruce McCaw bought out his half of the Coronado 25.

When Peggy Lou and I had started dating, Bruce got in my face and said to me, "McEniry, don't go pulling your usual…this is a real Lady, and you better treat her right!" He was very fond of Peggy.

It wasn't idle chit-chat, he meant it. We had spent a lot of time together, Bruce, Jim England, Peggy and I….boating, partying. It was a fun period.

Anyway, *there I was*…on the beach again.

# TWENTY-FIVE    M U S I C

W hen Peggy Lou and I were first courting we spent many of our dates at "The Great American Disaster", down on Bel-Red Road. It was a large restaurant, bar and pool hall. They made great hamburgers. Our date usually consisted of a hamburger, salad and a couple of games of pool. In fact, one evening I discovered a very active green worm in my salad. Jerry Hardin, the owner, came over when I asked for him. He was very apologetic and the meal was gratis, of course. We got to know Jerry pretty well. We didn't have any more worm-dramas.

The restaurant had a stage along one wall that hadn't been used in years. I often told Peggy Lou that it would be fun to bring a group into the room. She said that she thought that I hadn't played for over twenty years. She was right, of course but, "So?"

One afternoon some of Woody's friends were downstairs in the "Rec" room jamming (playing rock music, I think). I became tired of hearing a hundred and twelve measures of "E" and went downstairs. I asked the lads if they would at least play some blues. I ended up having to show them the structure. They were quick to learn. I joined them on piano, in order to show their piano player, the structure and how it should go.

The listening became easier.

Sometime later the guys came to me and asked if I would help form a band. I asked them if they knew what they were getting in to. It would take a lot of work. They agreed to the commitment. We started a 'twice-a-week' rehearsal schedule. Interestingly enough, Woody wasn't part of the effort, having secured a drummer's spot with a working band. His best friend Brad DeRouchey took over his spot. The other lads were Doug Richardson on guitar, Steve Armor, piano, and Blaine Lawrence on electric bass. I would be playing the vibes and flute.

Doug had recently joined the Army and was stationed at Ft. Lewis. He commuted, and sometimes spent the night.

I went to Jerry Hardin, owner of The Great American Disaster…later referred to as "GAD", and discussed bringing music into the club. We came up with a plan. Jerry had been thinking about some kind of an amateur contest. I didn't want my group to apply since I didn't feel that they were amateurs. But how about we could play our one set at the end of the contest while the judges were deciding the winner. It seemed like a good plan.

The 'group' would occasionally go sailing on our Coronado 25. Steve Armor, the piano player, was a bit overweight and I would call him "Ballast" and direct him to sit where he would provide stability... The lads decided it would be a great name for the group…so "BALLAST" was about to debut its musical career.

The amateur contest attracted quite a few applicants, more than was expected. It was a huge success. The club was filled to overflowing, with more than three hundred people in attendance.

It became our turn. The guys were very nervous but rose to the occasion as true 'show folk'. We played our seven or eight tunes with enormous applause between them. When we finished the applause was deafening. All that energy coming over the footlights is a fantastic drug

264

and easily one to get 'hooked on'. The guys couldn't believe it. It was difficult to get them back into rehearsals.

Brad DeRouchey, already a great drummer, was learning keyboard and applying it to his study of the Vibes. I had studied Vibes, as my primary instrument, while attending Weslake College of Modern Music in California. Brad and I exchanged ideas and he let me use his Vibes until mine arrived from 'Jolly 'Ol England'. I had ordered a set of "Premier Vibes", the company was also makers of up-scale drum sets. A friend, Steve Craiger, owned a music store in Bellevue and wanted to carry the Premier drum line. He had offered me a set of vibes at his 'dealer cost' if I would select Premier's instead of a domestic brand. It was a good deal for both of us.

After the success of the amateur contest Jerry decided that it would be fun to start a Wednesday night "open mic" jam session. Brad DeRouchey became the house drummer and I filled in on piano sometimes.

One night a guitar player, Larry Hayes by name, along with a bass player, by the name of Brian Kercheval took the stage with Brad. After a couple of tunes as a trio I joined them for the tune "All Of Me".

Peggy and I had started a company, "P & M Productions," intending to do recording. Peggy was tape-recording the Wednesday night sessions. When reviewing the tapes later, I was really impressed with what we had done with "All Of Me". I asked Brad to try to get hold of Larry and Brian. He did and we got together to listen to the tape. We decided that it was good enough to warrant putting together a group. It would become BALLAST II.

Brian was a phenomenally gifted musician. He could sit down at the drums and put Brad to shame, walk over to the piano and perform.... stop long enough at my vibes to create envy and pick up Larry's guitar and bring tears to our eyes. –we hated him!

Jerry was impressed with that Wednesday night performance also and asked if we could do a paid gig and then booked us Friday & Saturday nights for four weeks. It was a great run. I played piano, vibes and flute. –well, sorta. One night I called for "Black Orpheus", and would be playing flute. Well I played the initial eight measures with *first overtone*, which would be about a fourth tone over the intended. I finally got my embouchure together and finished the tune with the right notes. It was the last time that I performed flute on stage. I had decided that if I didn't know what was going to come out of it when I blew into it I had no right to play it when performing for money.

Peggy Lou was recording every performance of our four week, eight-night gig, so we got some wonderful tape.

The gig over, Larry Hayes started playing with a rock band and Brian left Bellevue to become a soundman for a traveling rock group.

After the success with BALLAST II I came to the conclusion that I should confine my efforts to seasoned players.

Along the way I met David Arntson, a piano player and Lon Alsman, a stand-up bass player. A fellow Raisbeck executive, Kim Frinnel, got us a gig in downtown Seattle at a new, and very exclusive restaurant called "Lafitte's". We played the Sunday morning brunch for many weeks. The club folded and then reopened under another name, "Duncan's". We played Friday and Saturday nights for a few weeks for the re-named club. We also did quite a few private parties. I don't remember the name we used for the group. I think it was billed "The David Arntson Trio with Mike McEniry". (Woody was the drummer.)

266

David and I had a falling out and I started working with Julian Catford. Julian was a wonderful classical, Latin, or jazz guitar player. I found another bass player, Barney Brazitis, when Lonny got a "road gig". Woody played drums on quite a few gigs, subbing for our usual drummer, Jeff Downing.

That band became SEA BREEZE. We did four weeks, Friday & Saturday night engagements at "Andy's Auburn Station" in Auburn.

Halloween weekend the management asked us to play in costume. I came as 'The Devil'. Peggy Lou did a wonderful job making me up...with red face, horns glued to my head, a cape, etc. It really looked good. *—bad?*

Driving home, about three in the morning, after performing in costume, I came upon a Mazda coupe that had just rolled over and stopped, inverted. I pulled over to see if I could help the driver. He was still strapped in, hanging from his seat belt. I released the seat belt...he fell on his head...I helped him out of the upturned vehicle and about then an on-coming car's headlights hit me full face and the driver, still woozy, facing me at the time, saw my costume and really jumped. (He was probably just dazed from the accident and landing on his head.) --his reaction was noteworthy. I had always intended to submit that to "Reader's Digest".

The downstairs Rec room in Peggy's house *(my home)* had a workshop on the other side of the wall. We walled off the far end of the shop and put in a dual-pane window between the soon to be control room and the Rec room. We now had the makings of a real live recording studio. Hey, its only money.

## A family music project

The entire Robinson-McEniry family was very musical. I played piano, flute & vibes, Peggy Lou played the guitar and sang, Woody was our resident professional, a drummer, Debi played viola and flute, my daughter Kathy played the piano and the flute, son Scott played the piano and saxophone and little Erik played the cello but was beginning to take an interest in both the guitar and drums.

In the fall of 1977 we, the family, embarked on a plan to do a special in-house Christmas program. It would be recorded but performed in our home just for us. As it turned out, our special friend, Bruce McCaw joined us as "the audience".

Erik (10), would be doing *Jingle Bells* on the cello, then Scott (12) performing *O Come All Ye Faithful* on sax, with my accompanying him on piano. Kathy (16) and Debi (23) as a flute duet, performed *Joy to the World* and then I joined them for *O Little Town of Bethlehem* making it a flute trio. Kathy and I did *God Rest Ye Merry Gentlemen* as a flute duet and then *My Favorite Things* with Kathy on piano while I played the vibes. Kathy and Debi did another flute duet on *O Holy Night* with my joining them on the vibes.

C'mon, bear with me.... this was a major production.

Doug Richardson performed *I Believe In Father Christmas*, and *A Christmas Song*, singing and accompanying himself on guitar. Then Doug, playing guitar, accompanied me playing flute on *Greensleeves*. Peggy Lou sang *A Christmas World* with Doug playing guitar and singing with her. Peggy then sang *A Christmas*

268

*Wish* while accompanying herself on guitar. Peggy and I played Bach's *Jesu, Joy of Man's Desire,* as a guitar duet. (Woody surprised us by not doing anything. He had a 'paying gig'.)

The cast and Bruce McCaw, our audience, finished the performance, singing *Silent Night.*

There were many hectic practice sessions among the various performers. It was fun...the house was full of music. And it seems that everybody was experiencing heavy "performance-anxiety" as show time neared. It got totally 'nuts' on the afternoon and night of the performance. One would think that we were going to be playing at the Opera House, later to be remodeled and re-named "McCaw Hall", after Bruce's Mother. It was an incredible event. The recording turned out great and it is a treasured, *produced,* CD remembrance of a family 'in music'. –our first "album".

The CD is labeled "CHRISTMAS 1977 AT ROCK CREEK RANCH". *(Copies are available from P & M PRODUCTIONS at a very nominal cost.)*

Bruce McCaw, while attending the exclusive "Poncho Auction", had bid and won 'the use' of the Steinway Concert Grand Piano that is kept in Seattle for visiting pianists that are on a Steinway contract. He decided to cash in his winning bid 'for use' at his insurance company's new building, open-house. He asked me to play but explained the piano thing and could I get a piano player instead of using the guitar player that I had been working with.

I asked around and remembered hearing Eddie Creed play one night, in Seattle. He was a remarkable player, sensitive playing on ballads and burning solos on jazz or bop tunes. I called him and asked if he would be available for a gig. He asked hours, money and where. I told him and then suggested rehearsal. His replay was that "I don't rehearse, Man."

The Steinway people delivered and tuned the piano. Eddie had to sign the Log Book, which held names of some famous classical performers. Eddied signed as *"Eddie Creed, jazz player"*.

We've been together, with a few personnel changes ever since. The group was called THE CHAMBER JAZZ QUARTET. Eddie replaced Bassist Lon Alsman with Steve Sanders. Steve has a great background having done a lot of 'studio work' in Los Angeles. Woody became our drummer even though he always complained that we should go get a real jazz drummer, that he was really a 'rock & roll' guy.

Woody worked out just fine. Woody had attended CENTRUM a couple of times and was able to study with the likes of Jeff Hamilton and Mickey Roker, jazz drummers. It was great working with my stepson, fellow sailor, and good friend.

We'd get together for recording sessions and rehearsals from time to time. But we knew the material so well and each other's' playing that a lot of rehearsal wasn't necessary. Eddie and Steve live fairly close to each other in Seattle and get together often to go over new material. Then Eddie would call me and direct me to the tunes so that I could dig 'em out and get familiar with 'em. Quite often I'd play a new tune with Eddie for the first time on an actual gig. It worked out.

The CJQ works quite a bit doing corporate gigs and things like Bellevue Square's Chalk Walk weekend. It's been slow going of late without many jazz gigs around. It comes and goes in that industry. And then it stopped.

The "Wall Street Debacle" had shut the door. There was little or no music work...especially for a jazz group.

After some period of time I got a call from our Agent, ENTCO, asking if we'd like to play some one-hour gigs in retirement homes around the city. I told him I'd check and get back to him.

When I called Eddie, he said, "I don't want to play for a bunch of *old geezers!*" (He had recently started drawing Social Security.) The drummer said he didn't want to 'set-up' for just an hour. And Steve Sanders was moving to Wenatchee, but would come back over for a *decent* gig. (Meaning a hundred or so in his pocket.) I started looking around for some other players.

Working with the State of Washington's CENTRUM organization, my good friend Bud Shank started the BUD SHANK JAZZ WORKSHOP, held at Ft. Worden State Park located in Pt. Townsend, Washington. The first seminar was July 19th to the 25th, 1981. I attended as a student and ended up teaching a couple of classes as assistant to Barney McClure. He would assign me the very beginners to introduce them to blues and improvisation.

A couple of years I was able to get Woody a free ride serving as "house mother" in one of the dorms. I didn't have to pay either due to the teaching thing.

One day in late spring of 1985, Bud Shank called and asked if I would be attending the Jazz Workshop that year. I said that I wouldn't be able to make it due to office workloads. He said that Milt Jackson was going to be there. (Milt Jackson, the Vibist with "The Modern Jazz Quartet".)

I turned to my lady and said that Milt Jackson was going to be at Centrum...her reply was "So are you."

I turned back to the phone, telling Bud what she had said and that I would be attending...then went on to say I

271

thought Jackson hated "honkies". Bud laughed and said, "Oh don't worry, you'll wear him down!"

The Centrum Bud Shank Jazz Workshop takes place annually at Fort Worden, in Port Townsend Washington. (It is where "Officer and A Gentlemen" was filmed.) It would run from June 30$^{th}$ through July 4$^{th}$, 1985. The group headlining would be Milt Jackson - Vibes, Cedar Walton - Piano, Ray Brown - Bass and Mickey Roker on drums.

Other members of the faculty were Jeff Hamilton-Percussion, Bobby Shew-Trumpet, George Cables-Piano, Bill Ramsey-Saxophone, and Mark Murphy-Vocals, to name a few. --and, of course, Bud Shank.

I would be Milt's only student.

Monday morning dawned and I reported to the building where we would be studying. It would also be the building with a room large enough to hold the Master Class. Jackson and I were the only ones assigned to the building during the workshops. My vibes were set up on a low stage that also held a small grand piano.

The day came and went…without a Milt Jackson.

The following day, after about an hour wait, Milt showed up. He came in, sat down, and looked up at me. He said, "What do ya want from me?"

Now, I was fifty-eight years old at the time…with a little gray in my hair, but I replied, "Mr. Jackson, I have followed your career since before the formation of the Modern Jazz Quartet. I almost feel that I'm in the presence of a deity and find it a little intimidating. I would be quite content to just listen to you talk about how you approach a tune, what to look for in soloing…how can I improve my playing…or anything that you wish to talk about."

Milt just looked at me. It was as if he wanted to make sure that I wasn't jiving him. It seemed to take a long

272

time. Finally, he nodded, got up and started to walk over to the piano. He turned and said, "Shit, let's play some blues."

He sat down at the piano and started an intro into a blues…no mention of key or count and I was expected to find the key and join in. After a few embarrassing attempts I eventually made it. That was the morning. No conversation…just playing one blues after another, various keys, tempos and structure…often switching to ¾ time or even a 24 bar structure. It was great!

We broke for lunch and I spent the rest of the afternoon knowing what to work on.

The following morning, I was out on the veranda having a smoke when I noticed Milt walking down the long veranda smoking a joint. He came up to me, nodded and motioned, 'did I want a hit'…I nodded 'okay' and shared the rest of it with him.

He asked my name again and then said, "Michael, are you ready for some more blues?" I replied in the affirmative and we got to work.

This time he had brought his own mallets. I asked if I could try 'em. He nodded and handed them to me. They were different than the Musser M-8's that I had been using. I asked where I could get a pair. He said that he had them custom made by a company in Chicago…and he would send me a pair. I said that would be great but where could I find the company. He had me write down *Balter in Chicago*. I wrote it on the back of a study guide that Centrum had furnished that year.

The week went by way too quickly. On a couple of days, I recorded conversations that we had. They are priceless now. The week was wonderful working with Milt Jackson at Centrum's Bud Shank Jazz Seminar. I remember that I mentioned to him that I thought that jazz was coming back. He snorted and said, 'Hell Michael, jazz ain't coming back…jazz ain't ever been anywhere!"

But like they say, "it ain't over til it's over".

Finally, Friday came and in the afternoon, the Master Class.

I sat right down in front, ready to record the session with this great quartet. After a few tunes, Jackson looked down at me and said, "Michael, get your ass up here!"

Now the Master Class consists of the entire faculty and student body. –a tough house! I was petrified. Cedar turned to me and asked what I would like to play. I suggested a blues. He asked the key. I replied, trying to be so cool, *"—three down."* (Meaning the key of Eb.)

Cedar responded, "What is that in English?"

Ray suggested that we make it a 24 bar structure….and asked Cedar to bring it in.

I stood, ready to play. –it came time to come-in and I hadn't. Ray, standing behind me, reached over and poked me in the back. I just started flying all over the Vibes, eventually getting it around to making some kind of sense. It finally ended with the student body giving me a standing ovation…not for my playing, but for knowing full well what I had had to overcome.

It was a moment to cherish in memory.

Milt never did get around to sending me those mallets. The years passed.

In 2003, I had been working with a young recording engineer, Greg Crosswhite, who was helping me with my home studio, having recently upgraded to 'digital'. I was going through some music files, looking for some things on 2-5-1, when I turned over a mimeographed study guide and there it was written on the back, *Balter in Chicago!!*

Now this being the age of the Internet…it didn't take long to find "MIKE BALTER MALLETS", along with a

274

phone number and E-Mail address. I opted to call, and after asking, was put in touch with Mike Balter. I told him the whole story about my week with Milt Jackson.

I not only ended up with some fantastic mallets, but had also found a new friend in Chicago. He made a custom set for me and refused payment. –any friend of Milt's would be his friend also.

Bud Shank's seminars were replaced with another jazz artist's seminars in 2004. Bud and Linda left Pt. Townsend, moving down to Arizona. We are still good friends and speak on the phone frequently. Bud is crowding eighty years of age now and still playing all over the world. Last year England, France and Sweden, plus concerts in the states. He told me the other day that his schedule in 2006 is almost as hectic. Good-oh!

The kids stayed with their music. Woody is our most professional musician, working a lot with other groups besides the CJQ.

Scott gave up the saxophone and has concentrated on the piano. His classical playing has exceeded my own. He does some Bach things that I didn't ever get finished. Christmas of 2005 he gave a recital for the whole family. Scott added some of the Peanuts Christmas Album to his classical performance. He received a well-earned standing ovation. (The recorded tape 'master' is archived.)

Debi still plays some flute, but has given up the viola.

Erik plays a lot of guitar and performed drums with a group and they "cut a 45 RPM record". He gets family credit for doing the first _real_ commercial recording…done in a pro studio and all. And copies were sold at their performances.

All of us have recordings done in our own studio and both Woody and I have tapes done on-site.

A friend, knowing I was looking around for some players, put me in touch with Ted Yellman, a piano player. We met and I found out he was *one hellava* piano player! I told him that I just happened to know a Bass player. Lon Alsman, I called him, we three got together and the "Chamber Jazz Trio" was born.

We formed up to play the retirement homes and do so for $150 for the one hour. We've done downtown Seattle jazz clubs...Vito's and also Club New Orleans, long gigs and having to deal with parking. Well, whatever the gig calls for, an hour or three hours...at least it's playing.

We get together and rehearse, play...jam, weekly. Thanks to modern technology I can easily record, on-site anywhere, thanks to a product called the "ZOOM h4n" recording device. It records onto an SD card, powered by two AA batteries and will record for 'only' 30 hours. Hello?

We've put out a lot of CD's for ourselves and for the retirement folk.

We're ready to do a CD for 'sales'. –maybe this year. Music is keeping me young.

-o-

An apology is forthcoming. I have wandered a bit from aviation by sharing, with you the passion of playing music. I'm still not through flying, the passion has merely assumed another form. However, *"passion"* is still ***"passion"***.

276

# TWENTY-SIX     LIFE GOES ON

I found myself 'on the beach' again. I decided to give Sundstrand Corporation a shot. I called and got an appointment with the Vice-President. The interview went well and he decided to find a place for me. The Ground Proximity Warning System (GPWS) was getting started and I took on the Project sales slot.

It was an interesting assignment. Essential to the project was the analysis of commercial airplane crashes that had FAA Crash Investigation documentation. We reviewed all of the available "Cockpit Voice Recordings" from the time that the FAA required them in commercial aircraft. As memory serves me, I think the oldest was from the fifties.

In some cases I knew a member of the flight crew; the DC-7 crash in Cold Bay, Alaska and most noteworthy the Alaska Airline Boeing 727 crash in Juneau, Alaska.

You may recall a previous chapter where I included the short story, DEBONAIR. I had hired a pilot, Jim Carson,. He had asked to give only a week's notice, since Alaska Airlines had hired him.   –he was the Flight Engineer on the 727 Juneau crash.

Jim had a very distinct speaking voice. It was as if his jaws were wired shut. Reviewing the CVR tapes from that crash I could hear Jim's distinctive voice in the background, I couldn't tell what he was saying only that it was him saying something. Sad.

Probably the worst heart-rending recording was the DC-9 mid-air collision with a small Cessna in the San Diego area. The Co-Pilot knew that the CVR would pick up his comment, so said, "—goodbye Mom, I love you!"

There wasn't a dry eye in the room listening to that one.

As a matter of interest, usually the last thing heard on a tape was, *"Oh shit!"* --and said in a manner of resignation, not fear.

I was responsible for the first GPWS sale. It was to Texas Airways. My victory was short-lived. Bendix had acquired one of our units, did a little reverse-engineering and came out with their own model.

Sundstrand had screwed the airlines over the years with the pricing associated with the Sundstrand Constant Speed Drive, a unit that was on every jet engine in the commercial fleet. The industry wouldn't put up or allow another "sole source" product from Sundstrand.

The industry quickly turned to Bendix for their GPWS…now FAA mandated, buys. Sundstrand lost a great deal of money.

I was "last hired, first fired".

A friend got me into an employment agency. It was straight commission but it put me in touch with job opportunities. One such arose so I put *my* resume in. Cutting to the quick, the job was Regional Manager for Kollsman Instrument Company. They flew me out to New Hampshire for interviews. I was hired.

-o-

I had joined Kollsman Instrument Company as the Northwest Regional Manager. My office was in our home. My job was sales and marketing to The Boeing Company, the airlines up in Vancouver, B.C. and United Airlines Maintenance Base in San Francisco. It was wonderful and gave me a lot of free time. For example, Boeing discouraged sales calls on Fridays and also Mondays. I did manage to stay busy enough to far exceed my sales forecast, plus give the company their *last* "huffer-puffer" Central Air Data Control System. It would be for the United Airlines 737 fleet. The industry was changing, moving in the direction of 'digital' systems.

There were a couple of lads down at Yarrow Bay Marina, where we moored, that had purchased two kit boats. They were assembling a forty-three foot and thirty-six foot sailboats. I helped with the thirty-six footer to see just how hard it would be. I was amazed at how easy it was and, most important, how much money it saved.

Bruce and I were ready to get something that we could stand-up in and also that had a reliable inboard engine that wouldn't *stop running* when put in reverse. The latter created all kinds of excitement while trying to go through the locks to get from Lake Washington to Puget Sound. Many's the time that the out-board quit when switched from Forward to Reverse gear.

One of the fellows doing the two 'kit' boats was importing and selling teak to Islander Yachts. He told me that Islander was putting their thirty-foot Mk II on the 'kit market'

After much planning and fact-finding, we decided to custom build the Islander 30, Mk II. Bruce thought it a good idea to put deposits on two kits. The plan was to build the first one to sell and then the second one to keep. Bruce arranged the financial loans with the bank. I would be doing the assembly work and managing the contract work. It was a fair deal. I still had some good connections in the marine industry, from my work with Airmarc. We would be able to buy at discount prices for most of what we needed.

Somehow the Islander Dealers found out that the "30" was in the kit market and they became very upset.

The result was that Islander withdrew the model from that market. When they reviewed the orders they found that Bruce and I had two kits on order and said that we couldn't do that. Bruce said, "I'll handle this. Not to worry."

Well, he did a wonderful job of it. He got our money back for the one kit, a deal on things like a complete wiring harness.... already made up...for $15, interior cushions, cabin lights and the permission to contract with Islander's mill foreman and other concessions. It was a hellava deal! Thank you Bruce, you sure did good!

With the concessions gained thru Bruce's negotiations with Islander Yachts we were ready to move ahead with just the one boat. The manufactured assemblies; hull, deck, Inner liner (The inner liner forms the galley, head, bulkhead locations and forward stateroom), plus a small diesel engine and rudder, were purchased and moved about a mile down the road from Islander to a private boat-yard in Costa Mesa. Bruce also arranged to hire the Mill Forman and a couple of lads from Islander. In their off-time they assembled the pieces, bedded the engine, installed the rudder and finished the thru-hull fittings. The Mill Foreman's quote was too good to pass up. His quote for the wood bulkheads, drawer assemblies and doors was less money than what I had figured for woodworking tools, etc.

The boat could be transported to Seattle and placed in the water for further outfitting. This factor saves the cost of dry moorage at the marina.... while still paying for a 'wet' moorage slip. We anxiously awaited delivery.

The year was 1975 and our sailboat had just been delivered to Seattle. My work schedule with Kollsman gave me a lot of time to do my share of the work.

I was really impressed with Bruce McCaw's skills in financing and negotiation endeavors, I didn't have any problems stepping aside and letting him lead.

We closed the books for the construction loan, at $26,200. including Main and Jib sails, mast, boom, spinnaker pole, winches and all the spinnaker gear, less the actual spinnaker sail. It also included life jackets, VHF Marine Radio, Depth Sounder and Wind Instrumentation. It was truly *"Fully Found"*. On that date, the Islander dealer, out at Shilshow had an Islander 30 Mk2, in stock, selling for $45,000....'bare boat'.

(My reason for putting this information in this narrative is to alert you to the savings that can be realized when going 'kit' vs. 'new purchase'.)

Our boat had been off-loaded at a yard in Seattle. We filled the 30-gallon diesel fuel tank and motored over to Yarrow Bay Marina. I would be doing the finishing work in our mooring slip at Yarrow Bay Marina.

With the hull in our moorage slip, I installed wheel steering, life lines, swim ladder, wind instrumentation and depth sounder. Then adding the head, sinks, pressure water system, a galley gimbaled stove and cabin heater with fuel tank. It was easy and fun. Galley stove and heater would be kerosene fired, fed from one remote tank.

The outfitting was pleasurable work and went quickly, we were soon sailing over the 'boundary main'.

Three years later, Kollsman decided to close their regional offices. I was offered a transfer back east to Nashua New Hampshire. I declined, having made many trips back to the home office, various times a year…experiencing spring, summer, fall and winter climes and didn't think it would be a good idea to up-root the family and make the move. Besides, I was worried about

281

Kollsman being able to make the change-over to the new digital world of aircraft instrumentation. They were really way behind the industry. So, I declined. They offered me 'two-weeks' severance pay. I mentioned that since I had made annual sales forecast in six months, with the sale to United Airlines, so perhaps they had better sharpen a pencil and in the meantime I would be talking to my attorney.

That did it. They came through with a nice 'parachute' and were even gracious about it. My boss asked me if I would have *really* gone to an attorney. I just smiled and didn't answer him. He handed me the check.

***...and there I was***...on the beach again.

**Islander 30, Mk 2   Commissioned "UNO MáS" October 1, 1976**

We took part in the "Friday Night Anthony Home Port" sailboat races on Lake Washington during the summer months.  My crew was essentially unchanged for about seven years.  This is almost unheard of.  It was probably due to our "strict" rules; *absolutely no drinking until within 24 feet of the vessel...no screaming or shouting at crewmembers or the Captain...and polite suggestions are always welcome.*  The official beverage on-board was "Mickey's Big Mouth" Ale....and since the lid screws back on, your beer won't be spilled when we 'come about'...and

283

PLEASE, no red wine!  (--stains horribly.)  Very good rules!

Woody became "First Mate"; Jim Tyler was "Chief Of The Boat".  Other members were Marc Lagen, Step-daughter Debi, Erik, Scott (when in town) and Tom Dorgan, plus his 'squeeze', Roxanne.  Other occasional members became "Able-Bodied", "Grinders", *Mickey's-fetchers* and other tasks as they occurred.

Of all the years that we raced we only received one trophy and that was for *"Perseverance".*  I may have told you earlier that the Islander 30 liked heavy air.  Most of the Friday night winds on the lake were light and variable.

Well this one night we had our kind of wind and the result was that we arrived at the first mark ahead of the race fleet.  In our surprised excitement, during the attempt to raise the spinnaker, we lost the halyard....it got away and went to the top of the mast.  We quickly got the Bos'n Chair out...started to hook up the Jib Halyard to the chair....and it got away to the top of the mast.  We only had the Main Halyard left.  God help the crewmember that loses that one!  So we lowered the Main sail, attached the Bos'n Chair and sent the most recent culprit up to fetch the two halyards that were flopping around up near the mast top.

In the meantime, the entire fleet came sailing by with hoots of laughter and raspberries.  We finally got halyards and sails squared away, the spinnaker flying and took off in pursuit.  We finished DFL.  ("dead *f\*#king* last!)

There was one cruise to Pt. Townsend that won't be soon forgotten.  I had brought along a large pot of "Carroll Shelby's Chili" makin's.  The crew ate a lot of it but by the time we were ready to leave Port Townsend they had had enough!  I ended up giving the rest of it to a nice couple that had the slip next to ours. Funny thing, though…they were never heard from again.

On March 1st of 1989 we had a surprise snowstorm. Over ten inches of heavy, wet snow. The weekend prior we had taken Jim Tyler on a short cruise over to Lake Union, at the request of his wife who was preparing a 'surprise birthday party' for him. We did a bit of drinking on the way over and back. Made it to the slip and secured the boat.

Our head pumped overboard, not into a holding tank. If the Inlet valve to the head is not securely shut off, the lake water will come in and fill the toilet bowl to within an inch of the top. And that's what happened. But then the *ten inches of heavy snow* lowered the boat more than an inch…and the inlet started filling the boat with water.

Even with my loss of attention, due to drink, I still had "armed" the bilge pump. (It had a float valve that would activate the pump if incoming water moved the float up.)

Well, dear reader, the float valve was 'gucked-up' with crud and the float didn't move 'up' to activate the bilge pump. The eight-dollar float valve had failed. Uno Mas had sunk in the slip and was hanging on her mooring lines.

Walking down the dock and discovering that your boat was sunk was almost as bad as finding your wife with her lover. —an experience I wouldn't wish on my worst enemy.

And, '*there I was*', in trouble with my Lady, my partner, the insurance company and myself!

Well, I *had* to redeem myself. I asked Bruce if it would be okay if I did most of the interior work…and then took my proposal to the insurance company. They had done a complete Marine Survey that came up with "replace with new" for over 90% of water-damaged items, for example, interior cushions, overhead leatherette, VHF radio, FM-Stereo player, clock, wind instruments, and even curtains and rugs.

I've always admired the interiors of yachts like the very expensive Hans Christian Models. Essentially, they had teak & holly cabin sole, tongue & groove planked over-head with teak crossovers on four-foot centers with knobby things on each end where the crossover meets the sides. Upholstery a green plush mohair, brass fixtures, brass lamps, and lots of teak. We already had the lots of teak in the bulkheads and galley trim, doors and drawers. I was determined to replicate that 'stately interior.'

I got quotes for the "replace with new" items and used that money for the Teak & Holly cabin sole, the overhead planking, two brass hanging lamps, new brass electric cabin lights, curtains and the teak 'cross-overs'

I asked the contractor who had installed the Teak & Holly cabin sole how much he would charge to do the six knobby things. He said $400. I thought I could do 'em. I bought some Styrofoam blocks to make patterns, since each one would be slightly different. I worked for a couple of nights on the FIRST one…still hadn't gotten anything but a pile of Styrofoam sawdust. The following day I called the contractor and asked if his offer was still good. Laughing, he replied okay.

Finally, she was finished. I called Bruce and arranged to meet him at the boat. He arrived, went below, carefully looking around then slowly turned to me and said, "Well done, McEniry, well done."

We had lost a summer of sailing but ended up with a beautiful boat. I was proud of the results of my handiwork, especially the planked overhead.

Planked 'over-head' with 'knobby-ends' on the teak cross-overs

287

# TWENTY–SEVEN BACK TO RAISBECK

$I$ was talking with Bruce McCaw one afternoon commiserating about the fact that my "parachute" wouldn't last forever and that I had to find something to do. He said that his insurance company handled Raisbeck's Product Liability Insurance and suggested that I should go talk to him. Jim Raisbeck's company, THE RAISBECK GROUP, was just finishing a Sabreliner wing modification project and about ready to go to market. They would soon be spooling up with folk.

When I replied in a somewhat negative manner Bruce said that he thought that we, Raisbeck and I, had made peace on the boat.

"You're right, of course, and it is 'Aviation'."

I remembered. We were going to be taking the boat over to the Sea Fair races and Bruce had asked if he could invite a friend. No problem…the friend turned out to be Jim Raisbeck.

Motoring over to the race area, Bruce at the helm, I made my way up to the bow. A short time later Raisbeck joined me.

"Mike, I think I owe you an apology,"

"Oh?", came my quiet reply.

"Yeah, it's about your 'associate-dealer' thing from our Robertson days. I later took your suggestion, raised the prices a bit and gave it a shot. It really worked. Where did you come up with that?"

"Jim, it was back when I worked for Pacific Airmotive selling airplane parts. P-A-C competed with other suppliers and some bright lad down in Burbank come

288

up with the scheme. The Associate Distributor program was just an additional 10% <u>after</u> their 25% normal dealer discount, but it was also linked to order quantity, and it really worked! I've always thought it was a great marketing tool."

Raisbeck thought about it for a moment and then replied, "Well it sure put the *'why isn't Cessna doing it'* to rest....it was a good idea."

At that moment I thought that Jim Raisbeck was 'okay'. Bruce's comment had brought it all back to me.

With resume in hand I made my way down to Boeing Field and to the *concrete Quonset Hut.* West Coast Airlines had built the large structure for their maintenance hangar. They, having moved on to Sea-Tac, Raisbeck took it over.

When I went up to the second deck, to the offices. I found my way on down the length of the building, to Jim Raisbeck's office. I told his secretary that I was hoping to see him, that I didn't have an appointment.

He was right in the middle of a staff meeting and when he noticed that I was outside his office, motioned me in.

Shades of Robertson STOL.... what did I want?

I explained that I was there looking for a job. And just like the time before at ROBERTSON STOL, he asked what I could contribute to The Raisbeck Group. Naturally I pursued the sales areas but he said that the project didn't need sales efforts since folk were lining up and competing for a 'position' in the modification schedules. But he asked me to call him later that evening and maybe he could find something for me to do.

I made the call, we chatted a bit and he offered me a position as his Personal Staff Assistant, at a ridiculous salary to start. I declined his offer, stating I didn't care for

289

the position or the money. He asked me to give it a try that I wouldn't be a 'spy' for him and to trust him on the money part. He indicated he was having some problems with his staff. They were having inflated ideas about staffing up, and he wanted to make a point. He asked me to trust him.

I accepted his offer. Hey! –we'd been in the trenches together via Robertson STOL…on the edge.

Jim had decided that I had a lot of varied experience and wanted to put it to use. He assigned me to various departments, one at a time, to help them with the start-up problems that they were encountering. He made it clear that I wasn't there to spy but to help.

He was true to his word on the money part, giving me substantial raises every two months until it was up to a reasonable level. It worked out. My main contribution was in inventory control and combined "used-on" parts tracking, by hand, this being long before *EXCELL*.

Things were smoothing out.

One day we had an interesting visitor. Milt Pugsley was a Vice-president and Chief Pilot for the Chrysler Corporation. Milt had worked with Jim in years past when Jim had the Howard-Raisbeck Learjet 20 Series program. Milt now had a current problem and had flown out to Seattle to meet with Jim and discuss a possible solution.

Jim called me into his office to meet Milt and to be present to hear about the problem. Pugsley had recently inherited Lee Iacoca from The Ford Motor Company.

A major part of the Chrysler air fleet consisted of Lear 35 and 36 models. They were the perfect fit for the Chrysler operations.

There had been two very dramatic Lear 35/36 loses. One in Alaska, that had made headlines since the Governor's wife had been aboard, and the other a Ford Company Lear 35 crash in Detroit that had a large contingent of high level Ford executives on board. The latter had a very crippling impact on Ford.

The problem was determined to be caused by irregular wing icing.

An explanation is in order.

The airplane operates most efficiently in the 40,000-foot realm. It's very cold at the high altitude environment. The airframe becomes "cold soaked". The FAA Approach Control inadvertently caused both of the accidents by 'rapid handling'. They had been cleared for a fast let-down to the 'Initial Approach Altitude'. In order to make the rapid descent the power had to be pulled back to "idle". The wing de-icing system, for these models of Learjets, was "Hot-Air-Bleed" from the engines. The airplane descended into the weather, accumulated wing- ice and when power was applied during the instrument approach, the ice didn't come off the wing equally, causing severe stall and subsequent crash.

Lee Iacoca had told Milt to get rid of the airplanes and replace them with something else.

There wasn't anything else on the market that fit their operational profile and Milt wanted to keep the Lears'. But the differential icing problem would have to be solved and he knew that Raisbeck could do it.

Jim tried to explain that he was up to his ears in the Sabreliner project, under *exclusive* contract to North American, and didn't have the time or capital, to take on another modification project.

Pugsley said that he would furnish the airplane, flight crew, fuel costs and any outside purchase items if Jim would provide the engineering and certification expertise necessary to solve the problem.

Raisbeck turned to me, saying, "Well, 'Special Staff Assistant to the President', what do you think? He was smiling.

Being up to date on the various departmental capacities, I replied that I felt that it could be done without impacting the Sabreliner project. Jim said, "Fine, you do it."

I became the Project Manager, in function, for the Raisbeck Mark VI Learjet 35/36 Wing Modification.

We achieved FAA Certification in a record twenty-eight days! It wasn't my effort, but the team under Kim Frinnel that made it happen. I merely kept track of the paper-work.  --James was still smiling.

This effort, being "a pilot's memoir', should include my introduction to the Learjet 30 Series. My impression was that it flew and felt like a fighter. I later learned that it was indeed, the wing and tail of a Swiss fighter. Bill Lear had acquired manufacturing 'Rights', added a cabin and 'viola', the Learjet 20 Series are born.

The airplane could be a real challenge for a pilot without military training. But it's still just an airplane.

The "Dee Howard–James Raisbeck" Lear Mk IV wing modification tamed that 'fighter-wing', improving handling and increased safety margins. It saved some lives.

I was able to get a significant amount of flight time in the Lears, riding as co-pilot. I did make the required day and night landings, to qualify legally. It wouldn't have mattered during the various flight tests since they were conducted under FAA "Experimental" category flights. But I was called upon to both pick up and deliver some of airplanes, in which I had to be legally qualified to act as co-pilot.

The Lear likes a 'low-degree angle', somewhat flat approach profile. My first jet experience, the Lockheed T-33, was like that. They're quick, but fun to fly.

Raisbeck's staff decided that our Northridge California operation should be brought up to Seattle. The operation at Northridge was part of the Howard-Raisbeck Lear Mk IV modification program. The Northridge plant provided large wing sections to Dee Howard. They were nearing the end of the contract and our staff wanted to move the operation to Seattle, along with the large wing tools and jigs. They would be put to use on the Sabreliner project. In fact, a few of the jigs down in Northridge were already set-up with the Sabreliner configuration.

Jim called me into his office and asked me to go have a look at what it would take to move the tools and fixtures and any personnel that would be willing to make the move up to Seattle.

I made three or four trips down to Northridge and came up with a budget proposal, working with Ted Cedarbloom, the main brain down there. As I recall, Ted and I came up with a budget in the neighborhood of $65,000, and without any fat. If one of the twenty-four families had a flat tire driving up to Seattle it would not be covered in the budget.

I submitted the budget to Raisbeck. Sometime later he called me into his office and queried me as how sure I was that the move could be accomplished within the submitted budget. I was confident of my numbers and said so. He then told me that his "group" of vice-presidents had said that it would be at least a quarter of a million. He said that if that didn't change my mind, to go ahead.

Cutting to the chase, the move went according to plan. The budget came in with about a $250 over-run, or something like that, from the $65,000 initial budget.

293

Cederbloom did a fantastic job, building the wing sections ahead, even factoring the troop's over-time accomplishing the 'build', into the budget equation. The large wing-tools were moved, set up in Seattle, and didn't miss a beat finishing the Dee Howard contract. Raisbeck was delighted. I made it clear to Raisbeck that it happened due to Ted Cedarbloom's efforts.

Peggy Lou and I drove a truck, called "Green Thing" up from Northridge, California. It was loaded with the last of the equipment and several workbenches.

We went down to Laguna Beach to spend the night so that I could show Peggy around my old stomping grounds...then off to Seattle, via Sausalito. We were to meet Jim's brother, Clifford, and pick up a few cases of wine from a winery where he was an investor. –a few cases.

The *few* cases filled all of the available spaces under the benches. I don't recall how many there were but it was a considerable amount. In fact, pulling onto a truck scale on our route home, it would kinda "glug" when I braked.

Raisbeck told me that my efforts were worth at least a $5,000 bonus, but he wouldn't be giving it to me since I would probably just use it to pay bills or some such. Instead he would let me give something to Peggy Lou that her first husband hadn't been able to.

Raisbeck had worked with Peggy's husband, Kearney Robinson, at Boeing. Kearney had traveled internationally for Boeing. It was severely frowned upon, by company policy, for an employee to take his wife, even if paying their way, on any Boeing business trip. Of course Raisbeck knew about that policy. He explained this to me and went on to say that he wanted me to take Peggy Lou to the Paris Air Show, followed by a cruise on the French

294

canal system in Burgundy Province. It would be the trip of a lifetime.

Leaving Seattle, Raisbeck had gone ahead since he had meetings in London with the Lloyds of London insurance people. (In the aircraft modification arena, Product Liability insurance is a major issue.) Peggy and I followed a few days later.

We stayed at a very old hotel near the Louvre. We were both suffering from the time change, having been up all night on airplanes. PanAm's polar flight to London and then an Air France flight to Paris. We strolled around the neighborhood, picked up a quiche-to-go and returned to the hotel room for the snack and sleep.

The following day I took a train out to the Paris Air Show. Peggy had decided that she would stay at the hotel and maybe visit the Louvre, right across the street.

I met Jim Raisbeck at the North American-Rockwell hospitality pavilion, as we had arranged. Jim told me that he had found a potential European distributor for the Raisbeck Mk VI Lear 35/36 modification program. Jim led me over to a Boeing 707 that was on static display, showing an executive interior. There we met with Carl Hirschmann, owner of Jet Aviation Ltd. He had service facilities in Zurich, Bern, Munich and Saudi-Arabia.

Jim had primed Mr. Hirschmann, but had allowed me to make the final pitch and closing. It was a gracious gesture on his part. I closed the deal, subject to final signing of contracts that would come later.

That evening James, Peggy and I were to meet with Bruce McCaw at a restaurant near the Eiffel Tower. It did get a 'trifle damp' out due to various spirits that were consumed. Bruce did his usual nap at the table. (I had always wanted to have a bunch of stick-on labels made up that said, *"Bruce McCaw Slept Here"* and distribute them around the world.) However, it was always a short nap and then he was ready to party on.

Jim, Peggy and I decided to walk back to the hotel, down the Champs-Elysées. This would be from the Eiffel Tower to the Louvre, a distance of about a mile or so. Peggy said that she wanted a portable radio, so we stopped at an all-night drug store and she purchased one. She was delighted that it spoke French. Now, mind you, the three of us were well into our cups. When we got to the Place de la Concorde I removed my sport coat and proceeded to "cape" cars as they came around the traffic circle. We finally made it to the hotel and collapsed for the night.

The following morning it was up at, or before, dawn. We had to catch a train from Paris to Auxerre where we would be picking up our boat to cruise the canal system in Burgundy Province.

There is no way that I can describe our collective hangovers. They were beyond description! We had to pack, stumble down and check out…grab a croissant, find a cab and head for one of the four train stations serving Paris. Ours was the southeast one. We already had our tickets, so it was just a matter of finding a porter for our luggage and finding the train. We found one.

The porter looked at our tickets and with a look of amazement headed out briskly for our train. His "briskly" soon became a dead run. We had a hard time keeping up with him…. but finally made it.

We got on the train, gathered up our luggage and went from car to car trying to find our compartment. At one of the vestibules I let one of the doors go and it hit Peggy Lou on her face. (I think 'they' remember every 'slight', short or tall.)

We made it to our compartment and collapsed.

The train stopped at small town stations along the way. At one stop I noticed a bar. I told Raisbeck, "Let's go get some wine." God! I needed a drink. We all did, for that matter.

Peggy Lou was nervous about both Raisbeck and I leaving her alone on the train. She said, "Dammit, you two...don't miss this train or I'll kill you!" She meant it!

I found out later in life that Peggy Lou's recurring nightmare was being abandoned in a foreign country, unable to speak the language and no idea of her location. (And I left her alone on a French train as I ran to buy some wine... I'm surprised our marriage lasted thirty-five years!)

We made it in quick-time, bringing back several small bottles of wine. It helped, until Peggy noticed that one of the bottles had a dead bee floating in the bottom. That didn't make us feel much better. Indeed, the evils of drink. Oh well.

Auxerre. We off loaded with baggage and hangover and met the manager of the boat company. He took us over to a store so that we could provision for the trip. He checked me out on the operational details of the boat. It was like a trailer on a small barge, forty feet long and about eight feet wide. We would be "self-operating".

Originally the boat was to have Jim Raisbeck's girlfriend and Jim, Bruce and his girlfriend and Peggy and I. Bruce decided to fly a DC-3, powered by three turbo-props, back to the states. Jim's girlfriend cancelled at the last minute so it was just the three of us on-board. Thank the Lord. It would have really been crowded with six folk milling about in forty feet...

The following day we had a restful breakfast and Jim went over the mail, the TWX's and memos that I had brought with me for him. One of the pieces of mail was a complaint from Rockwell that Raisbeck had taken on

297

another project that had been specifically spelled out as a no-no in the Sabreliner agreement. They were adamant in their demands that he divest himself of the Learjet project and concentrate on their joint venture.

Reminiscent of our early relationship where I had been his Staff Assistant, he turned to me, read the memo regarding the Learjet project and Rockwell's attitude and said, "Well *Mr. Staff Assistant* what shall I do with the Learjet Mark VI Project?"

I said, "Sell it to me."

His replay was, "You don't have any money."

I said, "You don't know that." and went on to say that I would put a check on his desk thirty days after returning to Seattle, covering my proposed offer that included commissions.

When he balked at that I reminded him that he had been lucky to get ten percent out of his other projects...facts that I knew. (I really didn't know that, I was guessing.)

He laughed and said that I was probably right and okay we had a deal.

The boat trip was a beautiful, restful experience. The canal wasn't very wide. It was wide enough for boats to pass with comfortable clearance. When we would come to some place of interest, we merely pulled over to the bank, drove a couple of steel stakes into the soil and tied the boat to 'em. Leaving the boat unlocked we could walk up to see a church, get more provisions or just a look-see.

The River Yonne fed the canal that we were on. We had to "lock" frequently. The locks were constructed in the late 1700's and early 1800's. The canals were the freeways of Europe, to move the goods of the time. The locks had a small stone cottage at each of them. Pensioners lived in the cottages and manned the locks. The cottages had beautiful roses and other flowers in abundance. The Lock Keepers were very friendly and helpful. I couldn't help but think how smug most Americans are thinking about the progress in the United States. Here the French had these 'freeways' while we were still fighting Indians.

We ran into another American couple that were also cruising the canal. He was retired Air Force and she was very much with the English-European accent. I asked her was she from Omaha or Wichita? --startled, she responded Omaha. (Chuckle… hello.)

A Sunday afternoon found us out of wine, so decided to go up to this small town and try to find something open. No luck. Along the way we came across a dog that Jim must have startled because it bit him pretty hard. Hard enough to draw blood. Nothing was open but we came across three Frenchmen. We tried to explain that we needed something for Jim's dog bite and that we were also looking for some more wine. They didn't speak English and we didn't speak French. Jim spoke a little German and one of them could understand some German and a bit of what Raisbeck was talking about. They came with us back to the boat.

One went home to get some medical items and wine. We all sat on the fantail of the boat and drank Scotch. The Frenchmen loved the Scotch. Soon one was back with medical supplies and a couple of bottles of wine, maybe three bottles. Anyway it would be enough to last us until the following day when France would be open.

Peggy Lou asked them about one of the packages in our provisions. After much pidgin Anglo-French, one of them finally said, "Gobble-gobble". The mystery was solved.

This short chapter can't do the canal trip justice. It was way too wonderful, marvelous and everything else.

Jim Raisbeck was exceptionally gracious and charming, adding to the experience. Not only was the scenery grand but we also just had a lot of fun.

Carl Hirschmann, President and Owner of Jet Aviation, our new European Distributor, had invited us down to his summer place at Cap Martin, near Monaco for the weekend. We finished our canal cruise and boarded a train for Menton, the closest train station to Monaco. Upon arrival we telephoned Hirschman and he sent a car to pick us up.

Hirschman's little summer place was about ten acres out on the tip of Cap Martin, which is the Eastern point of the Monaco harbor. He had recently refurbished the estate to the tune of ten million dollars! It was something else and reflected the monies wisely spent.

I started out our stay as "ugly Americans" by putting our trash in what I thought was an incinerator, but was, in fact, a Chinese oven. –oh well.

At lunch one day we were served small fishlets that had been baked in that same Chinese oven. One picked them up by the tail and ate the whole thing, head and all. I asked Carl what kind of fish they were. He replied, *"Very small."*

The weekend was pleasant enough. Our quarters were elegant. Swimming in the pool that Carl had designed that seemed to be part of the Med by virtue of water that rose to the brim of the marble and the overflow was in a small trench that bordered the pool about a foot back.

Carl's son Tom took us over into Monaco to their ski boat. It was a Riva, a bit larger than a Chris-Craft runabout and powered by a Maserati V-8 engine. Wow. I was the only one that water-skied. The sound of that engine made my day, though.

The weekend over, we were driven to Nice and boarded one of Hirschmann's Learjets. This was Peggy Lou's first ride in a Lear. She was suitably impressed. We flew from Nice to Zurich. Being in the back was alright.

Peggy was supposed to go shopping with one of the Hirschmann girls but she didn't show up…probably tired of Americans. Jim and I were driven to Basel, where the main Jet Aviation Offices were. The car was a Mercedes-Benz 600 limousine. Jim and I could lean forward and see the speedometer reading 140-150 kilometers/hour. –they do drive fast over there.

The formal business didn't take very long, we signed all of the papers and headed back to Zurich.

Peggy Lou had nearly emptied the small drinks in the room's refrigerator out of boredom. She did forgive us, however.

The next morning, we boarded a plane to London and then PanAm on to Seattle.

The trip was a "once in a lifetime" affair but it was great to be home. Thank you James David Raisbeck.

I called Bruce, told him about my agreement with Raisbeck for the Lear Mk VI program. He said that he would cover me. As it turned out, I didn't need any of Bruce's money. I was able to come up with the money that I owed Raisbeck by selling modification 'positions'. However, I had made a deal, and I appreciated Bruce's expertise. I needed his skills.

Thirty days after returning to Seattle I placed a check on Jim's desk. So, there we were. Bruce and I owned the Raisbeck Learjet Mk VI wing modification program. Bruce McCaw was President and 51% owner and I was Vice President & General Manager and 49% owner. Our new company was Jet Air, one of Bruce's former

301

dormant companies where he still had a lot of forms and stationary. It was a seamless transition.

I kept my office at The Raisbeck Group, paying them rent. I hired the Lear installation crew from "Group" for each modification. I made prompt payments to Raisbeck. It was good for both of us.

We actually made a little money. I ended up getting a couple of cars out of the deal and a salary for a year or so. I'm not sure what Bruce got out of it...I didn't ever ask. Then a few years later, Lear came up with their own 'fix' and wanted all of the 35/36's to be so modified, including the dozen or so Mk VI's that we had done.

Lo and behold, this even took us off of the liability position that we had held. Bruce had often commented to me about how would we like to be Donald Douglas when a DC-3 crashed......hundreds were still flying! His liability insurance bill has to be in the thousands!

Like I've said before...there is a God!

# TWENTY-EIGHT A TASTE OF NIRVANA

Life does go on. This part of my life was enriched by a great marriage to the most wonderful woman I have ever known…. Peggy Lou Herring-Robinson-McEniry.

She had been very happily married to Kearny Robinson, a highly placed Boeing executive, who had suffered a massive heart attack at age forty-eight. They had three children, two boys and a girl.

When I first arrived in Peggy Lou's life, Debi was eighteen, Woody seventeen and Erik four. Woody was initially resentful of my intruding on their life, still struggling with the loss of his Dad, but eventually became my best friend and even the drummer in my jazz group, The Chamber Jazz Quartet.

When Peggy and I bought our first real boat Woody and I would wait for rough weather and then go sailing. The purpose was to find out either the boat's limits or our own. –we didn't ever find the boat's limits.

Debi was very supportive of my marriage to Peggy Lou, wanting her Mother to find happiness in a relationship again. Erik, being only four, didn't remember much of his Father even though I encouraged him to never forget his Father.

1980 was a tough year with the loss of my daughter, Kathy. At age twenty she went down to Houston to marry Michael, a neat lad and a helicopter mechanic. A few days before their marriage they were at a party and Kathy went into the bathroom with another girl. She came out, staggering, and collapsed from having injected cocaine. She was DOA on arrival at the hospital. Her death was especially hard on Scott. He and Kathy had been more than

303

close. But the whole family suffered equally. Scott and Michael (Fiancé) took Kathy's ashes up to Roach Harbor and scattered them under the rose bushes in front of the old, famous hotel there.

Erik was hit hard with losing his Dad, then Step-Sister Kathy and, about the same time his Grandmother, Nana. Peggy and I were concerned about his getting through all of that. Life can get tough!

Scott attended Bellevue Community College for two years and then transferred to Western University in Bellingham. He became the only real college graduate in the family. His major was History and for a time thought that he might teach. He gave up that idea when it became apparent that you couldn't hit those smart-ass kids anymore. Oh well…. WTFOver.

The family grew. Debi was the first to marry. It wasn't a good one. Her groom was in line for a promotion at Fred Meyer Stores and was told that he should be married. He proposed to Debi, they married, he got the promotion and then two months later wanted out of the marriage. It was very hard on Debi….and she didn't deserve to be treated that way.

She met and married John Cole. He was a decent sort. They were married about twenty years when John was diagnosed with cancer. Thankfully, he didn't suffer long. After his death, Debi got to know Lynn Gahringer who had been a fishing and hunting buddy of Johns'. Both Debi and Lynn being single, were drawn together and eventually married.

Woody was next. He married Laurie Lundine September 3rd, 1982. (My band, *"Seabreeze"*, played at their reception. I was honored that they asked me to play.)

They gave us our first grandchildren. "Anthony Michael Kearney Robinson" was born in 1986 and "Sidne Marie" followed three years later.

Woody and Laurie were divorced in 2006 but remain good friends and still share some holidays with us. Scott married a girl that he had met in Bellingham while attending Western Washington University. That marriage lasted just over a year. They had acquired a really nice wooden sailboat. It had to go due to the divorce proceedings.

A year or so later Scott married Kay. They produced another grandchild, "Liam Michael McEniry", born April 29$^{th}$, 1997. (The birth date is significant since Peggy's birthday is April 26$^{th}$ and mine, April 27$^{th}$.)

Scott got into the Navy Flying Club at NAS Whidbey. He got his Private License and then stopped for now due to the cost. He felt that not being able to fly very often wasn't conducive to maintaining proficiency. I was sure proud of him for following in Dad's footsteps, though. –and he has stayed in Bellingham, getting a good job in technical sales. (Another footstep?) He works for a company called Blue Seas Systems. They manufacture electrical systems equipment for the Marine and RV industries.

Scott and Kay divorced last year and as this writing, Liam is eighteen`. Scott and Kay share custody so we get to see Liam frequently. And yes, I did sit him down at about age five and explained the fact that he was now the "eldest Son of the eldest Son"…and there was a family castle!

Last but not least was our youngest, Erik Lee Robinson. He met and courted Kiyomi Uehara. Kiyomi's father was a Major in the U.S. Air force, a bombardier-navigator on B-52's. Her mother, Sally Uehara, had been a

U.S. Naval officer, a Lt.(jg) when she met and married Jerry Uehara. Kiyomi was born in Thailand in 1967.

After eight years of happy married life they decided to add to their family: they got a dog. We were very happy for them and so maybe now Erik will get his 'stuff and car' outta here......oh well.

Along the way were family health issues. Peggy had some serious surgeries...removal of part of her colon, breast cancer, skin cancer on her eyelid and a blood condition that was a serious, but slow-acting blood cancer.

For my part came the discovery of cancer on my right kidney. It was removed laparoscopically, making it an easy recovery. And then in 2005 I had a ruptured diverticula resulting in emergency surgery, followed a few months later with more surgery and finally another one a couple of months after that. –but, we made it through all of that and still kicking.

Bruce McCaw became our boat partner on the Coronado 25 and then he and I custom-built Uno Màs, our Islander 30. We all had great experiences on that boat, culminating in Bruce giving me "his half" when he and his brothers became "zillionaires" with the sale of their cell phone company to AT&T. The gift was not expected and difficult to accept. (He said that he was just tired of paying half the moorage.)

Then later Peggy and I sold Uno Más and bought a used Limited-Edition Itasca-34 motor home. Peggy Lou hadn't really enjoyed sailing that much, but enjoyed the RV life. It was a ball. And the best part is that you slept in your own bed, ate the right amount of food, went where you wanted to go and when...it is a real treat to travel that way.

I had seen many of the country's attractions from the air and now became an opportunity to see them on the ground "Jellystone" Park, the Grand Tetons, Mt. Rushmore, and even Ft. Jones. ---huh?

Ft. Jones is a small town, surrounded by mountains and located in Northern California. It has an OMNI beacon and is a reporting check-point on VICTOR 23, (the I-5 of the air.) It is located between Medford, Oregon and Red Bluff, California. I have flown over it many, many times. It always looked like, what I imagined "Shangri La" could appear, with the mountains all around and the isolation. I wanted to see it from the ground.

It turned out to be a very unwise choice. It was horribly hot. Barely breathing, I turned the RV around and headed out of town.

Fate wasn't through quite yet, we had mechanical problems with the motor home on our way out. A bad experience. I firmly believe that if I hadn't turned around to leave, without stopping in Ft. Jones, Peggy Lou would have beaten me senseless! --oh well. We can almost laugh about it now.

Along the way, over the course of the many years of our life together, were the dogs. The family dog when I arrived in the Robinson Household was "Linka", followed by an insane animal, an Afghan, called "Nico". He didn't last long taking to snapping at visiting young children. Then we acquired "Murphy", plus a little later adding "Athos", a black Lab that happened to *just follow* Scott home from school one day. (Scott had taken an interest in Fencing; 'Athos'…. the Three Musketeers…hello?)

I didn't want any more dogs after our having to put down Murphy and then later Athos. I didn't want to go through that grief again.

Yeah, right! It lasted about three months and then Peggy Lou found an Akita on the internet in PAWS, waiting to be rescued. The animal was still with her first owners. The owners had a recent baby and didn't feel that they could give the dog the time that she needed. We drove up to Everett to see the animal. We were sitting in the house and "Caira" (Akita-Golden mix) came over to me and sat down <u>on</u> my feet. I looked over at Peggy Lou and said, "I lo-ov-ve her."

That was all that it took. We had a new (about 2 years old) dog. And what a dog she turned out to be. Absolutely the best dog that either Peggy or I have ever had. Bar none! We acquired the motor home shortly after and Caira took to traveling like a champ. Her favorite place was the RV Park up at NAS Whidbey. We would let her chase the rabbits.... but to no avail. (Whidbey Island is over-run with rabbits.) They were really quick. She also liked to chase squirrels in our backyard and on our street. In all the years of chasing she only caught one, that I recall.

RV's are a lot of fun for not a lot of money. They do burn fuel at a high rate. We cruised at 65-70 mph, burning 6.5 miles per gallon. She had a Main & Aux fuel tank for a total of 90 gallons, giving one a 500-mile range. (--with an 85-mile Reserve) To the 'Gypsy' in my genes it satisfies an itch that's fun to scratch.

The righteous and Golden part of this period of my life was family and seeing the growth, the marriages the first Grandchildren. I felt like an honored Patriarch. I was in Heaven....Nirvana.

-o-

An *afterword* about friendship:

We had received word about Kathy's death in the early morning. Later that day Bruce McCaw called and before he could tell me the reason for his call, I told him about Kathy. The following day he was at our front door.

308

He was there to share our grief and support us in any way that he could.

I am so proud to say..." Bruce McCaw is my friend." I found out later that he had called to tell me about the death of <u>his</u> friend that was attempting to set a 'water speed record' on Lake Tahoe. Bruce had been involved in the record attempt; to what degree I'm not sure, but he had lost a good friend.

# TWENTY-NINE   COMPANY INVOLVEMENT

**I** know, I know.... this is supposed to be about airplanes, but you can only stay airborne so long and there has to be some non-flying stuff to bridge the flying parts together. Most of the following is not too far afield from Aviation.

I was helping Jim Raisbeck rebuild his life after he lost The Raisbeck Group to Rockwell. They had some differences that ended up in court; the result was that it looked like Jim lost his company.

Jim had been doing some serious thinking about modifying the Beech King Air turbo-prop fleet. There were a bunch of them ranging from the model 90 to the model 200. It was a very large fleet of airplanes and just ripe for Raisbeck's magic improvements. I say that without sarcasm. Jim Raisbeck had *a gift for recognizing a need, picking the right market and supplying that need. He was not only a fantastic marketer but a genius when developing modifications that would improve handling, extend range, increase payload and make it faster, higher or whatever the crying need.*

He was a product of Purdue's aeronautical engineering program. James polished his craft at Boeing, developing the 727 short field performance envelope. It was there that he met Jim Robertson and became interested in Robertson's moonlighting company, ROBERTSON STOL. Week-ends found him working with Robertson, almost as a hobby, fascinated with the general aviation market. Robertson had picked the Cessna 172, 182, 180 and 206 models to apply STOL modifications. When Jim

Robertson died, Raisbeck was offered the Presidency. It was there that I met him.

Now, much later, I was helping him put together a presentation to attract investors to pursue the King Air Project. We were making the presentation to a financial group in a downtown Seattle boardroom, atop one of the big office buildings. Jim was standing at the head of the table, pontificating and going over the market, his proposed answer to the industry's clamoring needs and other details. I was sitting halfway down the table next to a white haired gentleman that had been introduced to me as "Sid Woodcock". The name rang a bell but I couldn't put it together. I was trying to remember where I had heard it. Then it came to me.

I had gotten involved with the Central Intelligence Agency back when I had been running my own company. The short story is that when I was buying and selling airplanes I would run into some strange requests like being asked about actual wing guns for a P-51 restoration project. I remember thinking that somebody downtown should be interested in 'arms sales'. Since my caller was a German national, I called the Central Intelligence Agency instead of the F.B.I.

I explained my position as a broker and what had taken place. They asked for details, including names and places. When I told them the name of my caller.... told them it was Otto Schlutter. (not the real name) it spiked their attention. The "name" was someone of interest and he was currently under investigation. I was asked to continue to work with him, and try to arrange a meet in Seattle.

The meeting took place at the Sheraton in downtown Seattle.

What impressed me was the "wire" that was placed on me. It was the size of one of those green metallic-wrapped 'after dinner' mints. It was placed in my dress shirt pocket, a hole punched in the back of the pocket and a wire running down inside my clothes, down into my pant leg. I was impressed with the size of the bug. It would work with my suit coat over it as well.

The meeting went well, the Agency got what they wanted. They didn't restrain Otto. I was dismissed with thanks and appreciation and so forth. I thought that was the end of it.

Not too long later I was 'recruited' by a local Air Show pilot, to do some flying for El Salvador during their dispute with Nicaragua over a Soccer game that evolved into armed conflict. I would be flying a F4U Corsair, one of my all-time favorite airplanes.

The problem was resolved; peace fell over the area before I had a chance to do any flying. Bummers.

Anyway this all led to some involvement working with an Agency project involving El Salvador. Woodcock's name had been associated with that project.

I turned to him at the table and said sotto voice, "Sid Woodcock, Sid Woodcock, have you spent any time down south?"

You could hear the click of his eyeballs as he turned partly toward me and said, "How far south?"

I answered, "El Salvador?"

He smiled and said. *"We'll have lunch"*. (Meaning we would get together sometime later.)

We had that lunch. Sid knew my background since the Raisbeck presentation included backgrounds of key personnel that Raisbeck would be bringing to the package.

Sid asked me if I was currently working for Raisbeck. I replied that no, I was helping him get another project going and currently, at liberty.

He asked about Raisbeck's design work. I told Sid that Raisbeck really could do what he was claiming…that the man had a real flair for identifying a problem and designing the fix.

"Well, it sounds like you have a little time on your hands. I have a small company with a few production problems that you might find interesting."

After lunch we went over to his company, located down off Kamber Road, in Bellevue. The company was DETONICS 45. It was a gun manufacturing firm. I looked things over and ended up telling Sid that I would give him a year, on a contract. We put together an agreement.

I really enjoyed my General Manager's position. The folk were a strange bunch. Very intense. Lots of waxed mustaches, 'camo' clothing, short hair, etc. This was a group of semi-military *wanna-bees*…. or rather, more to the point, "gun people", not *'wanna-bees'*.

After I had been introduced as the new General Manager I asked that department heads meet with me in the conference room.

When I walked in I said, *"Gentlemen, and Lady, this is the eye of the storm. I don't want you to think of me as your new General Manager but as God, and when I speak it will be words from the 'Burning Bush'!"*

(The current movie playing at that time was The Great Santini and that was the speech that Santini gave to the pilots of the screw-up squadron that he had inherited as Commanding Officer. Three Detonics staff members had seen the movie and kinda smiled, --eyes got very big on the other two.

I went on to say that there would be a staff meeting at 0700 hours the following day and those that wished to remain employed would be there, on time and ready to go to work.

The following day, when I walked in at 0700 hours, exactly, I motioned them to keep their seats. (I don't know if they were getting ready to stand or not.)

I told them where yesterday's speech originated and that I intended to run the company like the 'fighter squadron' that I hadn't ever had the privilege of commanding. We had our laugh and they thought that it was a great idea...the 'squadron' thing.

Most of my department heads had sort of grown into their positions without developing skills appropriate to the task, but got the job done. I was able to help develop the missing areas and we really built a team turning that company around. It was a great pleasure.

Fun moments, like when I would post a memo, someone would come along and write "BB" on the bottom of it. (*Burning Bush*)

I stayed six months beyond my one-year contract. When I left the company my crew presented me with a Detonics 45; engraved on the slide are the words, *"To The Great MacTinni from his boys in the squadron"*. I still have and treasure that gun.

A few years later I wrote my first novel, THE JANITOR, by J.M. (Mike) McEniry. (Amazon Books, ISBN 9781499521047) The main character was modeled after Sid Woodcock, who was former OSS in War2 and who later did "contract work" for the Agency. He specialized in 'janitorial services'. There was a lot of call for that sort of work in the sixties. The novel is about El Salvador when some Catholic Nuns were assassinated.

-o-

Raisbeck had gotten his new company, now called RAISBECK ENGINEERING, off the ground and offered me the Vice-President of Sales position. It didn't take very long to get the King Air project coining money. I did most of the sales efforts along with a bit of test flying as co-pilot. I hadn't been through any formal training on the airplane but picked up the skill 'on-the-job'. The King Air is a delightful airplane to fly, surprisingly light on the controls, yet a solid instrument platform. I enjoyed it. I really felt that in order to hurt yourself in a King Air it would have to be 'on purpose'.

One of our trade shows was in Atlanta. During the show our Chief Pilot had an emergency at home and had to return. He couldn't take our airplane since it was on 'static display' showing our products..

I was left to fly the airplane back to Seattle when the trade show was over. I hadn't ever been *really* checked out in the King Air but I had made a few landings and was fairly comfortable. I didn't know that much about turbo-prop engines but I was okay about the flight. I told our Chief Pilot not to worry. It's just another airplane.

When first traveling Internationally I had picked up an American Express Gold card, that being the card of choice in Europe and the Americas' at the time. I hadn't been traveling much or using the card lately, now I was going to spend a bit of money.

I had to pay the tie-down fees for the week in Atlanta, and then refueling. On the way home I landed in Wichita for refueling and couldn't get one of the engines started and had to 'call out' a mechanic to come and change an igniter.

Since I was in Wichita I called Peggy's brother, Bob Herring, and he being a pilot, wanted to come out to meet me and to see the King Air. We hit it off. (I was able to get to know him a few years later when Peggy Lou and I drove out to Wichita and stayed with Bob and his wife

Carol. –neat folk! They owned a company called LORAC manufacturing custom motorcycles, among other things.)

Then more expenses with tie-down and fuel in Denver. All in all, I ran up about $5,000 on my American Express Gold Card in a couple of days...

They called a few days later. The very polite, very nice. A young lady carefully asked subtle questions to determine that I was indeed the one that had made the charges.

I told them that I appreciated the follow-up.

There was some kind of conflict with Beech that resulted in our sales drying up. Reluctantly I had to leave the company.

I ended up working for the Brown Brothers, who had a company in the automotive collision repair market. I managed the sale and installation of 'down-draft, high-tech paint booths'. Part of it was okay. The brothers treated me well but I hated the industry. It was like dealing with a bunch of used car salesmen on a daily basis. Arggh!

My immediate boss was Dave Brown, who was also a Private Pilot. When I did an installation down in Roseburg Oregon, we rented a Piper Cherokee out of Tacoma Industrial airport. (Bud Rude had suggested Tacoma when I asked him the usual "how, where and when" to find an airplane.) On the way back to Tacoma we experienced a complete electrical failure. It was a clear flying day and we'd be back before dark. The only problem would be contacting the tower for landing.

All was not lost, Dave Brown had an early "Brick Phone", (early Cell Phone). He had to call Information, try to get them to tell him the number that *isn't given out*, then call the tower's telephone number to get landing clearance. Some kinda drill, but it worked. The tower operator

316

expressed surprise at our use of a phone for permission to land.

Dennis Martin called one day, inviting me to lunch. He had a new company and offered me the National Sales Manager position. He was looking to build a national Dealer network. It sounded like an interesting project. I took it. I spent a great deal of time on the road, trying to take the company national.

Dennis sold the company and I was soon out of a job since the new owners had their own sales personnel. It was my last corporate position.

I drew Unemployment for a while. The clerk at the State office asked if I was going to retire. I answered in the negative. –then he went on to ask how many job offers I had. I got his point. Nobody wants an *old guy*. It was an awful feeling. I decided to go ahead and draw my Social Security. I didn't feel good about that. I couldn't believe it was all over. WTFOver.

A few years ago, Darlene took ill and lapsed into a coma. She hadn't remarried, so Scott had to make the decision to disconnect the life support systems that were keeping her alive. Scott was informed that she was brain dead and knew that she would not want to be "kept alive", making it an easier decision. Still, not easy. He took her ashes up to Roche Harbor and scattered them in the same rose bushes where Kathy's ashes are.

I bummed around doing 'temporary' office jobs.

On one of the jobs I saw a way to improve the operation I was assigned to work on. I took my suggestions to the man-in-charge. He kept my notes and didn't hire me back the following day. Temp work…. certainly different.

They don't want you to 'help manage', just do the mundane role you were hired for.

And I did some handyman stuff for a neighbor and then stumbled into a painting job at Vintage Racing Motors.

McCaw had joined a small group of investors acting as 'Patrons' to János L. Wimpffen, a research writer, working on a two book project covering "Five Decades of Long Distance Racing", the World Sports Car, Grand Touring and Manufacturers Championships. The project was titled "TIME AND TWO SEATS". I had met János at his office at Vintage, and was trying to do some 'proof-reading' for him. I wasn't a very good proof-reader because I would get too interested in the narrative and miss the 'proofing'. Peggy Lou got involved and did a great job for him, since she could care less about the subject matter. János listed her in the credits when he published.

I had been hanging out at Vintage, and Thor Thorson, president of Vintage, after asking me if I had anything else to do, ended up making me a nice 'part time' offer. As of this writing I have been with Vintage Racing Motors for close to twenty years. The company is one of the McCaw Holdings. I'm carried on the rolls as a "consultant", thanks to my Marine Corps retirement, I don't need benefits. Anyway, that's how I happened to become a part-time Consultant.

One morning Bruce's Chief Pilot called and said let's go flying. He told me that Bruce had told him to get "McEniry's butt back in the air". We flew a Piper Aztec over to Pt. Townsend for lunch then flew back. My landing at Pt. Townsend was a greaser.... the one back at Seattle wasn't. When we were filling out the Flight Sheet I said "Let's see, I got one VFR landing and one Night landing."

He said, "What night landing?"

I replied, "Well if my eyes are closed, doesn't that make it a night landing?"

My "Last Flight" was with my Son Scott, having acquired his Private Pilot rating, and it was July 26th, 2009.

**My last Log Book entry shows a total of 7,544.0 hours.**

I'm seriously considering doing some more aviating but I'll need a Medical. It's just a thought...still a bit of 'passion' left in these aching bones.

# THIRTY        FINAL APPROACH

**O**n Tuesday, the 16<sup>th</sup> of September, 2008, we brought Peggy Lou home from the hospital. Her blood cancer had taken a turn for the worse and she knew that she was dying. The day before she had decided that she wanted to die at home and asked that all medications be discontinued. Once home, Hospice helped getting her settled in to a rented hospital bed and started morphine injections. Peggy was not in any pain but that is what Hospice does when they're called in. It certainly made her discomfort easy to bear but it didn't leave a whole lot of 'lucid' time. I was able to enjoy two periods where it was just she and I together, alone.

She looked over and said, "James Michael, you do not do very well by yourself. You're still a good looking man and there's someone out there for you. Just be careful, find someone *'Nice'.*"

Peggy Lou was very fond of our Veterinary Nurse, Catherine Duesenberg, whom she had known for over twenty years…always referring to her as "nice". So much so that it seemed as if "nice" was Catherine Duesenberg's middle name. I knew full well who she was talking about.

The other time where it was just the two of us, and we were alone, she smiled and said, "Neener, neener, neener…I'm outta here! You get to deal with all the **stuff**!"

The back story to that was, at one point we were seriously considering "down-sizing" and looking at what was available. The accumulation of "**stuff**" in the house was almost overwhelming…her former husband's photo lab and dark-room equipment….my accumulated music recording equipment…the kid's things that were still in the downstairs storage area and so forth. It was too much. We just decided to stay put. Now she was opting out. With any luck I'll get to do the same 'leaving-it-to-the-kids' to sort out and deal with. –neener, neener..

On the following Saturday, the 20$^{th}$ of September 2008, Peggy Lou left me. I had known grief, the loss of a daughter, a Mother, and now a mate…losses beyond endurance, a part of life to be endured, but this was beyond that scope. Poets have attempted to paint the magnitude of personal loss, grief, --musicians have written songs about loss, and, of course, there are "*Blues*".

The song "Autumn Leaves" is one that I associate with the loss of my beloved. The tune started for me when Bruce asked if I would perform for his wedding reception. Did he want the Chamber Jazz Quartet? No, just me. When I asked how, he said that he would be hiring the Fred Radtke Orchestra from the Olympic and I could use the 'rhythm section' (piano, drums and bass) …. they knew all the tunes. I asked what he would like me to play.

"I don't know, how about 'Autumn Leaves'?" He asked.

Well, I hadn't been playing much so I had a few weeks to do some 'wood-shedding' on the one tune.

Let me explain something, when one has a couple of weeks to practice one tune…one will end up knowing that tune inside and out…all the sweet places and the places to avoid. It went well, I nailed it. (We musicians really should know ALL tunes that well!)

In fact, Bruce had asked our mutual friend, Bud Shank to perform as well. As I was coming off the band stand and he was coming on, he remarked, "Michael, I didn't know you could play like that…we should do something!"

321

I was ten feet tall returning to our table at the reception. Bud Shank had liked my playing! Wow!

Some years later, driving down the road listening to one of our local jazz radio stations, I heard some girl singing "Autumn Leaves" and damn near drove off the road! I couldn't believe her 'take' on the tune. I pulled over and called the station and was told that it was Eva Cassidy, performing at the Blue Note, a Washington D.C. jazz club.

I immediately drove to a record store and bought the album only to discover that she had died of cancer at a young age. What a loss. I contacted the estate and learned that some of her arrangements were available and ordered "Autumn Leaves".

During the Spring and Summer of 2008, I was working with a friend of the family, Greg Crosswhite, a wonderful guitar player. Peggy Lou was quite ill during that period, eventually going into the hospital in late summer.

When Greg and I were working downstairs in the studio on the Eva Cassidy arrangement of "Autumn Leaves", Peggy would ask that I keep all the doors open so she could hear and enjoy what we were doing.

The next time you hear some performer singing the song, listen to the words *"... the falling leaves drift by my window,...the falling leaves of red and gold...I see your lips, the summer kisses, the sun-burned hands I used to hold. Since you went away...the days grow long, and soon I'll hear old winter's song. But I miss you...most of all my Darling... when autumn leaves, start to fall...".*

(By Joseph Kosma, 1945)

322

We play the tune with the trio and sometimes I choke up pretty hard getting through it…in fact, it's hard to just type the words.

Her obituary read:

*Peggy Lou set a new standard for a Renaissance Woman. She was a wonderful mother, an outrageous life companion, lover and friend. Her artistic talents were exposed through her work with wood carving, oil painting, wreaths & dried flower arrangements, to name a few. She then applied her talents to the recording side of our music endeavors. She was the "P" in "P & M Productions". Her impeccable taste was evident in her recording and mixing, creating a finished product equal to commercial efforts. She sang beautifully and played the guitar fairly well but would only perform for her family. —we have some recordings. Peggy Lou's life trip with Michael covered many chapters that included not only her artistic depth but sail boating and the travels in their caravel. She shared thirty-five years of her life with him, enjoying their 35th anniversary last August 16th. Her main focus in life was her family and close friends. All of those she touched were forever in awe of her compassion and graciousness. She was a wonderful lady and is so sorely missed. She left behind a massive hole in this earth!*

**Peggy Lou Robinson-McEniry**

April 26, 1933 –to- September 20, 2008

# THIRTY-ONE FOLLOWING ORDERS

**W**hen Peggy and I were first married I was pretty heavily involved with the Marine Reserve. We attended several functions and it was suggested that she should be a "Colonel" so there wouldn't ever be any doubt who was in command, since I was merely a Major.

Well Peggy Lou's death-bed suggestion was certainly right. Catherine Ann Duesenberg was a Veterinary Nurse and me being an "old dog", it appeared to be the right thing to do. We started dating and I asked her to marry me. She accepted.

When we applied for our Marriage License, they wanted to know where Catherine's Mother was born. Catherine had to go home, open her 'lock-box' and retrieve her Birth Certificate. I happened to notice the 'lock-box' also contained a five by seven-inch brown envelope with a scoop on top to make it easy to pull out a photo. Catherine said to go ahead and take a look. The photo was Fred Duesenberg in an Officer-Cadet uniform, going through Officer Candidate School....*in the Wehmacht*, --the German Army.

We went to my 'lock box' and I have the same type envelope with my picture as a Navy Midshipman, taken while attending Naval Aviation Cadet training.

It was like the same company was doing all the world's Cadets. Probably not the case but it seemed like it.

Upon his death, Fred Duesenberg had left his home in Bellevue to his wife, Catherine. When Fred died the Mortgage Insurance had paid off the Home Loan, leaving Catherine the house free and clear.

Peggy Lou had left me her estate, in the same manner, as well.

Catherine and I decided to do a "Prenuptial Agreement" to protect our individual estates for our kids. It was easy enough to do and I'm sure that kids from both sides of our respective families felt a bit of relief.

Catherine's daughter "Cricket" (Mary Catherine) was living in the home and would continue to do so. This allowed Catherine to move in with me and we're trying to live "happily ever after". So far, so good.

**Catherine Ann Duesenberg-McEniry**

Here's my favorite Nurse! A most wonderful compassionate and loving Lady. How can one man be so lucky twice in a row! (And note closely, the last pair of 'Wings', have found a good home!) I love this girl.

Catherine hadn't ever been to Disneyland so I rented an RV, to see how she'd take to the RV life style, and headed South.

It was a wonderful trip. Catherine enjoyed Dizzyland but enough already. RV'ing, on the other hand, she felt was the only way to travel. As it has turned out, it's a good thing since Catherine has never been up in an airplane and the thought of doing so terrifies her. However, we can't 'drive' to Hawaii! So vacations will be road trips.

Catherine knew our Akita-Golden "Caira" pretty well from working with her at the Veterinary Clinic, agreeing that an Akita-mix was a good choice of animal. Caira was long gone. We talked about rescuing another one. Akita's are a Japanese breed. They were bred to hunt the small Japanese black bear and also wild boar! It kinda gives them an attitude, making them a wonderful loyal guard dog. Mixing breed cools them down, as was the case with Caira. We decided to pursue it.

It took a bit of time but we found one over in the Tri-Cities area of Eastern Washington.

The woman who had listed the dog with PAWS was anxious to find a home for him. We decided to go have a look-see.

"Sipher", named by her son who was the original owner, was an Akita-Boxer mix, tan colored with white chest and paws. He had to 'kennel' Sipher when at work and when the son died unexpectedly, the mother had taken the dog. However she had cats and Sipher became an 'outside' dog. He lived in a plastic dog house with bales of straw packed around the dog house for attempted insulation. By the way, we're talking about Eastern Washington in the winter time....it gets cold. The yard was

327

full of dog poop. It was pretty bleak and time for a 'rescue'. We were happy to provide that blessing....for the Mother, for the dog and for us. We scored second, to Sipher's good fortune.

Keeping track of the RV market I stumbled across what looked like a "good deal". A thirty foot Itaska at a very low price, so what the hell, why not. I thought it would be fun to fix up. I did fix it up...it wasn't so much fun as it was expensive. We named her "POS" for the usual reasons.

We did a couple of local weekenders and then an Oregon trip. While everything was working we sold her.

Not long after we stopped at a consignment lot that I knew about and Catherine spotted a real beauty; a thirty-four foot, 1998 Holiday Rambler Endeavor. That RV was pure "castle", a real beauty. Absolutely trouble-free, drove like a dream and made RV'ing what it should be. We enjoyed her for over five years. Many trips, one with Aunt Patsy down to Reno to visit Patsy's daughter Robin and husband Richard.

Finally, it was time for it to go. I sold it to a fellow Marine, now a "Pastor". (Really.... I wouldn't lie about that.) They would have to live in it until his new church assignment came through. Nice couple.

-o-

Well, that's about it, Folk. Thank you for reading my story. My life has been a fantastic trip, achieving my childhood dream from age seven, flying airplanes from the lowly Piper J-3, to SNJ's, jet trainers, biz-jets and fighters...big hairy prop-driven dive bombers and then transports. I found the real niche that played to my core, in General Aviation and fell totally in love with it. The grass-roots of aviation. —you won't make a whole lot of money but it's a worthwhile trip.

The real life lesson learned and lived, is *"passion"*. With it life can be good…..it was good to me.

### IT WAS A VERY GOOD YEAR

…But now the days grow short,
*I'm in the autumn of my years.*
*I think of myself as vintage wine,*
*From fine old kegs*
*From the brim to the dreg*
*It pours sweet and clear*
*It was a very good year.*
*It was a bunch of good years!*

(by Ervin M. Drake)

**James Michael McEniry, a Pilot**

# High Flight

Oh, I have slipped the surly bonds of
earth,
And danced the sky on laughter-
silvered wings,
Sunward I've climbed and joined the
tumbling mirth
Of sunlit cloud, and done a hundred
things you
Have not dreamed of.......
And wheeled and soared and swung,
High in the sunsplit silence hovering
there,
I've chased the shouting wind along
and flung
My eager craft through footless halls
of air.
Up, Up, along delirious burning blue
I've topped the windswept heights with
easy grace
Where never lark nor even eagle flew.
And while with silent lifting mind I've
trod

*The high untresspased sanctity of space,*
*Put out my hand………*
*And touched the face of God.*

By John Gillespie Magee, Jr.

(A Battle of Britain fighter pilot, from
Canada, killed on a training flight.)

*…and there I was.*

**The End**

Made in the USA
Columbia, SC
02 July 2019